CS- Great

BRITISH CULTURAL STUDIES

Media and Popular Culture

A Series of Critical Books

SERIES EDITOR
David Thorburn
Director of Film and Media Studies and
Professor of Literature,
Massachusetts Institute of Technology

In recent years a new, interdisciplinary scholarship devoted to popular culture and modern communications media has appeared. This emerging intellectual field aims to move beyond inherited conceptions of "mass society" by recognizing the complexity and diversity of the so-called mass audience and its characteristic cultural experiences. The new scholarship on media and popular culture conceives communication as a complex, ritualized experience in which "meaning" or significance is constituted by an intricate, contested collaboration among institutional, ideological, and cultural forces.

Intended for students and scholars as well as the serious general reader, **Media and Popular Culture** will publish original interpretive studies devoted to various forms of contemporary culture, with emphasis on media texts, audiences, and institutions. Aiming to create a fruitful dialogue between recent strains of feminist, semiotic, and Marxist cultural study and older forms of humanistic and social-scientific scholarship, the series will be open to many methods and theories and committed to a discourse that is intellectually rigorous yet accessible and lucid.

Communication as Culture
Essays on Media and Society
JAMES W. CAREY

Myths of Oz
Reading Australian Popular Culture
JOHN FISKE, BOB HODGE, and GRAEME TURNER

Teenagers and Teenpics
The Juvenilization of American Movies in the 1950s
THOMAS DOHERTY

Comic Visions
Television Comedy and American Culture
DAVID MARC

Reporting the Counterculture
RICHARD GOLDSTEIN

Shakespearean Films, Shakespearean Directors
PETER DONALDSON

British Cultural Studies
An Introduction
GRAEME TURNER

Additional titles in preparation

British Cultural Studies

AN INTRODUCTION

GRAEME TURNER

Media and Popular Culture: 7

ROUTLEDGE
New York London

First published in 1990 by Unwin Hyman Inc.

Reprinted in 1992 by
Routledge, an imprint of
Routledge, Chapman and Hall, Inc.
29 West 35th Street
New York, NY 10001

Published in Great Britain by
Routledge
11 New Fetter Lane
London EC4P 4EE

Printed in the United States of America on acid free paper

Library of Congress Cataloging-in-Publication Data
Turner, Graeme.
British cultural studies : an introduction / Graeme Turner.
p. cm. — (Media and popular culture)
Includes bibliographical references and index.
ISBN 0-04-445424-4. — ISBN 0-415-90688-1 (PB)
1. Great Britain—Popular culture—History—20th century. 2. Mass media—Great Britain—History—20th century. I. Title.
II. Series.
DA589.4.T87 1990
306.4'0941—dc20

British Library Cataloguing in Publication Data
Turner, Graeme, *1947–*
British cultural studies : an introduction. – (Media and popular culture ; no. 7)
1. Great Britain. Cultural studies, history
I. Title II. Series
306.07

ISBN 0-04-445424-4
ISBN 0-415-90688-1 (PB)

Contents

PART II *Central Categories*

List of Photographs

Series Editor's Introduction

Graeme Turner's lucid account of the history and key arguments of British cultural studies has rare virtues, particularly in a time of high theory and fancy terminologies. His book discusses theory seriously and responsibly, but also readably. The intellectual movement he writes about has already strongly influenced historians, media scholars, and literary critics beyond Britain, in the United States and elsewhere. But its lineage and central, fashioning figures—E. P. Thompson and Raymond Williams, preeminently—remain less well used by American scholars than various European schools and writers. One hope I have for Turner's thoughtful primer is that it will help to rectify this relative neglect, inciting readers to deeper, sustained encounters with many of the authors he examines, and especially with the adventurous and powerful founding figures: Paddy Whannel and Stuart Hall, Richard Hoggart, Williams, Thompson.

Turner is perhaps right to see the first phase of British cultural studies, the work of these men, as theoretically naive. But their resistance to grand theory, their insistence on the local and the specific, on the *experienced* concreteness of real life, continues as a guiding, steadying influence on all forms of cultural interpretation. The respect for Chaplin and his audience articulated so thoughtfully—and against such a weight of Leavisite and High Modernist scorn for industrial commercial culture!—in Hall and Whannel's *The Popular Arts* (1967), for example, anticipates contemporary media scholarship in many respects. Hoggart's and Thompson's sensitivity to the richness of working-class experience lies behind—both nurtures and, too often, judges—the ramifying contemporary scholarship devoted to audiences and to the cultural experiences of groups defined as marginal by the dominant culture.

And in Raymond Williams, as Turner helps us to see, one can recover a complex, elaborating articulation of one of the great enabling principles of cultural studies: the recognition that culture is a process, not any fixed thing at all, but a shifting, unequal, endless contention among traditional and emerging voices, institutions, and ideologies.

Turner is quick to acknowledge that "British cultural studies" is a limited category, a kind of fiction, but I think his book proves the fiction useful and even true. Repeatedly in the theory and scholarly practice outlined in these pages we can hear, I think, a distinctive tonality, an undersong of the ordinary and the particular, call it a residual empiricism or something even plainer: respect for the real.

—David Thorburn

Introduction

If it had been written 30 years ago, a book with this title would almost certainly have been expected to deal with "high culture": the elite art forms seen to provide the best that has been written, spoken, or performed over the ages. An index of how large a shift has occurred in that 30 years is that I will deal primarily not with elite but with popular culture. This book will chart some of the reasons for this shift, while outlining cultural studies as a set of key sites of investigation, key methodologies and theoretical orientations, and a critical practice.

The term *cultural studies* is now well known as the title for an important set of theories and practices within the humanities and social sciences. As its international journal, *Cultural Studies,* puts it, the field is "dedicated to the notion that the study of cultural processes, and especially of popular culture, is important, complex and both theoretically and politically rewarding." While the field is now achieving recognition, it is not a discrete or homogeneous theoretical formation, nor is it easy to define. It is not surprising that although there are many readers and collections of articles dealing with specific aspects or applications of cultural theory, this book is the first to attempt to introduce it, accessibly and comprehensively.

As Paul Willis (1979) has said, the "culture" that is the subject of British cultural studies is "not artifice and manners, the preserve of Sunday best, rainy afternoons and concert halls. It is the very material of our daily lives, the bricks and mortar of our most commonplace understandings" (pp.

184–85). What we wear, hear, watch, and eat; how we see ourselves in relation to others; the function of everyday activities such as cooking or shopping; all of these have attracted the interest of cultural studies. Emerging from a literary critical tradition that saw popular culture as a threat to the moral and cultural standards of modern civilization, the work of the pioneers in cultural studies breaks with that literary tradition's elitist assumptions in order to examine the everyday and the ordinary: those aspects of our lives that exert so powerful and unquestioned an influence on our existence that we take them for granted. The processes that make us—as individuals, as citizens, as members of a particular class, race, or gender—are cultural processes that work precisely because they seem so natural, so unexceptional, so irresistible.

The work of Raymond Williams, Richard Hoggart, Stuart Hall, and in particular the Birmingham Centre for Contemporary Cultural Studies (CCCS) has established the consideration of popular culture—from the mass media to sport to dance crazes—on an academic and intellectual agenda from which it had been excluded. This exclusion had exacted a great cost; what it regarded as peripheral and meretricious included the most basic and pervasive of social processes, practices, and meanings. It is from these "peripheral" networks of meaning and pleasure that culture is constructed, for "it is one of the fundamental paradoxes of our social life that when we are at our most natural, our most *everyday*, we are also at our most cultural; that when we are in roles that look the most obvious and given, we are actually in roles that are constructed, learned and far from inevitable" (Willis 1979, 184). Willis's concluding phrase is the one that bites: if the roles we take for granted should *not* be taken for granted, then their exclusion from academic inquiry is, at least, unwise. So, the focus on popular culture has quickly become a focus on how our everyday lives are *constructed*, how culture forms its subjects. No idle interest, the aim is to locate the social and political effects of these formations.

The following chapters present a history of the development of these ideas, specifying what seem to me the central principles of British cultural studies. The book is organized in two parts. Part I sets up the basic theoretical principles in

Chapter 1, and sketches a history of British cultural studies in Chapter 2. Part II looks in more depth at the central categories within the field: texts, audiences, the social production of everyday life, and the problem of ideology. The first chapter, necessarily, has some heavy ground clearing to do, and those who are already familiar with semiotics and structuralism may wish only to skim through it on their way to Chapter 2. Throughout, I present descriptive accounts of the significant contributions to each topic; in many cases, this work is quite daunting to read in its original form, and my account aims to guide both those who intend to seek out the original book or article and those who do not. As often as possible, I have chosen to allow the original works to speak for themselves, and have quoted liberally. For the conceptual organization of the material, of course, I alone am to blame.

Before proceeding with this account, however, there are a number of admonitory points to be made about the "tradition" constructed through this history, its "Britishness," and the status of the theoretical formulations made in the process of constructing it. The title *British Cultural Studies* is itself a touch too precise. While I am going to concentrate on *British* work in the wide and shifting field of cultural studies, and while I am also going to examine the *British* roots of British cultural studies, it is important to recognize that this tradition is not sealed off from other influences. While I may argue that the role of Williams and other British researchers is seminal, the work of the European structuralists—Lévi-Strauss, Saussure, Lacan, Barthes, Foucault—and certain inflections of European Marxism—Althusser, Gramsci—are also central to the formation of what is now recognized as British cultural studies. Further, although I will not deal with these corollary movements, readers should be aware that there are other important, non-British, traditions in cultural studies: the work emanating from the sociology of Bourdieu or de Certeau in France, for instance, or the American anthropological tradition James Carey (1989, 61) identifies with Clifford Geertz and calls "cultural science." This book is not aimed at appropriating the whole of the field and incorporating it into the category of British cultural studies; rather, it looks at one, relatively discrete but particularly influential, corner of this emerging intellectual terrain.

The distinctiveness and usefulness of the British tradition of cultural studies could be said to lie in its relatively accessible applications of European theoretical models to specific cultural formations. It is unusual in the degree of emphasis it has given to "concrete" or applied studies—applying complex social theory to, say, the process of leaving school or organizing a lift home from the local dance. Richard Harland (1987) may be too sweepingly dismissive, but he is also roughly correct when he claims that "Anglo-Saxon Semioticians are largely indifferent to matters of philosophy; their interests are more practical, focusing upon various specific studies in various specific fields of communication" (p. 4). Far from limiting the tradition's appeal, this practicality has expanded its usefulness and contributed to the influence it has enjoyed.

A reason for caution in writing such a book as this is that cultural studies is preeminently a critical field: there *is* no orthodoxy in this field, and many have warned against the dangers of such an orthodoxy developing. When the Birmingham Centre for Contemporary Cultural Studies launched its journal, *Working Papers in Cultural Studies*, it "refused" to define the field, choosing instead to embark on what Hall (1980a) calls a "sustained work of theoretical clarification" (p. 15). While not every product of the Centre could be said to achieve this objective (and resisting an orthodoxy can certainly limit the achievement of clarity), such work continues, and it would be wrong to see these pages as describing a stable, fixed field of theory or practice. This book, I hope, offers instead a kind of narrative in progress, proposing ways of conceptualizing where the field of study has been and where it might be now.

This dogged and perhaps slightly curious resistance to the establishment of a theoretical orthodoxy in cultural studies is a product of two of its defining characteristics: the complexity and comprehensiveness of the theoretical issues it has confronted in order to deal with the problem of culture, and its commitment to critical, political objectives. The first characteristic creates real problems in a book such as this, since the issues dealt with are genuinely complex and difficult to simplify for the purposes of an introduction without sacrificing accuracy or comprehensiveness. This is also a problem for the tradition itself, and has led to accusations of "theoreticism," an elitist fondness for the intricacies of theory for their own sake. Such theoreticism is seen to produce a particularly self-regarding kind of writing, couched in an exclusive and intimidating jargon that is deployed as proof of the academic seriousness of the field of study and its objects. Readers of this book will have to judge for themselves how successfully I have compromised between the demands of simplicity of expression and an appropriate complexity of conceptualization.

The second issue, however, is more substantive. Work in cultural studies has consistently addressed itself to the interrogation of society's structures of domination. It has focused most particularly on the experience of the working class and, more recently, on that of women as locations where the action of oppressive power relations can be examined. In its theoretical tradition, it is inextricably linked with a critical European Marxism that seeks to understand how capitalist societies work and how to change them. This means that while cultural studies' subject matter may be popular culture, and while this may even be dealt with in ways that involve an element of nostalgia, for instance, the objective of cultural studies is not simply to recover aspects of social experience that were dear to the researchers' own hearts. It is all too easy to characterize work on the media, or on youth cultures, or on the music industry, as a kind of "slumming" by middle-aged academics who want to legitimate the activities of their youth. Such motivations are at odds with the basic enterprise of cultural studies. As Richard Johnson (1983) says, it is important to recognize the inadequacy of studies of popular culture that occur for "purely academic purposes or when enthusiasm for . . . popular cultural forms is divorced from the analysis of power and of social possibilities" (p. 9). Popular culture is a site where the construction of everyday life may be examined. The point of doing this is not only academic—that is, as an attempt to understand a process or practice—it is also political, to examine the power relations that constitute this form of everyday life and thus to reveal the configuration of interests its construction serves.

This political dimension is one legitimate reason there is concern about the establishment of a cultural studies orthodoxy, about cultural studies' inclusion within the traditional academy, or about the incorporation of its work and its challenges within more conventional academic discourses. Cultural studies defines itself in part through its disruption of the boundaries between disciplines, and through its ability to explode the category of "the natural"—revealing the history behind those social relations we see as the products of a neutral evolutionary process. It is understandably worried at the prospect of becoming a "natural" discipline itself.

Nevertheless, a book like this is necessary to provide an accessible introduction to an important body of theory that is in many cases unavailable outside journal articles and that is not easily assimilable by undergraduates. So, while I am under no illusions as to what the fate of a book like this might well be—it *could* support the installation of an orthodoxy within teaching programs if not in research—there seems no alternative if I want the material it contains to gain a wider currency. Therefore, I offer what must look like something of a ritual disclaimer: this book does not set out to offer *the* definitive account of the tradition, nor do I feel we need such an account. The aim of this book is to provide a guide for students entering this important and complicated field, to enable them to search out the appropriate primary sources relevant to their interests or needs.

There could be substantially different accounts of this tradition from what follows. While I have dealt with all aspects of the field that seem significant, I am aware of placing some emphasis on the textualist/structuralist aspects; those who work in, say, history and use cultural studies theory may feel that my literary and media studies background has skewed my definition of the field in this direction. I would acknowledge that possibility, and invite alternative accounts. Cultural studies is a various and vigorously contested field, yet this very fact makes it necessary for students to have some kind of map that will organize the territory at least provisionally so that they may then begin to explore it and reframe it in their own ways. This book is intended to be that map.

For permission to use illustrations, I would like to thank the BBC, AAP, Methuen/Routledge, John Fairfax and Sons, and the Brisbane Courier-Mail. For their part in the production of the book, through conversation, comments, or encouragement, I would like to thank John Hartley, Richard Johnson, Philip Neilsen, Lisa Freeman, and, most particularly, my editor, David Thorburn. My wife, Christine, deserves my gratitude for bearing with me once again, and for attempting to make up for the fact that my children don't seem to take any of this seriously at all.

PART I

First Principles

1

The Idea of Cultural Studies

Writing in 1983, Richard Johnson, a former director of the Birmingham Centre for Contemporary Cultural Studies, revised the grammar in the title of his paper "What Is Cultural Studies Anyway?" to read "What *are* cultural studies anyway?" (p. 1). It is a significant shift. There are many ideas about what constitutes the center of cultural studies. Seemingly, many of the arguments about the shape of the field and the appropriateness of specific practices within it are driven by the original disciplinary orientation of individual contributors. Thus, historians tend to be suspicious of the textual analysis practiced by those who originally trained as literary critics; the literary critics in turn are often suspicious of the way in which sociologists or ethnographers accept statements from their subjects without sufficient analysis and interpretation. It would be a mistake to see cultural studies as a new discipline, or even a discrete constellation of disciplines. Cultural studies is an interdisciplinary field where certain concerns and methods have converged; the usefulness of this convergence is that it has enabled us to understand phenomena and relationships that were not accessible through the existing disciplines. It is not, however, a unified field, and much of this book will be taken up with mapping lines of argument and division as well as of convergence.

All of that said, cultural studies *does* contain common elements: principles, motivations, preoccupations, and theoretical categories. In this chapter, I will outline the most basic of these at an introductory level. I will return to develop them more fully in later chapters.

Language and Culture

In Chapter 2, I will sketch out the beginnings of British cultural studies within English literary studies, looking at the contributions of Raymond Williams and Richard Hoggart in some detail. At this stage, only a couple of points need to be made about the way in which this tradition began.

Customarily, cultural studies is seen to begin with the publication of Richard Hoggart's *The Uses of Literacy* (1957) and Raymond Williams's *Culture and Society 1780–1950* (1958) and *The Long Revolution* (1961). Both Hoggart and Williams can be placed within a tradition of English literary criticism generally identified with F. R. Leavis and noted for its concentration on the forms of literary texts and on their moral/social significance. What was impressive about both Hoggart and Williams was their ability to mobilize their methods of textual criticism so as to "read" cultural forms other than literature: popular song, for instance, or popular fiction. But there were clear limits: both writers suffered from the lack of a method that could more appropriately analyze the ways in which such cultural forms and practices produced their *social*, not merely their aesthetic, meanings and pleasures. To reconnect the texts with society, with the culture and the individuals that produced and consumed them, involved a fundamental reorientation. One was required to think about how culture was structured as a *whole* before one could examine its processes or its constitutive parts.

As Iain Chambers (1986, 208) has suggested, "Explanations based on the idea of totality, on the rational frame that connects the most distant and complex parts, are characteristic of the great Continental schools of thought": Marxism, classical sociology, psychoanalysis, structuralism, semiotics. The European influence on British cultural studies largely came, in the first instance at least, from structuralism. Structuralism has many variants, but its common characteristic is an interest in the systems, the sets of relationships, the formal structures that frame and enable the production of meaning. The original structuralist stimulus registered within British cultural studies was not, however, a theory of culture, but rather a theory of language. Within most of what follows, language looms as the most essential of concepts, either in its own right or through being appropriated as a model for understanding other cultural systems.

Ferdinand de Saussure's theory of language is our starting point.[1] Commonsense understandings of the function of language would see it as a system for naming things; seemingly, an object turns up in the material world, we apply a name to it and communicate this to others, and the word enters into usage. Saussure sees it differently. For him, language is a mechanism that determines how we decide what constitutes "an object" in the first place, let alone which objects might need naming. Language does not name an already organized and coherent reality; its role is far more powerful and complex. The function of language is to organize, to construct, indeed to provide us with our only access to, reality.

This distinction might become clearer if we refer to Saussure's proposition that the connection between a word and its meaning is not inherent, or natural, but, in most instances, quite arbitrary; the word *tree* means what it does to us only because we agree to let it do so. The fact that there is no real reason *this* word should mean what it does is underlined by the fact that there are different words to express the same concept in different languages. Further, there is no "natural" reason the concept itself should be expressed at all. There is no universal law that decrees we should distinguish between trees and, say, flowers, or between trees and grass; that we do so is a matter of convention. Australian Aboriginal cultures discern a multitude of differences among various conditions of what white Australian culture sees as empty desert; their language has many words differentiating what whites simply call "bush" or "scrub." Even the way we "see" the world is determined by the cultural conventions through which we conceptualize the images we receive. When the first colonists arrived in Australia, their early paintings of the indigenous peoples resembled current European aesthetic conventions of "the noble savage." They bore little resemblance to what we now see as the "real" characteristics of Australian Aborigines. Those early painters represented what they saw through the *visual* "languages" of their time. So, even our idea of the natural world is organized, constituted, through the conventions of its representation: through languages.

When Saussure insists that the relation between a word and its meaning is constructed, not given, he is directing us to the cultural and social dimensions of language. Language is cultural, not natural, and so the meanings it generates are too. The *way* in which language generates meaning, according to Saussure, is important. Again, he insists that the function of language is not to fix intrinsic meanings, the *definitions* of those things it refers to, as we might imagine it should. Language is a system of relationships; it establishes categories and makes distinctions through networks of difference and similarity. When we think of the word *man*, we attribute meaning by specifying the concept's similarity to, or difference from, other concepts; crucially, we will consider what such a word tells us this object is *not*: not boy, not girl, not woman, and so on. Cultural relations are reproduced through the language system: to extend the previous example, the word *man* might also generate its meaning in opposition to other concepts—not weak, not emotional, not sensitive, for example—that go to build up a particular cultural definition of the male role within gender relations.

The insights contained within Saussure's theory of language have a relevance beyond linguistics because they reveal to us the mechanisms through which we make sense of our world. Specific social relations are defined through the place language allocates them within *its* system of relations. Such an explanation of language endows it with enormous determining power. Reality is made relative, while the power of constructing "the real" is attributed to the mechanisms of language within the culture. Meaning is revealed to be culturally grounded—even culturally specific. Different cultures may not only use different language systems but they may also, in a definitive sense, inhabit different worlds. Culture, as the site where meaning is generated and experienced, becomes a determining, productive field through which social realities are constructed, experienced, and interpreted.

The central mechanism through which language exercises its determining function is explained through the notions of *langue* and *parole*. Saussure divides the structure of a language system into two categories: *langue* is the full repertoire of possibilities within a language system—all the things that can be thought and said; *parole* refers to the specific utterance, composed by selection from the *langue*. Although *langue* is an enormous system, it is also a determining, limiting system in that it sets up specific sets of relations that are impossible for any one speaker alone to change (although, as we shall see, the system does contain the potential for change). Any utterance composed within the system is also constrained by it, restricted to the categories it recognizes, the conventions it establishes. In speaking a language we find it immensely difficult not to reproduce its assumptions, its version of the world:

> The individual absorbs language before he can think for himself: indeed the absorption of language is the very condition of being able to think for himself. The individual can reject particular knowledges that society explicitly teaches him, he can throw off particular beliefs that society forcibly imposes upon him—but he has always already accepted the words and meanings through which such knowledges and beliefs were communicated to him. . . . They lie within him like an undigested piece of society. (Harland 1987, 12–13)

The great contribution of Saussure's theory is that it directly relates language and culture; some may say it works too well, making it difficult to separate them.

Saussure's next step is outside the specific domain of linguistics. He argues that the principles that structure the linguistic system can also be seen to organize other kinds of communication systems—not only writing, but also non-linguistic systems such as those governing images, gestures, or the conventions of "good manners," for instance. Saussure proposes an analogy between the operation of language and the operation of all other systems that generate meaning, seeing them all as "signifying systems." This analogy has been widely accepted and adopted. The reasons for its attraction are pretty clear. Language is a signifying system that can be seen to be closely ordered, structured, and thus can be rigorously examined and ultimately understood; conversely, it is also a means of "expression" that is not entirely mechanistic in its functions but allows for a range of variant possibilities. Saussure's system thus acknowledges or recognizes the power of determining, controlling structures (analogous to *langue*), as well as the specific, partly "free," individualized instance (analogous to *parole*). It offers enormous possibilities for the analysis of cultural systems that are not, strictly speaking, languages, but that work like languages. The structuralist anthropologist Claude Lévi-Strauss adopted Saussure's model to decode the myths, symbolic systems, even the customary practices employed in the preparation of food, of "primitive" societies; and the French semiotician Roland Barthes (1973) applied it to the analysis of the codes and conventions employed in the films, sports, and eating habits (among other topics) of contemporary Western societies in *Mythologies*. For such followers, there was little doubt that "culture . . . was itself a . . . *signifying* practice—and had its own determinate product: meaning" (Hall 1980a, 30).

Semiotics and Signification

That cultural product—meaning—is of crucial importance. If the only way to understand the world is through its "representation" to us through language(s), we need some method of dealing with representation, with the production of meaning. In his *Course in General Linguistics* (1960), Saussure suggests the establishment of a "science which would study the life of signs within society" (p. 16). Semiology "would teach us what signs consist of, what laws govern them." Semiology was to be the mechanism for applying the structural model of language across all signifying systems and for providing a method of analysis that would be "scientific" and precise. While it is not entirely scientific, semiotics—as we shall call it here—has become a most useful method, the terminology of which is basic to cultural studies and needs to be outlined at least briefly in this section.

Semiotics allows us to examine the cultural specificity of representations and their meanings by using one set of methods and terms across the full range of signifying practices: gesture, dress, writing, speech, photography, film, television, and so on. Central here is the idea of the sign. A sign can be thought of as the smallest unit of communication within a language system. It can be a word, a photograph, a sound, an image on a screen, a musical note, a gesture, an item of clothing. To be a sign it must have a physical form, it must refer to something other than itself, and it must be recognized as doing this by other users of the sign system. The word *tree* is a sign; the photographic image of Tom Cruise is a sign; the trademark of Coca-Cola is a sign, too. Less obviously, when we dress to go out for a drink, or to see a band play, our selection and combination of items of clothing is a combination of signs; our clothes are placed in relation to other signs (the way we do our hair, for instance) that have meaning for those we will meet there. We intend that these signs will determine our meaning for those we meet, and we fear that the meanings we have attempted to create will not be the meanings taken: for instance, instead of being seen as a part of a particular social scene, we may be "read" as *poseurs* or phonies. In this, as in other situations, we signify ourselves through the signs available to us within our culture; we select and combine them in relation to the codes and conventions established within our culture, in order to limit and determine the range of possible meanings they are likely to generate when read by others.

In order to understand the process of signification, the sign has been separated into its constituent parts: the signifier and the signified. It has become conventional to talk of the signifier as the physical form of the sign: the written word, the lines on the page that form the drawing, the photograph, the sound. The signified is the mental concept referred to by the signifier. So the word *tree* will not necessarily refer to a specific tree but to a culturally produced concept of "treeness." The meaning generated by these two components emerges from their relationship; one cannot separate them and still generate meaning. The relationship is, most often, an arbitrary and constructed one, and so it can change. The mental concept conventionally activated by the word *gay*, for instance, has shifted over the last decade or so, articulating an entirely new set of relations. The ways in which such a shift might occur are of crucial importance to cultural studies, because it is through such phenomena we can track cultural change.

We need to understand the social dimension of the sign: the ways in which culture supplies us with the signifier, the form, and the signified, the mental concept. A conventional system of classification is of some relevance here: the distinction between literal and associative meanings—or denotation and connotation. According to such a system, we have the literal (denotative) meaning of a word, such as *mugging*, and the wider social dimension (connotation), where the accretion of associations around the word extends and amplifies its literal meaning. Of course, *mugging* is not likely to produce utterly literal meanings, free of connotation; there is really only the theoretical possibility that such a thing as a connotation-free, or unsocialized, meaning might exist. Stuart Hall and a group from the Birmingham Centre for Contemporary Cultural Studies have written a large book, devoted almost solely to the public understandings of this one word—*mugging*—in Britain, and the cultural and political means through which those understandings were constructed (Hall et al. 1978).

Roland Barthes (1973) has, in effect, extended this system of classification into semiotics. In his essay "Myth Today," he has outlined an incremental signifying system in which social meanings attach themselves to signs, just as connotations attach themselves to a word. This culturally enriched sign, itself, becomes the signifier for the next sign in a chain of signification of ascending complexity and cultural specificity. So, for example, the word *outlaw* has acquired social meanings that will be called up and that will acquire further and more specific accretions when used, say, in a western film or in the lyrics of a song played by a heavy metal band.

Similarly, the meanings Sylvester Stallone has accrued in his *Rambo* films become part of what he signifies in subsequent performances. Barthes's particular concern in "Myth Today" is with the way cultural associations and social knowledge attach themselves to signifieds. He calls these attachments "myths," not meaning to suggest that they are necessarily untrue, but that they operate, as do myths in primitive societies, to "explain" our world for us.

Photo 1.1. Ferdinand and Imelda Marcos (*Reprinted with kind permission of John Fairfax and Sons.*)

It is easier to demonstrate the function of semiotic methods in practice than to explain them in the abstract. The accompanying news photo (see photo 1.1) was taken on the last day of Ferdinand Marcos's presidency of the Philippines. It combines a number of signs: the figures of Marcos himself and that of his wife, Imelda, are the most important, but the microphone and balcony rails also combine to provide us with a context—probably the balcony of the presidential palace. At the time the photo was published, there may have been varied responses to it, particularly in the United States, where support for the Marcos regime was becoming politically embarrassing. Let us see what semiotics will tell us about this photo.

The image of Marcos is a signifier that immediately activates cultural knowledge about Marcos himself. The signified of Marcos is, presumably for most of us, highly charged: our "reading" of it might include our assessment of his dictatorship, the allegations of corruption and extortion, and the contested history of his dealings with political opponents—in particular, Benigno Aquino. For most readers, the signified would be informed by what Barthes would call myths about the link between corruption and power, by explicitly political attitudes about U.S. foreign policy, perhaps by a (not necessarily unified or noncontradictory) selection from the competing myths that "explain" the Marcos persona, and possibly by racist notions of despotic Third World leaders drawing on the implicit assumptions of such popular fictions as *Mission Impossible* and *Romancing the Stone*. So, for Western readers, this photo will not have a neutral, purely denotative meaning; Marcos's cultural meanings are inevitably invoked as we recognize the signifier.

There are also other signifiers to notice here: Marcos's posture and gesture. We might recognize these generally as signifiers of defiance, of power, or of political resistance; when combined with the specific signifieds, the combination of gesture and posture is easily read as the sign of a futile, despotic thirst for power. When these signs are combined with those signifying Imelda Marcos, such a reading is reinforced. Facial expressions can be signifiers, too, and Imelda looks anxious. The arrangement of the signs—the images of Ferdinand and Imelda Marcos—within the frame is also important. The relation between them is such that her anxiety, while subordinated in the composition, undermines the power of his resistant and defiant gesture. The photo's compositional construction of an interplay between man and wife, between dictator and consort, domesticates the moment somewhat by turning a major political event into an individualized family drama. Here myths connecting men, power, and the secondary role played by their women are offered as an almost irresistible invitation to interpret the contrast between her expression and his. It is a rich and ambiguous photo, and thus a wonderfully appropriate choice for a newspaper to use at such a juncture; with Marcos liable to fall at any time, this picture could be used to signify the futility of his attempt to retain power, or the determination with which he was managing to hang on. The headline and caption in the newspaper when it appeared would partly determine which set of meanings readers would most likely construct.

If we turn to another example, the practices of advertising provide a clear demonstration of the processes of signification. Advertising could be said to work by fitting a signifier to a signified, both cooperating with and intervening in the semiotic process. Advertisers typically deploy a signifier, already conventionally related to a mental concept they wish to attach to their product, as a means of providing their product with that meaning. So, the manufacturers of Ski yogurt in Australia run a series of television ads featuring a particular life-style: sailboarding, hang-gliding, surfing, skiing. The arrangement of signifiers within the images places great emphasis on the natural environment in which these activities take place: water, snow, air. There is no obvious connection with yogurt, but the life-style shots are intercut with shots of the product being consumed by the same suntanned young things who were sailboarding. The process of semiosis means that we stitch the signs together, connecting the yogurt with the life-style depicted. It is similar to the process of metaphor in writing or speech, in which two otherwise unconnected ideas are syntactically linked and thus bleed into each other; each takes on some of the meanings of the other.

The result, for Ski yogurt, is the product's incorporation into an idea of the natural, into the existing myths of youth, and of a healthy outdoor life-style. As a consequence of advertising like this, yogurt is now a "life-style product" as much as a food; this campaign emphasizes the product's place within a set of social, subcultural, fashionable, life-style relations more than it emphasizes Ski's taste as a food—its place within a culinary (if still fashionable) set of relations. Finally, the ads are informed by a myth that links youth, health, and nature, as if youth were not only more healthy and vigorous but also more "natural" than other physical states. This operates in tandem with the apparently unshakable myth that certain aspects of one's physical appearance are the key to all other states of well-being, from employment to love to personal happiness and success. Such myths may seem transparently false, but (like myths in primitive societies) they do have surprising explanatory force. Television programs such as *Lifestyles of the Rich and Famous* reinforce such myths by knitting fame, financial success, and glamour together in every segment. To see the successful as exceptionally gifted, and implicitly to see oneself as ordinary and therefore in need of the signifiers of success that life-style products might provide, is to accept the mythic explanation offered for an inequitable and discriminatory economic and social structure.

These last comments foreshadow the next of the common elements within British cultural studies, its political objectives. But before we leave semiotics, it is important to reemphasize its usefulness as a methodology. At the most elementary level it supplies us with a terminology and a conceptual frame that enables the analysis of nonlinguistic signs. For this reason alone, semiotics has become part of the vocabulary of cultural studies. The method is widely deployed in the analysis of film and television. Clearly, its value lies in its ability to deal with sound, image, and their interrelation. In television studies, particularly, semiotics' break with an aesthetic mode of analysis and its relative independence from notions of authorial intention are valuable. There is a link, however, between aesthetic analysis and semiotic analysis: the strategy of calling the object or site of one's analysis *a text.* The term is appropriated from literary studies and depends upon an analogy between the close analysis conventionally applied to literary texts and the close analysis cultural studies applies to popular cultural texts. The objectives of cultural studies' analyses of texts may differ markedly, however, from those of predominantly evaluative modes of literary studies, such as the tradition associated with F. R. Leavis in Britain. While many individual or groups of cultural texts may be particularly interesting to us—the Madonna video for "Like a Prayer," for instance, or a ground-breaking situation comedy such as the British show, *The Young Ones*—the point of textual analysis is not to set up a canon of rich and rewarding texts we can return to as privileged objects. Structuralist influence on the application of semiotics to popular cultural texts has insisted that analysis should not limit itself to the structures of individual texts, but should use such texts as the site for examining the wider structures that produced them—those of the culture itself. As Richard Johnson (1983) has emphasized, while textual analysis is, as we shall see, a major current within cultural studies, the text is still "only a *means* in cultural study"; it is "no longer studied for its own sake . . . but rather for the subjective or cultural forms which it realises and makes available" (p. 35).

Johnson has been skeptical of the value of textual analysis, and arguments around the practice will be taken up in Chapter 3 in greater detail, but he is right to stress the importance of the text as a site where cultural meanings are accessible to us, rather than as a privileged object of study in its own right. The precise nature of cultural studies' interest in these meanings is important, too; at its most distinctive, cultural studies analysis is aimed toward a particular end—that of understanding the ways in which power relations are regulated, distributed, and deployed within industrial societies. This introduces the next topic, and I approach it by acknowledging the philosophical and political roots of British cultural studies in British Marxism.

Marxism and Ideology

British Marxist thought underwent radical transformations during the 1960s. When Raymond Williams published *Culture and Society* in 1958, he was able to scoff at English Marxist critics as essentially irrelevant to any wider community of ideas. This attitude was increasingly inappropriate as the 1960s developed and the influence of European Marxist thought provoked a break with traditional Marxism and an embracing of what has been called a "complex" or a "critical" Marxism (see Bennett 1981, 7; Hall 1980a, 25).

Stereotyped representations of Marxist thought conventionalize it as a monolithic and revolutionary body of theory. This European tradition is neither of these things; its standard discourse is the critique, and it spends as much time dealing with issues and divisions *within* the field as outside it. The influence of such European theorists as Lukacs, Benjamin, Goldmann, and Sartre was extended through English translations of their work in the mid-1960s, affecting a large range of academic disciplines and political formations. Crucial, for cultural studies, was the way in which this tradition reframed the place and function of culture:

> The Marxism which informs the cultural studies approach is a *critical* Marxism in the sense that it has contested the reductionist implications of earlier Marxist approaches to the study of culture. These, especially in Britain, often tended to view culture—whether we mean this in the sense of works of art or literature, or the ways of life of particular social classes—as being totally determined by economic relationships. The Marxist approaches that have informed the development of the cultural studies perspective, by contrast, have insisted on the "relative autonomy" of culture—on the fact that it is not simply dependent on economic relationships and cannot, accordingly, be reduced to or viewed as a mere reflection of these, and that it actively influences and has consequences for economic and political relationships rather than simply being passively influenced by them (Bennett 1981, 7).

Traditional Marxism had devalued the importance of the idea of culture; culture was part of the "superstructure" of society, and thus simply a product of the economic and industrial base. Yet, as Saussure's account of the social function of language suggests, this ignores the way in which language exercises a determining influence over the "real"—including the material bases of capitalism. Historians, too, have argued against such a view as too simple an account of history and its formation. Cultural studies employed critical Marxist theory to launch attacks on the "economism" in previous explanations of how existing power relations have been instituted and legitimated. Drawing in particular on Louis Althusser's (1971) argument that key "ideological" apparatuses (the law, the family, the education system, for instance) are every bit as significant as economic conditions, cultural studies insisted that culture is neither simply dependent on nor simply independent of economic relationships. Rather, as Althusser argues, there are many determining forces—economic, political, *and* cultural—competing and conflicting with each other in order to make up the complex unity of society.

Marx's aphorism that "men make their own history, but not in conditions of their own making" has become an often-repeated dictum in this field. The problem of *how* the conditions in which we make our own history are determined is a central one for Marxist and for cultural studies theory. Althusser's answer is to argue for a network of determinations, differently articulated at different points and for different people, that exercises an overseeing, or "overdetermining," control over social experience. The mechanism through which the process of overdetermination works is that of ideology.

Ideology, in earlier Marxist formulations, had been seen as a kind of veil over the eyes of the working class, the filter that screened out or disguised their "real" relations to the world around them. The function of ideology was to construct a "false consciousness" of the self and of one's relation to history. Althusser's work marks a conclusive break with this way of conceptualizing the term. Just as Saussure had argued that language provides us with access to a *version* of reality, rather than to *the* reality, Althusser's definition sees ideology not as false but as a conceptual framework "through which men interpret, make sense of, experience and 'live' the material conditions in which they find themselves" (Hall 1980a, 33). Ideology forms and shapes our consciousness of reality. For good or ill, the world it constructs is the one we will always inhabit.

Clearly, ideology must saturate language. The formation of the categories through which we understand experience, as mentioned above in the quotation from Harland (1987), begins before we can resist them. The language system, with its constitutive ideological frameworks, is always already there waiting for the child to insert him- or herself into it. This is why feminists have been so critical of sexist language—the ways in which ideologies of domination are institutionalized through the use of *Miss, Mrs.*, or the assumption that every committee must have a "chairman." Althusser also insists that ideologies must be examined not only in language and representation, but also in their material forms—the institutions and social practices through which we organize and live our lives. John Fiske (1987a) explains how Althusser's ideological state apparatuses (the media, the legal system, the educational system, and the political system) achieve ideological ends by establishing and legitimating social norms:

> These norms are realized in the day-to-day workings of the ideological state apparatuses. Each one of these institutions is "relatively autonomous", and there are no overt connections between it and any of the others—the legal system is not explicitly connected to the school system or to the media, for example—yet they all perform similar ideological work. They are all patriarchal; they are all concerned with the getting and keeping of wealth and possessions, and they all assert individualism and competition between individuals. (p. 257)

Since ideologies are observable in material form only in the practices, behaviors, institutions, and texts in society, the need to examine these material forms seemed to be extremely pressing. There is now a rich literature of inquiry into the material, social, and historical conditions of ideological formations. These range from histories of the media to the histories of discourse identified with Michel Foucault, histories of the notion of discipline, or of Western sexuality, for instance, that see such concepts as entirely culturally produced.[2] However, within British cultural studies, the primary focus of ideological analysis has been on the media, in particular, on their definitions of social relations and political problems, and on their implication in the production and transformation of popular ideologies (Hall 1980a, 117). This has been a central concern for the Birmingham Centre.

These critical Marxist accounts of ideology insist on culture's determination by specific historical forces, legitimated by specific ideological formations, and in specific material interests. There is nothing natural or inevitable about their view of history. Althusserian Marxism does not stop there, however. Ideology not only produces our culture, it also produces our consciousness of our selves. Another essential category moves into our sights now—the category of the unique individual, possessed of innate, intrinsic qualities expressed and realized in the idea of the self. This category, this romantic idea of the individual, is the next target of cultural studies theory.

Individualism and Subjectivity

Marxism has always seen the notion of individualism as a central supporting mythology for capitalism; the placement of the individual at the center of history has thus been vigorously resisted. Althusser's and, later, Jacques Lacan's critiques of individualism, however, are significantly different from those that preceded them.

Althusser argues that ideology operates not explicitly but implicitly; it lives in those practices, those structures, those images we take for granted. We internalize ideology and thus are not easily made conscious of its presence or its effects; it is unconscious. And yet, the unconscious has, within many philosophical frameworks, been seen as the core of our individuality, a product of our nature. If Althusser is right, then, our unconscious, too, is formed in ideology, from *outside* our "essential" selves. For Althusser, the notion of an essential self disappears as a fiction, an impossibility, and in its place is the social being who possesses a socially produced sense of identity—a "subjectivity." This subjectivity is not like the old unified individual self; it can be contradictory, and it can change within different situations and in response to different kinds of address. We rely, in fact, on language and ideology to instruct us in how we are to conceive our social identities, in how to be a "subject."

The post-Freudian psychoanalyst Jacques Lacan takes this notion further. Lacan appropriates the model of structural linguistics from Saussure, and argues that our unconscious is a sign system, too, that functions like a language. (Dreams, for instance, offer an example of this.) The *langue* of our unconscious is not produced by a unique individual, but by culture. Just as we learn to speak in the language and customs of our culture, and are thus in a sense constructed through them, our unconscious too is formed through the perceptions and language of others. Our view of ourselves is composed from a repertoire given to us, not produced by us, and so we are the subjects, not the authors, of cultural processes.

Dizzying as this can seem when first encountered, such perspectives have been extraordinarily productive. For instance, consider how such a view of the individual/subject might have affected the first feminist critiques of the social construction of the feminine. Alibis against accusations of sexual discrimination customarily invoke the problems inherent in "natural" female attributes: women are not given managerial jobs because they are not "risk takers," or they tend to get too "emotionally involved." Their consignment to the home and family is justified because these are seen as their "natural" place, and this is reinforced by their "natural" interests in children, sewing, homemaking, and so on. Even women who might have to admit to such interests, or such personal attributes, could now argue that there is nothing natural about them: they are socially produced. What to do about this is a little more difficult; women cannot be granted an exemption from cultural processes, but they can interrogate their function so that women's subordination no longer has the alibi of being "natural." For recent feminist theorists, post-Freudian notions of subjectivity have been widely used to examine the social construction of the feminine and to frame attempts to intervene in that social process.

More widely, the notion of subjectivity has provoked studies into the construction of subjectivities by and within specific historical movements. Media studies and screen theory have looked at the way the medium, and in many cases a particular text, constructs a specific range of subjectivities for the reader or viewer. There is a rich controversy around this work, particularly that published in *Screen* magazine, but it has been useful in underlining the fact that we respond to the invitation of a text by inhabiting a designated or constructed subjectivity. This subjectivity may well be quite different from what we construct for ourselves in reading other texts. Socially produced subjectivities do not need to be consistent (Morley 1986, 42).[3] David Morley's research on people's use of television found that viewers could adopt internally contradictory positions in response, say, to particular items within one television news program, inhabiting a range of competing and apparently inconsistent subjectivities. Nor would a viewer's response to a television news program be framed solely by that program; clearly, a range of social, economic, and cultural forces will "over-determine" the way in which the viewer sees him- or herself as the subject of that program's address.

This foreshadows an area that will be followed up in Chapter 3—the degree to which texts construct the subjectivities of their audiences. Morley's work is opposed to that of the majority of the *Screen* critics in insisting that the reader is a social, as well as a textual, subject: that is, the text is not the only or even the major mechanism producing the reader's subjectivity—even while he or she is reading the text.

Texts, Contexts, and Discourses

As will have become plain by now, cultural studies is a complicated field in which the role of theory is crucial. The problem of conceptualizing the social relations that make up our popular cultures defeats small-scale empirical analyses. One really does have to develop some overarching theoretical position that can organize one's practice coherently. However, the complexity of the field has meant that while all the variant approaches share a view of culture as a political, historical process, constructing everyday life, their specific approaches and their chosen subject matter can look very different.

Current work in cultural studies includes histories of popular movements, particularly in the Britain of the nineteenth century, that focus on subcultures and the gaps in official histories; Lacanian studies of subjectivities, particularly the construction of feminine subjectivities in particular contexts and through particular media; "ethnographic" studies of subcultures within contemporary urban societies, attempting to analyze the subcultures' interpretations of their own cultural experiences; the analysis of specific media, such as television, in an attempt to understand the structure of their "languages," and their relation to ideologies; the analysis of particular textual forms—from popular fiction to music video—in order to pin down their formal and ideological characteristics; studies of media economy, drawing on the major traditions of the 1960s and 1970s in Britain, and tracking the production of culture through media institutions and government cultural policy; a combination of textual analysis and ethnographic audience studies that attempt to find out how, primarily, television audiences use the medium; and the continuing enterprise of theoretical clarification of the whole field of study. This is not an exhaustive list, but it at least suggests the breadth and depth of the field.

To see that such diverse activities belong to the same broad enterprise is not easy, but it is important to recognize that despite this variety of topics and perspectives, the object inspected is the same: culture. The methodologies I have outlined—structuralism and semiotics in particular—and the central terms I have glossed—signification, representation, texts, subjectivity, ideology—are applied throughout the field, too. Nevertheless, it was customary for quite some time to perceive cultural studies as split by a broad methodological and theoretical division between structuralists and "culturalists."

The structuralism/culturalism split will occupy us again later, but for the moment it is worth outlining as a debate. Structuralists saw culture as the primary object of study, and approached it most often by way of the analysis of representative textual forms. The forms and structures that produced cultural meanings were the center of their attention, and so they tended to be less interested in the culturally specific, the historical, or the differences between forms than they were in tracking overarching characteristics and similarities. "Culturalists," and British historians in particular, resisted structuralism; it was too deterministic, too comprehensive a definition of the force of ideology. Identified particularly with Raymond Williams and E. P. Thompson, culturalism retained a stronger sense of the power of human agency against history and ideology; that is, culturalists argued that determining forces could be resisted, and that history could be affected by radical individual effort. The focus of their work was resolutely parochial—on the "peculiarities of the English." Where structuralism took on a particularly European, even "foreign" image, culturalism seemed to be the homegrown, British alternative.[4]

This structuralism/culturalism split always was a little too neat: it delimited as well as divided the field. It is now a much less applicable distinction, anyway, as Tony Bennett has argued in his introduction to *Popular Culture and Social Relations* (Bennett et al. 1986). Since the interest in the work of Italian theorist Antonio Gramsci, there is a real cause to suggest that the split no longer occupies as important a place as it once did. Gramsci's theories of hegemony will be explored further in later chapters, but suffice to say here that he resolves a number of problems seen to hamper the application of Althusser's theory of ideology. Most important, Gramsci offers a less mechanistic notion of determination, and of the domination of a ruling class. Where Althusser's explanation implies that cultural change is almost impossible and ideological struggle futile, Gramsci explains how change is built into the system. He acknowledges the power of the individual human agent within culture by analyzing not only the overdetermining structure that produces the individual, but also the range of possibilities produced for the individual. Finally, Gramsci's work is historicized, addressing the construction of cultural power at specific historical moments.

In practical terms, the differences between the major tendencies in cultural studies have revealed themselves in the ways through which individual authors have approached their subject matter. Here, too, we can see two broad, if not always mutually exclusive, categories of approach: one either works through a set of textual formations from which one begins to read constitutive cultural codes or one examines the political, historical, economic, or social context in which texts were produced and thus tracks the codes from the culture into the text. These days, neither approach is as discrete as once was the case, but the early days of textual analysis did tend to see texts out of context, to ignore their placement within a specific historical juncture, while contextual studies tended to deny the need to interpret specific representations at all. Now, however, since the active relationship between audiences and texts has been acknowledged, the boundary between textual and contextual work, between representation and history, is breaking down.

At this point, then, it is probably easier to talk of an agreed-upon set of cultural studies and practices and approaches from which analysts may choose than at any previous period. We now have wide agreement on the usefulness of the more sophisticated notions of ideology drawn from Gramsci; textual analysis is much more historical, more socially coded, because it now takes account not just of signs and signification but of their combinations in particular, culturally specific discourses. The development of the term *discourse* has itself been significant; it refers to socially produced groups of ideas or ways of thinking that can be tracked in individual texts or groups of texts, but that also demand to be located within wider historical and social structures or relations.

The range of discursive analyses is wide. Richard Dyer, for instance, has extended his useful work on the semiotic function of film stars—what they signify independently of the characters they might play—to the examination of particular star images and their social meanings. Dyer (1986) looks, for instance, at Marilyn Monroe and traces her enclosure within discourses of sexuality during the 1950s. These discourses constructed sexuality in what were then new ways: sex was connected with the core of the self; its expression was a mechanism for psychological health and its centrality to life a rebuttal of notions of sexual guilt and prudery. The key texts in which such discourses could be located are the early issues of *Playboy*, with their emphasis on guilt-free, innocent sexuality, and Monroe is enveloped within the *Playboy* ethic almost literally: she was the magazine's first centerfold. Other examples of discursive analysis, tracking ideological discourses across texts, institutions, and history, include Elaine Showalter's (1987) account of the nineteenth-century treatment of madness, which argues that the institutions and technologies employed were a consequence of insanity's construction as a "female malady," and Angela McRobbie's (1984) analysis of dance clubs and young girls, which examines the way in which the pleasures of dance are set aside as the licensed domain of the female.

Applying the Principles

In this section, I want to apply the principles I have been summarizing, to show them in action in a "reading" of a text. This will demonstrate what kind of knowledge actually emerges from a cultural studies approach, and might reinforce definitions of some basic terms. What follows is not, however, meant to be a definitive reading of its subject; rather, it is a set of notes that might indicate the shape of further interpretation.

Our topic is not a television program or a film, or a photograph, but a cultural and political figure—ex-Lieutenant-Colonel Oliver North. I want to suggest how we might employ cultural studies principles to interpret him as a sign. And, I stress, these suggestions may have little to do with a *material* Oliver North you could call on the phone; this is a reading of the cultural construction of Oliver North.

We could start with some account of North's placement within the institutions he served, analyzing the ideological formations through which he was inserted into the culture. Or we could provide a history of the patriotic/military discourses within which he makes the most sense; this would involve a study of state institutions and their political and social

Photo 1.2. Oliver North, with his wife Betty by his side, speaks to newsmen at his lawyer's Washington office (*Reprinted with kind permission of AAP.*)

histories. For our purposes here, I am content to start with a text, using it as a means of access to the codes, myths, discourses, and ideologies that give North his meaning. While this is only a beginning, I think we will find it can take us quite some distance.

Photo 1.2 depicts Oliver North at the press conference after his conviction on three of the twelve criminal charges connected with the Iran-Contra scandal. We might begin in the same way we did with our analysis of the Marcos photo, by noting the major signs and their arrangement within the frame. North and his wife obviously dominate the photo, but their relationship is significantly different from that of Ferdinand and Imelda Marcos in our earlier example. As the caption states unequivocally, Betty North is by her husband's side both physically and figuratively. The two are standing close together, North drawing support from his wife. He is still the dominant figure, but his wife could not look more committed to the cause of proving her husband's innocence. The positioning of the other major sign in the photo, the American flag, facilitates such a reading. North's relation to the flag and what it represents is, at least, ambiguous; he can be constructed, as we shall see, as either defending or betraying the ideals it symbolizes. Its inclusion in the photo, and its central position within the frame, integrates North and his cause with that of the United States, although one cannot dismiss the possibility of reading the photograph as massively ironic.

North's expression, that of his wife, and his posture are important signifiers too, but in order to make sense of them we need to move outside this text, and consider how its meaning is produced at least partly through its relation to other photos of Oliver North. The relations between this picture and others of Oliver North are called *intertextual* relations, and they frame our view of him in this example. Photos of North have exploited a limited repertoire of signifiers: early in his career as a newsworthy person, he customarily appeared in his uniform, his short haircut signifying his commitment to the defense forces and thus silently denying the possibility of dishonesty; he characteristically appeared in three-quarter profile, jaw thrust forward determinedly, often in mid-speech, as in this example; surprisingly often he has been shot from slightly below, looking slightly upward—this has an ennobling, mythologizing effect. The upward look, in particular, had the ambiguous consequence of signifying a respectful but dogged defiance while also invoking his willingness to serve his country, his deference to his superiors and ultimately to the flag. Given the specific nature of his defense (that he was "only following orders"), and given the role he developed as the representative of an interventionist foreign policy, the repetition of this posture is of some significance. He is certainly more newsworthy, more culturally resonant, within such constructions than he would be if he were to be enclosed entirely within discourses of, for instance, criminality: if, for instance, he was always shot from above, looking down, in disheveled clothing or hiding his face from the camera.

To take the reading a little further we need to move closer to the discourses implicated in the text. When we connect these signifiers with the mental concept they refer to, we immediately activate competing sets of "explanations" of, or myths about, North's activities. Photos of North, particularly those of him in uniform, touch off sharply opposed myths for different readers: crudely, what Oliver North signifies to one group is a dangerous, "Rambotic," military individualism, while to another group he signifies the plainspoken, innocent, and self-sacrificing hero of John Wayne (or Ronald Reagan!) movies. Interestingly, despite the divergent subjectivities producing these different readings, within both interpretations North emerges as a quintessentially *American* figure; hence, the inevitability of the flag in the photo. The myths and discourses of American nationalism are deeply implicated in North's cultural significance, and since they are themselves far from unified, we should not be surprised at their participation in the contradictions within the meanings of Oliver North.

When we "read" such texts we need to be aware that language is *polysemic;* that is, it can mean different things to different readers. In North's case, the informing myths aroused by the signifiers in this photo are not only various, but almost diametrically opposed. As a sign, North is a battleground of competing categories: from rogue to national hero to CIA conspirator to scapegoat.

The resolution of this battle has shifted over time: "Olliemania" probably peaked during the 1987 congressional hearings, but the degree of moral loathing directed at North was probably at its peak then too. As time has gone on, however, North's role has been most consistently constructed as the scapegoat for higher-placed figures, with Ollie-mania taking on the role of a sideshow. Support for North's acquittal, however, came from both those who felt he had done nothing wrong and those on the opposite side of the political fence who felt he should not pay for the crimes of his superiors. This might explain the figures published in *Time* magazine (May 15, 1989) reporting that 53 percent of a survey sample were against North going to jail, 45 percent thought he should be pardoned, and 67 percent believed George Bush had still to come clean on his own part in the scandal.

North himself has indicated some awareness of his own signifying function, and press images of him have been remarkably restricted in the repertoire of meanings activated. This photograph is itself an example of that: contributing myths connect him with his role as a family man, staunchly supported by his wife, unjustly accused of serving his country *too* well, but man enough to fight for his hearing without whining or attempting to blame anyone else. He has had help in this, in the media's tacit agreement to recycle images that ennoble him in order to maintain the heat on the administration he served. The most widely used photograph of North in the Western press was his taking of the oath at the congressional hearings, the perfect image of the model soldier. This encouraged the view of him as a scapegoat, a small but loyal player taking the rap for his superiors. The circulation of such an image prolonged and fueled speculation about just who North was serving: Who was the subject of that dutiful, selfless gaze? From North's point of view, such images can only have done his cause good, but those who would read this text in opposition to such a construction might be tempted to see it as further evidence of corruption and duplicity.

This reading, so far, has been relatively culturally specific in that it has suggested readings likely to be negotiated within North's own culture. From outside the United States, the meanings may take on different inflections: the major story outside the United States has been Ollie-mania, the status North enjoyed, and to a lesser extent still enjoys, with some sections of the American public, as a national hero. In these "foreign" constructions, North still operates as a signifier of a particular view of American politics and values: the difference, perhaps, is that very rarely are these values endorsed. Nevertheless, for the foreign press, North the personality is a minor figure compared to North the symbol of American foreign policy under Reagan; most of the Western press have used North as the location for a critique of that foreign policy.

This is a useful reminder. A text such as this, and a genre of such texts, always needs to be placed into a historical context. To outline the particular historical conjuncture that produced North's actions and his subsequent celebrity is beyond my brief here, but a reading of this text would not be complete without some consideration of such a context. In fact, there is probably little point in simply "reading" Oliver North if we do not explore the sources of his constitutive myths in American culture.

An example of such an exploration is Larry Grossberg's (1988) attempt to link North's celebrity with a revival of politically conservative ideologies within America and other Western societies; Grossberg talks of North as one of a new breed of American hero, a breed that includes Rambo, Han Solo of the *Star Wars* films, Sonny Crockett of *Miami Vice*, and—centrally—Ronald Reagan. John Fiske (1987b, 112) has linked the representations of lead characters in current TV cop and private eye shows (*Magnum, P.I.*, *Miami Vice*, *Simon & Simon*) with the representation of American experience in Vietnam (*China Beach* and *Tour of Duty*). He sees both trends as working to renovate images of masculine power, legitimating the power of those "in control of 'The Law' to impose that law upon others." This, too, could be part of the context into which our text can be placed. If Grossberg is right, or if Fiske is right, the appropriate intertextual context for this analysis may be not other photos of Oliver North but the representations of law and authority in American television drama, or the specific ideological effects of the reconstruction of the Vietnam War on TV and in popular culture generally. This may, in turn, connect us with the restatement of conservative (naturalized through the term *traditional*) values in American and British politics. Whatever we might conclude, it is important to stress that, ultimately, North's meaning has to be given a specific history, not just a set of texts.

Notes

1 This can be found in Saussure's *A Course in General Linguistics* (1960). A simple account of Saussure's work is found in Culler (1976).

2 See Chapter 5 for discussion of the media histories; for an example of Foucault's work, see *Discipline and Punish: The Birth of the Prison* (1979).

3 As Morley puts it, "The same man may be simultaneously a productive worker, a trade union member, a supporter of the Social Democratic Party, a consumer, a racist, a home owner, a wife beater and a Christian."

4 For the classical location of the discussion of this split, see Hall (1981).

2

The British Tradition: A Short History

My account of cultural studies' "first principles" has inevitably foregrounded the European theoretical influence. This should not obscure the fact that British cultural studies has very specific historical roots in postwar Britain, where the revival of capitalist industrial production, the establishment of the welfare state, and the Western powers' unity in opposition to Russian communism were all inflected into a representation of a "new" Britain. This was a culture where class was said to have disappeared, where postwar Britain could be congratulated for its putative discontinuity with prewar Britain, and where modernity and the Americanization of popular culture were signs of a new future. The precise conditions of British or, more particularly, English culture were subjected to especially keen scrutiny in the attempt to understand these changes and their cultural, economic, and political effects.

British cultural studies emerged from this context. But it was not the only product. Within the social sciences there was a substantial revival of interest in the nature of working-class culture and communities. Addressing the widely held thesis that the working class had become "bourgeois"—that is, that their living conditions and their ideologies had become indistinguishable from those of the middle class—were a number of studies of urban working-class life that documented the survival of working-class value systems and social structures. The work of the Institute of Community Studies, and a proliferation of participant-observer studies of working-class communities, attempted to get inside these structures, often abandoning the conventions of scientific objectivity in order to do so (for an outline of this movement, see Laing 1986, ch. 2).

Interest in British popular culture came from other quarters as well; in the early 1950s, the Independent Group (IG) was examining the visual arts, architecture, graphic design, and pop art, and establishing itself at the Institute of Contemporary Arts (ICA) in London. This movement, like cultural studies later, was primarily interested in everyday, not elite, culture and focused particularly on the influence of American popular culture on British life—an influence that was largely to the movements' adherents' taste. In fact, as Chambers (1986) points out, "the very term 'Pop Art', coined by the art critic Lawrence Alloway in the early 1950s, was intended to describe not a new movement in painting but the products of popular culture" (p. 201).

The IG's relish for postwar culture, style, and modernity was not, however, widely shared within the British academic world. Indeed, the major academic tradition I will trace into British cultural studies was implacably opposed to popular culture. The so-called "culture and civilization" tradition was concerned by the development of popular culture, and the concomitant decline of more "organic" communal or folk cultures that proceeded from the spread of industrialization during the late eighteenth and nineteenth centuries. Matthew Arnold's *Culture and Anarchy*, published in 1869, warned of the likely consequences of the spread of this urban, "philistine culture," which was accelerating with the extension of literacy and democracy. Where class divisions had once been sufficiently rigid to confine political and economic power to one class, industrialization and the growth of the middle class and an urban working class had blurred these divisions. The aesthetic barrenness of the culture of the new "masses" worried Arnold, who felt that such a culture must necessarily fail to equip its subjects for the social and political roles they would play within democratic society.

The "culture and civilization" tradition is most clearly defined, however, by its response to the twentieth-century technologies that radically extended the purchase of "mass culture"—in particular, those that enabled the mass distribution of cultural forms such as the popular novel, the women's magazine, the cinema, the popular press, the popular song, and, of course, television. Between the wars, general concern about the moral and aesthetic content of culture began to concentrate on its forms of representation (the mass media in particular) and to become identified with the work of a circle around the English literary critical journal *Scrutiny*: F. R. Leavis, his wife Q. D. Leavis, Denys Thompson, and L. C. Knights. Relating the "abuse" of language to specific social and moral effects, the *Scrutiny* group produced some of the earliest critiques of "mass culture": F. R. Leavis and Denys Thompson's *Culture and Environment* (1933) and Q. D. Leavis's *Fiction and the Reading Public* (1932), which looked at, respectively, advertising and popular fiction. T. S. Eliot, although often an opponent of the *Scrutiny* line in literary criticism, also analyzed the forms and content of popular culture in order to attack the classless "new" culture in *Notes Towards a Definition of Culture* in 1948.

These approaches were unashamedly elitist; from their perspective, popular culture was to be deplored for its deficiencies—for its lack of "moral seriousness" or of aesthetic value. The mass culture of contemporary England was unfavorably compared to an earlier, albeit mythical, folk culture located in some past formation of the "garden of England." Industrialization, mass communication, and technology were all seen to be inimical to this earlier, more organic version of British existence; it was as if the entire twentieth century were intrinsically "anti-British." The specific concern with mass culture was generalized in order to criticize other popular cultural forms, including many of the forms of everyday life within industrial societies. Within such a critique, the products of popular culture "existed only in order to be condemned, to be found wanting on one ground or another":

> as corrosive of the capacity for ethical and aesthetic discrimination, or—and most enduringly—as worse than whatever forms of popular culture may have preceded

> them, a corruption and dilution of an earlier and supposedly, sturdier, more robust and organic phase in the development of the people's culture. (Bennett 1981, 6)

The account of the everyday life of the ordinary citizen produced by these studies was extremely remote and patronizing. As Bennett (1981) says, it was a discourse of the "cultured" about the culture of those without "culture": "Popular culture was approached from a distance and gingerly, held out at arm's length by outsiders who clearly lacked any fondness for or participation in the forms they were studying. It was always the culture of 'other people' that was at issue" (p. 6).

This elitism was made to seem more "natural" and legitimate by the fact that those expressing it had similar class backgrounds; the prewar means of entrance to higher education more or less ensured this. However, the expansion of educational opportunities within Britain after the war, and the spread of adult education as a means of postwar reconstruction as well as an arm of the welfare state, eventually had an effect on the class origins of those who inherited this intellectual tradition. The "scholarship boys and girls" (those admitted to universities and colleges on merit, regardless of income or background) included a significant number from the working or lower-middle class. Key figures in the next generation of cultural criticism in Britain—Raymond Williams and Richard Hoggart, for two—were working-class, and had a personal involvement with this despised sphere of culture. As Bennett (1981) goes on to point out:

> This has altered the entire tone of the debate as a sense of liking for and, often, deep involvement in the forms studied has replaced the aloof and distant approach "from above", and as the need to *understand* the effects of popular culture on ourselves has displaced the need to *condemn* it because of what it does to "other people". (p. 6)

Certainly the influence of the scholarship students was important in recasting the examination of popular culture in Britain in the 1950s and 1960s. Even now, many of those working in cultural studies tend to foreground their origins as being in some respects from outside the mainstream of British academic culture. Links with the early foundations of cultural studies in adult education are also relevant here; Williams, Hoggart, and Hall all worked as adult education tutors early in their careers, and Williams acknowledges debts to this work in *Culture and Society 1780–1950* (1966), *Communications* (1962), and *The Long Revolution* (1975). Working as an adult education tutor brought one into touch with a range of subcultural groups not normally encountered at university, whose membership in a popular rather than an elite culture needed to be accepted and understood by their teachers. One can imagine how this might provoke some radical rethinking for a standard Leavisite of the time.

Others were also having to do some rethinking at this time. The cultural and ideological gap between schoolteachers and their pupils was widening as popular culture became more pervasive. The cultural development of the schoolchild became a battleground, defended by the "civilizing" objectives of the education system but assailed by the illicit pleasures of popular culture. The spread of commercial television across Britain in the late 1950s increased the urgency with which such concerns were felt. Stuart Laing (1986, 194) suggests that the 1960 National Union of Teachers (NUT) conference, titled "Popular Culture and Personal Responsibility," was a seminal event at which these debates were aired and structured.

The National Union of Teachers conference was aimed at finding ways of dealing with popular culture that did not dismiss it out of hand and thus acknowledged its place within the everyday lives of school pupils, but that nonetheless taught some principles of discrimination—the exercise of choice, the "personal responsibility" of the title—to guide pupils' consumption of cultural forms. This was a liberalization of the Leavis line—it made it possible to argue that certain popular forms (such as jazz, the blues, or the cinema) had recognizable aesthetic concerns and traditions. But it was still, residually, a high-culture view of popular culture, interested in aesthetic rather than social pleasures and meanings.

It was, however, an influential conference; Hoggart and Williams both spoke, together with the British home secretary, Rab Butler, Stuart Hall, writer Arnold Wesker, and film director Karel Reisz. Williams acknowledges the conference's implications in *Communications*, and two books emerged directly out of its deliberations: Hall and Whannel's *The Popular Arts* (1964) and Denys Thompson's *Discrimination and Popular Culture* (1964, rev. ed. 1973[1]). Hall and Whannel's book will be dealt with later, but Thompson's collection is a wonderfully clear demonstration of the confusion engendered by the combination of an elite method of analysis of and a democratic-humanist interest in the forms of everyday life. The essays in *Discrimination and Popular Culture* adopt extremely varied perspectives on the collective objective of counteracting the debasement of standards resulting from the "misuse" of the press, radio, cinema, and television. On the one hand we have the moral panic motivating David Holbrook's literary analysis of the "dismal" and "limited world" of popular magazines, while on the other hand we have Graham Martin's sober institutional study of newspapers, which notes how simplistic and misleading such literary analysis can be when applied to popular culture (Thompson 1973, 80). Rather than following Holbrook's lead, Martin relates the styles and contents of the different products of the press to their social roles. Other contributors attempt to legitimate the popular arts by discovering hitherto unnoticed homologies between popular and high art; this effort is almost parodic: "groups like Pink Floyd and The Who are concerned mainly with instrumental sounds, with developing their music along lines sometimes as abstract as those of the classical symphonist" (p. 144). It is a measure of the distance we have traveled in understanding rock music that this kind of comment rarely appears these days.

Of course, Denys Thompson's introduction is much more sensible than this, and the collection has been influential; it was still supporting courses on popular culture well into the mid-1970s. But the babble of competing voices it licenses to speak signifies the failure of the analysts of popular culture, in 1964, to articulate a clear sense of their objectives and methods. The NUT conference is a sign of the felt need for more appropriate ways of understanding the problem of culture; *Discrimination and Popular Culture* indicates that while the culture and civilization tradition may have asked important questions, it lacked the equipment to address them. It is time to begin tracing the development of alternative methodologies and objectives, and my starting points are the conventional but necessary ones: the work of Hoggart, Williams, Hall, and the Birmingham Centre for Contemporary Cultural Studies.

Hoggart and *The Uses of Literacy*

Richard Hoggart was born to a working-class family in Leeds in the last year of the Great War, was educated at his hometown university, and served in the British Army during World War II. From 1946 to 1959, Hoggart was an adult education tutor at the University of Hull, teaching literature. Laing (1986, ch. 7) suggests that this experience was crucial to Hoggart's definition of culture and the place of education within it. The typical participant in adult education (usually an individual who for economic, personal, or class reasons was denied or had forgone normal entry into higher education) is also the reader about whom, and to whom, *The Uses of Literacy* (1958) appears to have been written. Certainly, there were few opportunities for Hoggart to "convert" conclusively to another set of class positions; he was teaching those who had come from much the same background as himself, and interpreting for them a set of cultural standards that may have seemed foreign but nevertheless prevailed.

More than most academic books, *The Uses of Literacy* invokes the personal experience of the author—not always as direct evidence, it must be said, but often through the admission of a personal partiality, or even a worried ambivalence. This has some benefits; in those chapters that outline the "full rich life" Hoggart remembers as typical of the working class—in particular the linkages among forms of popular entertainment, the social practices of the neighborhood, and family relations—Hoggart's personal experience provides a sense of "authenticity" that is among the book's most distinctive attributes. *The Uses of Literacy* is not primarily confessional, however. The book's method is to employ the analytical skills provided by Hoggart's literary training, often to great effect: the analysis of the discourses and conventions of the performance of popular song, for instance, is interesting and persuasive, and the discussion of popular fiction still repays attention.

It is important to recognize Hoggart's achievement in applying, as successfully as he did, the analytical protocols of literary studies to a wider range of cultural products: music, newspapers, magazines, and popular fiction, in particular. The book's most significant achievement, however, is the demonstration of the interconnections among various aspects of public culture—pubs, working-men's clubs, magazines, and sports, for instance—and the structures of an individual's private, everyday life—family roles, gender relations, language patterns, the community's "common sense." Hoggart describes working-class life in the prewar period as a complex whole, in which public values and private practices are tightly intertwined. Subsequently, he tends not to separate out specific elements as "good" or "bad"; Hoggart acknowledges the social determinants of even the regressive aspects of working-class living, such as domestic and neighborhood violence. However, while Hoggart's account of traditional urban working-class life is admirable in this sense of its complex interconnectedness, it is nevertheless a nostalgic account of an organic, rather than a constructed, culture. In common with the rest of the culture and civilization tradition, Hoggart looks back to a cultural Fall, when earlier versions of working-class culture were lost. Hoggart differs from Leavis or Eliot only in that his Fall seems to have taken place during the 1930s rather than the nineteenth century, so that his description of the urban working class of this period bears all the attributes of a folk rather than a popular culture.[2]

Nostalgia is central to the book's project. Hoggart's establishment of the richness of prewar working-class culture in the first half of *The Uses of Literacy* is employed to heighten the second half's contrast with the newer "mass" popular culture of postwar England. This contrast stresses the latter's lack of organicism, its failure to emerge from specific roots within the lived cultures of ordinary people. In the analysis of *this* version of popular culture, Hoggart is less inclined to suspend aesthetic judgment, or to take the culture on its own terms. The book regards modern popular music, American television, the jukebox, popular crime and romance novels, and cheap magazines as intrinsically phony. They are accused of displacing, but providing no substitute for, a popular culture experientially connected to the social conditions of those who produce and consume it. Not only are the relations of production and consumption a problem, but—almost inevitably—the quality of mass-produced culture is, too. Hoggart spends much of the second half of the book invoking Leavisite aesthetic standards against these cultural products. Such a practice is not a significant feature of his portrait of the "full rich life" of the past, but he clearly feels authorized to criticize the newer, worrying trends. Indeed, Hoggart anticipates the readers' support in this enterprise; he admits to assuming their agreement with his judgment of the "decent," the "healthy," the "serious," and the "trivial" in his analyses of popular culture texts (p. 344). The result of Hoggart's critical practice is a book about the importance of such distinctions, of standards of discrimination, in the production and consumption of popular cultural forms.

The Uses of Literacy observes conflicting social and theoretical allegiances: to both the culture and civilization tradition from which its ideological assumptions and analytical practices proceed, and to a working-class cultural and political tradition that acknowledges significance in the *whole* of the cultural field. The contradictions thus produced are apparent in the book's method, as it moves from an affectionate account of the social function of popular culture to an evaluative critique of its textual forms, exposing both the author's ambivalence about the class he has left and the limitations of the theoretical tradition he has joined.

These problems are clearest when Hoggart deals with specific examples of this new mass culture. While he well describes the complexity of the constitution of the cultural field of his youth, he is blind and deaf to the complexity of, let alone the functions served by, the "full rich life" of contemporary working-class youths. A notorious example of his alienation from his subject is his description of "the juke-box boys":

> Like the cafes I described in an earlier chapter, the milk-bars indicate at once, in the nastiness of their modernistic knick-knacks, their glaring showiness, an aesthetic breakdown so complete that, in comparison with them, the layout of the living rooms in some of the poor homes from which the customers come seems to speak of a tradition as balanced and civilized as an eighteenth century townhouse. . . . the "nickelodeon" is allowed to blare out so that the noise would be sufficient to fill a good-sized ballroom, rather than a converted shop in the main street. The young men waggle one shoulder or stare, as desperately as Humphrey Bogart, across the tubular chairs.
>
> Compared even with the pub around the corner, this is all a peculiarly thin and pallid form of dissipation, a sort of spiritual dry-rot amid the odour of boiled milk. (pp. 247–48)

He goes on to describe the young men as "the directionless and tamed helots of a machine minding class":

> If they seem to consist so far chiefly of those of poorer intelligence or from homes subject to special strains, that is probably due to the strength of a moral fibre which most cultural providers for working-class people are helping to de-nature. . . . The hedonistic but passive barbarian who rides in a fifty-horse-power bus for threepence, to see a five million dollar film for one-and-eightpence, is not simply a social oddity; he is a portent. (p. 250)

As one group of critics has said, this prose could almost—"in its lack of concreteness and 'felt' qualities—have been written by one of the new 'hack' writers [Hoggart] so perceptively analyses" elsewhere (Hall and Jefferson 1976, 19).[3]

The book, nonetheless, has enjoyed substantial influence. Stuart Laing (1986, 184) has referred to Richard Dyer's proposition that Hoggart's construction of working-class life has influenced the long-running TV serial *Coronation Street*, which takes place in a fictionalized northern environment Reyner Banham satirically terms "Hoggartsborough." The book's most enduring theoretical value, however, lies in the fact that it reveals, in Critcher's (1979) words, the "network of shared cultural meanings which sustains relationships between different facets of culture" (p. 19), and the complexity of this network. If some of these meanings are subjected to inappropriate judgments, the book does nevertheless open up culture as a field of forms and practices, and asks us to understand them.

As a result of *The Uses of Literacy*, Hoggart became a highly visible contributor to public arguments about the media and popular culture, and is still invoked as an authority in the area. After a period of four years as professor of English at Birmingham, Hoggart became the founding director of the Centre for Contemporary Cultural Studies (CCCS) at the University of Birmingham in 1964. He remained there until 1968, when he left to become assistant director-general at UNESCO. Hoggart's work at the Centre continued, significantly developed and reframed by Stuart Hall, but his own writing since *The Uses of Literacy* has not exercised the same influence on the theoretical development of cultural studies. The role of the theoretical pioneer passed over to Raymond Williams; it is to his work we turn now.

Raymond Williams

Like Hoggart, Raymond Williams came from a working-class background—in his case, a Welsh village. Also like Hoggart, Williams spent most of his early career as an adult education tutor, for Oxford University, from 1946 to 1960. The influence of this role was considerable: Williams's involvement in the journal *Politics and Letters*, a journal that aimed at uniting left-wing working-class politics with Leavisite literary criticism, was directed toward an audience of "adult education tutors and their students" (Laing 1986, 198), and his first book, *Culture and Society* (1966), came directly out of an adult education class on the idea of culture in T. S. Eliot, F. R. Leavis, Clive Bell, and Matthew Arnold. *Communications* (1962) explicitly acknowledges its debt to Williams's time in adult education.

Williams's theoretical influence over the development of cultural studies has arguably been more profound than any other, and it began with the publication of *Culture and Society* in 1958. *Culture and Society* is a book of literary history, but with a crucial difference; its focus is not on literary texts for their own sake but for their relationship to an idea. Williams follows a thread in English thought and writing through the nineteenth and twentieth centuries in order to establish the cultural grounding of ideas and their representations. The book employs a version of Leavisite close textual analysis, and has certainly had a life on textbook lists as a consequence of that (in fact, that is how I first read the book myself). But its movement is back from the idiosyncrasies of the text to movements within the society, relating specific representations to the culture's ways of seeing. This is the real strength of *Culture and Society*: the reader's continual sense of an entire field of study emerging from the clarity and persistence of the book's pursuit of the connections between cultural products and cultural relations.

To read *Culture and Society* now is to be impressed by its prescience, and by how continually its insights and objectives outrun the supply of available theoretical support. That the book does not actually constitute the field itself should come as no surprise; most of cultural studies' constitutive theoretical positions—from structuralism, from critical Marxism, from semiotics—were simply unavailable to most British readers at the time it was written.[4]

Williams's work in this period enjoys a complicated relationship with the Leavisite tradition. It emphasizes practical criticism and offers a version of English cultural history that in many ways accords with Leavis's, invoking an "uncertain nostalgia for the 'organic', 'common culture'" of an England that "predates and is more 'English' than industrialised England" (Eagleton 1978, 40). However, Williams's view of culture cannot be entirely contained within this tradition; his celebrated opening account of the four meanings of the word *culture* includes that of culture as a "whole way of life, material, intellectual and spiritual" (Williams 1966, 16). Williams is interested in the whole of cultural experience, its meaning and "patterning": accordingly, he finds himself interested not just in literary or philosophical uses of language but in "actual language," "the words and sequences which particular men and women have used in trying to give meaning to their experience" (p. 18). He is unaware of structuralist explorations of language systems as a means to understanding the workings of culture, and so is unable to develop this interest further; as he says, with unconscious understatement, "the area of experience to which the book refers has produced its own difficulties in terms of method" (p. 17). In *Culture and Society,* Williams "still has to discover the idiom which will allow him to extend 'practical criticism' and organicist social positions into fully socialist analysis" (Eagleton 1978, 39). What he *does* discover is that culture is a key category, because it connects his two major interests—literary analysis and social inquiry.

The category of "culture," however, cannot be said to be fully developed in *Culture and Society,* although it pervades the book's arguments. Williams is still caught among the four definitions the book canvasses. This is most noticeable in the chapters dealing with the twentieth century, where Williams collides head-on with the culture and civilization tradition. His account of Eliot's formulation of culture as "a whole way of life" is critical, and his discussion of Leavis rejects the text-based approach to the mass media and popular culture upon which most Leavisite critiques depend. "It is obvious," says Williams, "that the ways of feeling and thinking embodied in such institutions as the popular press, advertising and the cinema cannot finally be criticised without reference to a way of life" (p. 251). And while he is both critical of and distanced from traditional Marxism in this book, he does imply the relevance of Marxist perspectives:

> The one vital lesson which the nineteenth century had to learn—and learn urgently because of the very magnitude of its changes—was that the basic economic organisation could not be separated and excluded from its moral and

> intellectual concerns. Society and individual experience were alike being transformed, and this driving agency, which there were no adequate traditional procedures to understand and interpret, had, in depth, to be taken into consciousness. (p. 271)

The economic basis of society, in short, was centrally implicated in any question of culture. Although Williams then moves into a ritual attack on economic determinism, it is clear that the Arnoldian definition of culture as "the best that has been thought and said" is subordinated to a more social, historical, and materialist view. Culture is talked of both as an idea, its history "a record of our meanings and our definitions," *and* as sets of material forms, their history that of the "changed conditions of our common life" (p. 285).

While Williams insists that "there are in fact no masses; there are only ways of seeing people as masses" (p. 289), his rejection of the mass culture critique is less than categorical. Like Thompson's contributors, Williams attempts to legitimate certain aspects of mass culture at the expense of others—the "good" against the "bad." The book is dated by this strategy, but to Williams's credit he sees that it is futile to attempt the analysis of a "whole way of life" with a set of standards and analytical tools developed in order to establish the preeminence of one small section of it. Eventually, Williams has to admit that democratic notions of equality are among the casualties of a Leavisite approach to culture: "An insistence on equality," he says, "may be, in practice, a denial of value." Value, the proposition that some things are inherently and permanently better than others, is not an innocent category; Williams warns against its function as dogma, as a means of legitimating existing ideological structures. Most important, he deplores the invocation of value as a means of denigrating the everyday lives of the vast majority of ordinary individuals. He characterizes this as an act of contempt, the sign of a lack of interest in "men and their common efforts" (p. 306). Such a position is the reverse of Williams's own.

Reading the concluding sections of *Culture and Society*, one can see Williams's own position hardening, focusing on culture as the preeminent object of attention, and laying the foundations for the more fully argued and conclusive establishment of the category in *The Long Revolution*. In this next book Williams finally breaks with the literary-moral tradition that inevitably compromises *Culture and Society*.

The Long Revolution was published in 1961, a year after the NUT conference, and it reflects the increasing intensity of contemporary debates about the cultural impact of the media.[5] While Williams uses the book to clarify his own interest in culture, and to move further away from the tradition of thought that struggles to contain him in *Culture and Society*, it is, nevertheless, also a book that more closely aligns him with Hoggart's pessimistic accounts of popular culture and, in particular, the media. Unlike Hoggart's, however, Williams's pessimism is not founded entirely on aesthetic grounds, as *The Long Revolution*—significantly—focuses on the cultural institutions, their ideologies and discourses, as well as on media products. Admittedly, the book is limited by internal contradictions; it lacks a theory of cultural structure and an appropriate method of textual analysis. However, its publication was, as Stuart Hall (1980a) has said, a "seminal event in English post-war intellectual life":

> It shifted the whole ground of debate from a literary-moral to an anthropological definition of culture. But it defined the latter now as the "whole process" by means of which meanings and definitions are socially constructed and historically transformed, with literature and art as only one, specially privileged, kind of social communication. (p. 19)

This shift is the strategic one, making the development of cultural studies possible.

The Long Revolution's opening premise is that British society has been engaged in a progressive and gradual revolution: through industrialization, democratization, and cultural transformation. Since the importance of the first two historical movements was generally acknowledged, the book took on the task of establishing the comparable significance of cultural change:

> Our whole way of life, from the shape of our communities to the organisation and content of education, and from the structure of the family to the status of art and entertainment, is being profoundly affected by the progress and interaction of democracy and industry, and by the extension of communications. This deeper cultural revolution is a large part of our most significant living experience, and is being interpreted and indeed fought out, in very complex ways, in the world of art and ideas. It is when we try to correlate change of this kind with the changes covered by the disciplines of politics, economics, and communications that we discover some of the most difficult but also some of the most human questions. (Williams 1975, 12)

Dealing with these questions occupies the first section of the book, which attempts to set up a theoretical framework for the analysis of culture. This framework is clearly much advanced from that operating in *Culture and Society*. What emerges is an impressive set of definitions of terms and practices:

> Culture is a description of a particular way of life, which expresses certain meanings and values not only in art and learning but also in institutions and ordinary behaviour. The analysis of culture, from such a definition, is the clarification of the meanings and values implicit and explicit in a particular way of life, a particular culture. (p. 57)

The objects of analysis are also outlined:

> Such analysis will include . . . historical criticism . . . in which intellectual and imaginative works are analysed in relation to particular traditions and societies, but will also include analysis of elements in the way of life that to followers of other definitions are not "culture" at all: the organisation of production, the structure of the family, the structure of institutions which express or govern social relationships, the characteristic forms through which members of the society communicate. (p. 57)

Williams insists on the need for seeing the cultural process as a whole, so that the textual analysis of media products (for instance) should be conducted in relation to an analysis of the institutions and social structures producing them. The analysis of culture, then, is "the study of relationships between elements in a whole way of life," attempting to "discover the nature of the organisation which is the complex of these relationships" (p. 63).

These definitions are still relevant today. Less enduring, perhaps, are the methods Williams used to carry them out. It is difficult to read the book's focus on the constitutive "patterns" of cultural relationships, for instance, without regretting the absence of structuralist methodologies. Further, as the book presents its account of contemporary England, one notices that the development of analytic methods is subordinated to the development of a particular critique of British culture. The book is not merely an account of the long revolution, but an argument for its continuation. The latter half of *The Long Revolution* is littered with calls for a "common culture," the rejection of class culture, and the conception of a society "which could quite reasonably be organised on the basis of collective democratic institutions and the substitution of cooperative equality for competition as the principle of social and economic policy" (p. 328). Behind this is a disenchantment with contemporary English life, which stirs up the residue of nostalgic organicism from Williams's first book. The analysis, then, does not establish a methodology.

The book does make a further contribution to a theory of culture, however, in its notion of the "structure of feeling." Williams suggests that all cultures possess a particular sense of life, a "particular and characteristic colour": "this structure of feeling is the culture of a period" (p. 64). Williams's own description of the term is notoriously slippery; Tony Bennett's (1981) is more accessible, if still tentative: "The general idea . . . is that of a shared set of ways of thinking and feeling which, displaying a patterned regularity, form and are formed by the 'whole way of life' which comprises the 'lived culture' of a particular epoch, class or group" (p. 26). Even this, as Bennett implies, is too general. One must admit that, while the idea has been influential, it is hard not to sympathize with Eagleton's (1978, 33) view that Williams's description of "that firm but intangible organisation of values and perceptions" of a culture is little more than a description of ideology.

The concept's function within Williams's theory of culture, perhaps, explains why it has remained in use for so long, despite its lack of clarity. It is important to realize that the structure of feeling of a period can run contrary to the dominant cultural definitions. Thus, British working-class culture survives despite its devaluation within successive dominant constructions of culture. Williams uses the category as a means of insisting on the existence of an *organic* popular spirit, closely linked to lived conditions and values, that may or may not be reflected (and that may be contested or resisted) at other levels of culture. As Anthony Barnett (1976) says, the structure of feeling is "designed exactly to restore the category of experience to the world, as a part of its mutable and various social history" (p. 62).[6] As we shall see, this is a strategic move that ultimately connected Williams with the British "culturalists," distancing him from the European structuralists and from formulations of ideology that tended to subordinate individual experience. The category, and the problems in defining it adequately, proceeds from the conflict between Williams's humanism—his insistence on the free agency of the individual—and his socialism—his awareness of the ways in which individual experience is culturally and politically constrained.

With all its faults, *The Long Revolution* establishes a comprehensive theoretical foundation for cultural studies, ready for the influence of European Marxism and structuralism to provide the methodologies for its further development. Williams's background in literary criticism gives both textual and historical approaches their due; the full range of later applications of cultural studies is foreshadowed at one point or another. Ironically, Williams himself may be said to benefit least of all from this; he founded a tradition that others, largely, have developed.

Both Hoggart and Williams offer slightly idealized versions of working-class culture as, in a sense, models to be emulated in contemporary British culture. What they value in the "common culture" of their respective pasts seems to be the complex unity of their everyday lives: the close social relations among work, organized politics, public entertainments, and so on. This is what Hoggart believed was threatened by the new mass-produced culture. Williams's argument for a progressive liberalization of culture and the spread of democracy in *Culture and Society* led him to a more optimistic vision: of the spread of working-class cultural values achieving the common culture of socialism. By the time he wrote *The Long Revolution,* however, this optimism was already fading, and his sense of the danger posed by the structure and practices of media institutions moved him closer to Hoggart's position. Laing (1986, ch. 7) suggests that their positions were finely connected in the NUT conference, and that progressively during the 1960s Williams's position was being revised.

During this period, Williams entered intramural teaching, as a lecturer at Cambridge. Laing (1986, 216–17) suggests that as Williams moved away from adult education he also moved away from an emphasis on "the lived," everyday culture. The 1960s saw an unprecedented explosion of popular cultural forms in Britain: "swinging Britain," the Liverpool sound of the Beatles and others, and the identification between the nation and a populist modernity are signified through the James Bond movies and the appropriation of the Union Jack as a pop icon on tote bags, T-shirts, and even shoes. Substantiated by the widespread adoption of the NUT conference's strategy of centering discussion of class and popular culture on the role of the mass media, such factors all contributed to the establishment of media analysis as "the central plank of the new field of cultural studies" for Williams as for others (Laing 1986, 217). In *The Long Revolution,* it is noticeable how the term *communications* competes with *culture;* the first conclusive sign of this shift in attention, however, is the publication of the first edition of *Communications* in 1962.

It is important to stress that Williams's discussion of the functions of modern communication technologies is not separate from the cultural project that informed *Culture and*

Society and *The Long Revolution*. The program of cultural change laid out in *The Long Revolution* reappears in *Communications*. Again, Williams (1962) insists that the cultural revolution is "part of a great process of human liberation, comparable in importance with the industrial revolution and the struggle for democracy":

> The essential values . . . are common to the whole process: that men should grow in capacity and power to direct their own lives—by creating democratic institutions, by bringing new sources of energy to human work, and by extending the expression and exchange of experience on which understanding depends. (p. 138)

The goal of a common culture is still there, shaping the second half of the book. This time, however, the cultural revolution will be accomplished through, rather than in spite of, mass communications technologies and institutions; reforms within the communications sector itself have the potential to democratize society.

Despite its primary focus on technologies and institutions, *Communications* is still caught in the web of complexities and contradictions that ensnares attempts to separate art and culture. On the one hand, Williams defends the permanence of literary value against the variations of history: "We must not confuse," he says, "the great works of the past" with the particular "social minority which identifies itself with them" (p. 110). On the other hand, although he continues to interrogate aspects of popular culture in order to privilege "only the best work," he is careful to separate himself from Leavisite positions and terminology: "If we look at what we call 'mass culture' and 'minority culture' [these are Leavis's terms], I am not sure that we invariably find one on the side of reality and one against it" (p. 113). Indeed, at the end of the revised edition (1975), he concludes that the whole controversy has now been displaced by the development of cultural studies: the "older kind of defence of 'high' culture, with its associated emphasis on minority education and the social privileges needed to sustain it, has not disappeared but is now clearly residual" (p. 183).

In general the move from the central category of culture to that of communication is potentially quite helpful, since it enables Williams to shed some of the baggage carried from the culture and civilization traditions and to begin to explore other traditions of theory and research. Unfortunately, the strongest influence on the book is from American communications research, primarily empiricist branches of sociology and political economy. The result is a strong collection of content analyses and media history—models for others to follow but almost entirely enclosed within an existing American theoretical tradition. Much of this tradition is now discredited within cultural studies, a casualty of the antiempiricist cast of structuralist thought, and Williams's dependence on these theoretical models makes *Communications* a dated book. That said, in *Communications* Williams does take a useful strategic step toward understanding the communication industries rather than simply deploring their products, and toward seeing communication as contained within culture rather than as secondary to it. And, possibly most usefully, the "Proposals" chapter offers sets of suggestions for the study and teaching of communication: these include proposals for the study of media institutions and media production, and for the development of a mode of textual criticism that can deal with *all* cultural forms. As so often with Williams's early work, one is surprised by how closely these proposals describe what has become established current practice.

Between *Communications* and Williams's next exploration of cultural studies, *Television: Technology and Cultural Form* (1974), Williams returned to literary studies, publishing two studies of drama, *Modern Tragedy* (1966) and *Drama from Ibsen to Brecht* (1968). His more personal account of British culture, *The Country and the City*, was published in 1973. By 1974 the study of the media was well established in British academia through media sociology, media economy, and the developing field of cultural studies. The CCCS had been working primarily in media studies for some years, and the Leicester Centre for Mass Communication Research had also produced ground-breaking research. Williams still had new things to offer media and cultural studies, however.

Television: Technology and Cultural Form is a powerful and original book, and although it offers resistance at strategic points to the influence of structuralism—of which Williams was by now well aware—it marks the beginning of a new breed of British accounts of television.

Television: Technology and Cultural Form breaks with Williams's previous work in two key areas: first, it rejects the accounts of technologies and their social effects produced by American mass communication research, research so influential on *Communications;* second, instead of focusing solely on the content of television programs, it analyzes the medium's technological structures and how they work to determine television's characteristic forms. While work of this kind was going on elsewhere, particularly in the CCCS, this was the first book-length study to employ such an approach to the medium.

Possibly the book's most widely quoted passage describes Williams's first experience of American TV, in a hotel in Miami:

> I began watching a film and at first had some difficulty in adjusting to a much greater frequence of commercial "breaks". Yet this was a minor problem compared to what eventually happened. Two other films, which were due to be shown on the same channel on other nights, began to be inserted as trailers. A crime in San Francisco (the subject of the original film) began to operate in an extraordinary counterpoint not only with the deodorant and cereal commercials but with a romance in Paris and the eruption of a prehistoric monster who laid waste New York. Moreover, this was sequence in a new sense. Even in commercial British television there is a visual signal—the residual sign of an interval—before and after the commercial sequences, and "programme" trailers only occur between "programmes". Here was something quite different, since the transitions from film to commercial and from film A to films B and C were in effect unmarked. (Williams 1974, 92)

What Williams takes from this is the recognition that, despite

TV guides, broadcast TV is not organized around discrete units—programs. Nor is TV's characteristic form a chain of program sequences regularly interrupted by advertising. Williams argues that the multiplicity of program forms within an evening's TV are not disruptive, but are incorporated into its "flow":

> What is being offered is not, in older terms, a programme of discrete units with particular insertions, but a planned flow, in which the true series is not the published sequence of programme items but this sequence is transformed by the inclusion of another kind of sequence, so that these sequences together compose the real flow, the real "broadcasting". (p. 90)

This flow effect is institutionalized in programming policies aimed at keeping the audience with the channel for the whole evening, hence the use of trailers to "sustain that evening's flow" (p. 93).

Notwithstanding John Ellis's (1982, 117–24) critique in *Visible Fictions*, which points out that the same principles can be used to describe formal patterns *within* television programs and develops the idea that television works in "segments," not programs, Williams's development of the notion of flow and sequence has been significant. Its great advance is that it attempts to understand how television, as a medium, specifically works. "Flow" and "sequence" aim to describe a characteristic of the experience of television, a characteristic produced by the complex articulation of production practices, technological and economic determinants, and the social function of television within the home, as well as the formal structures of individual television genres. It is a kind of analysis that is singularly lacking in *Communications*, and in most other full-length studies of the medium produced at the time.

The final section of *Television: Technology and Cultural Form* deals with the effects of the technology of television. It attacks empiricist mass communication research and technological determinism, and concludes by restating Williams's view of what "determination" is. While he admits the validity of certain forms of American "effects" research, Williams directs his strongest criticism at developments from such research that argue that the medium of television itself—not even the specific message—has a determining, causal effect on behavior:

> If the medium—whether print or television—is the cause, all other causes, all that men ordinarily see as history, are at once reduced to effects. Similarly, what are elsewhere seen as effects, and as such subject to social, cultural, psychological and moral questioning, are excluded as irrelevant by comparison with the direct physiological and therefore "psychic" effects of the media as such. (p. 127)

In other words, history is the determining force; it produces us *and* the medium of television. Williams offers accounts of the development of radio and television in which he demonstrates the difference between the invention of a technology and its diffusion in a culture. Invention itself does not cause cultural change; to understand any of the mass communication technologies we must "historicize," we must consider their articulation with specific sets of interests and within a specific social order (p. 128). Consequently, Marshall McLuhan's work is dismissed as "ludicrous" and Williams treats his privileging of the technologies of television with contempt: "If the effect of the medium is the same, whoever controls or uses it, and whatever apparent content he may try to insert, then we can forget ordinary political and cultural argument and let the technology run itself" (p. 128).

Williams accuses this tradition of media analysis of "technological determinism," that is, of ascribing to a technology a set of intentions and effects independent of history. In place of that relatively crude explanation for the determination of cultural practices, institutions, or technologies, Williams offers his own, subtler explanation:

> The reality of determination is the setting of limits and the exertion of pressures, within which variable social practices are profoundly affected but never necessarily controlled. We have to think of determination not as a single force,

> or a single abstraction of forces, but as a process in which real determining factors—the distribution of power or of capital, social and physical inheritance, relations of scale and size between groups—set limits and exert pressures, but neither wholly control nor wholly predict the outcome of complex activity within or at these limits, and under or against these pressures. (p. 130)

This formulation is still useful today.

Williams's work to this point in his career is marked by the struggle between his humanism and his socialism; none of the works examined so far has accepted the invitation of Marxist thought as a means of resolving the many contradictions within his thinking about culture, art, and communications. In *Marxism and Literature*, published in 1977, we have an extraordinary theoretical "coming out," as Williams finally admits the usefulness of Marxism and his place within its philosophical traditions.

Marxism and Literature begins with an autobiographical account of Williams's own relationship with and resistance to Marxism. He reveals he had a relatively unsophisticated knowledge of it at the time he wrote *Culture and Society*, but that his gradual acquaintance with the work of Lukacs, Goldman, Althusser, and, later, Gramsci had alerted him to a new critical mode of Marxism that was not crudely deterministic or economistic. He discovered a body of Marxist thought that challenged traditional Marxism's division of society into the base (the economic conditions) and the superstructure (the effects of the economic base, including culture). Critical Marxism complicated such a model by, for instance, insisting that culture was not merely a reflection of the economic base but could produce its *own* "effects." There, Williams (1977) found support for his formulation of culture as a "constitutive social process, creating specific and different 'ways of life'" (p. 19).

Williams, in effect, announces his conversion, and a whole range of theory becomes available to him that had hitherto been off limits. He admits the value of semiotics as a method of textual analysis (but still sees it as dealing with aesthetics!); he notes the importance of Saussure's work (but still worries at its rigid determinism); he acknowledges the importance of the economic determinations of culture, and outlines the means through which media institutions, for instance, can be studied; he offers a materialist definition of the category of literature, seeing it as a historical category of "use and condition" rather than as an ideal, essential entity. But the most important development in *Marxism and Literature* is that Williams finally outlines his view of ideology.

When Williams breaks with the traditional Marxist division of base and superstructure, he does so in order to foreground the role of culture. He concludes the discussion of this issue in *Marxism and Literature* by saying that it is not the base or the superstructure we should be examining, but rather the processes that integrate them—the processes through which history and culture are determined. The examination of determination leads, inevitably, to an examination of the mechanisms through which it is held to occur: mechanisms variously defined as the working of ideologies.

As Williams says, the problem of determination is the most intractable issue within Marxist thought, but his conclusions are characteristic. Rejecting more mechanistic schemes of determination, he opts for the Althusserian idea of "over-determination," a concept encountered briefly in Chapter 1 of this volume. Overdetermination allows for the "relative autonomy" of cultural forces, and consequently explains the achievement of ideological domination as a struggle between competing and contradictory forces. For Williams, the virtue of Althusser's view of ideology over earlier versions is that it is able to acknowledge the importance and complexity of individual, "lived" experience: "the concept of 'overdetermination' is more useful than any other way of understanding historically lived situations and the authentic complexities of practice" (p. 89). However, while this is true, Althusser finds it easier to explain how these relatively autonomous formations are necessarily subject to ideological forces than to explain how these forces can be resisted or dominant ideologies contested. Williams, like many others in the field, found an answer to this in Gramsci's theory of hegemony.

Gramsci's theory of hegemony holds that cultural domination or, more accurately, cultural leadership is not achieved by force or coercion, but is secured through the consent of those it will ultimately subordinate. The subordinated groups consent because they are convinced that this will serve their interests; they accept as "common sense" the view of the world offered them by the dominant group. (Such a process, for instance, might explain how working-class voters in Britain can see Margaret Thatcher as protecting their interests.) Gramsci's insistence on the production of consent implies a cultural field that is composed through much more vigorous and dynamic struggle than that envisaged by Althusser. Cultural domination is the product of complex negotiations and alignments of interests; it is never simply imposed from above, nor is it inevitably produced through language or through ideological apparatuses such as the education system. The achievement of hegemony is sustained only through the continual winning of consent. (Further discussion of hegemony will be presented in Chapter 6.)

For Williams, the attraction of Gramsci's theory is that it both includes and goes beyond two powerful earlier concepts: "that of 'culture' as a 'whole social process', in which men define and shape their whole lives; and that of 'ideology', in any of its Marxist senses, in which a system of meanings and values is the expression or projection of a particular class interest" (p. 108). The idea of hegemony connects, in a sense, the theory and practice of social process and provides us with ways of examining how specific formations of domination occur. Again, for Williams, the power of the theory is its ability to consider individual experience within history, to talk of culture as "the lived dominance and subordination of particular classes," thus stitching history, experience, politics, and ideology into the study of everyday life.

To develop this position further, and to emphasize the fact that domination is a process rather than a permanently achieved state, Williams identifies three kinds of cultural forces: the dominant, residual, and emergent forces discernible at any one point and within any one historical juncture. These terms roughly correspond to the ideological forms of, respectively, the present, the past, and the future. These cultural forces may be utterly antipathetic to each other's interests; by incorporating them into his schema,

Williams is installing the notion of conflict, difference, and contradiction as components within a theory of determination. As Williams says, domination must never be seen as total: "No mode of production and therefore no dominant social order . . . ever in reality includes or exhausts all human practice, human energy, and human intention" (p. 125). It is fitting to conclude this necessarily partial survey of Williams's work with his insistence on political possibility, on the power of the human agent to change his or her conditions of existence. This has been the overriding concern in his work from the beginning.

Williams's acceptance of Marxism had an odd effect on his role in cultural studies. It is as if he accepted his place within a Marxist tradition only to disappear into it; his value over the last decade has been as a pioneer rather than as a leader. Critiques of his work argue that he never came up with a thoroughgoing statement of his position, or that he never developed methods for its application. Even the honesty of his work, openly revising his position, has been attacked as a flaw (see Eagleton 1978, 33). But Williams's work remains strikingly original and compelling reading even now, and his commitment to the political objectives of theoretical work was exemplary. For Williams, cultural studies was a practice, not a profession, and his work remains an indispensable guide to the full range of developments to occur within British cultural studies during his lifetime.

E. P. Thompson and Culturalism

Raymond Williams is normally, if a little problematically, located in the "culturalist" tradition within British cultural studies; E. P. Thompson is a less equivocal representative of this tradition. Thompson's importance is not confined only to cultural studies, however. His book *The Making of the English Working Class* (1978a) has had a profound influence on the writing of British social history since its publication (it was first published in 1963) and has also been implicated in explorations of popular culture, class, and subcultures from within sociology, anthropology, and ethnography.

Unlike Williams, Thompson developed his theory of culture from within Marxist traditions. Although he left the Communist party around the time of the Soviet intervention in Hungary, the debates in which he engaged were debates within Marxism itself. However, there are many similarities between his position in 1963 and that of the Raymond Williams of *Culture and Society* and *The Long Revolution*: Thompson resisted simple notions of economic determinism, and the traditional base-superstructure model, in order to recover the importance of culture; he resisted simple notions of class domination and thus recovered the importance of human agency; he insisted on the importance of "lived" culture and of subjective experience; and he maintained a basic humanism. Culture, for both men, was a lived network of practices and relationships that constituted everyday life, within which the role of the individual subject had to be foregrounded.

Thompson, more than Williams, developed his theory through practice, through his history of the making of culture by its subjects. A more important difference between the two was the conflict-based view of culture Thompson proposed, in opposition to the consensualizing view Williams offered in *Culture and Society* and *The Long Revolution*. Thompson resisted Williams's definition of culture as "a whole way of life" in order to reframe it as a struggle between *ways* of life. Thompson's culture was constituted by the friction between competing interests and forces, mostly located in social class. Williams's residually Leavisite view of culture was countered by Thompson's unequivocal definition of culture as popular culture, the culture of "the people." The intellectual project for Thompson was to rewrite the history of this culture in order to redress the imbalance of its representation in "official" histories.

The Making of the English Working Class sets out its agenda explicitly in its opening pages; Thompson attacks orthodox labor and social histories for leaving out the working class, for remembering only the successful—"those whose aspirations anticipated subsequent evolution": "The blind alleys, the lost causes, and the losers themselves," he says, "are forgotten." Thompson sets out to rescue the casualties of ruling class history, "the poor stockinger, the Luddite cropper," from "the enormous condescension of posterity." His goal is not simply to recuperate the past:

> In some of the lost causes of the people of the Industrial Revolution we may discover insights into social evils which we have yet to cure. Moreover, the greater part of the world today is still undergoing problems of industrialisation, and of the formation of democratic institutions, analogous in many ways to our own experience during the Industrial Revolution. (Thompson 1978a, 13)

The result is a polemical, imaginative, and richly readable account of the formation of a class and the specific discourses that gave its members' lives their meaning.

The immediate beneficiary of this work was not cultural studies; Thompson saw his work as directly examining "the peculiarities of the English," and as such the project has been accepted and taken on (Johnson 1980, 48). There is now a strong tradition of British social history that is shaped by Thompson's work. Although Johnson (1980) has defined the historical and historiographic interests of the CCCS in roughly Thompsonian terms, emphasizing in particular the relevance of historical research to the analysis of the present, cultural studies has had reservations about Thompson's work and the work of historians generally. Furthermore, what reservations cultural studies had about the contribution of history were well and truly reciprocated in historians' distrust of European cultural theory. Thompson (1978b) himself proved to be an enthusiastic controversialist, and engaged in a decade of argument that culminated in *The Poverty of Theory* in 1978. This field of conflict has been conventionalized as one between structuralism and culturalism.

Structuralism encouraged cultural studies theorists to see Thompson's (and, for that matter, Williams's) concentration on individual experience and agency as romantic and regressively humanist. Since consciousness is culturally constructed, why waste time dealing with its individual contents when we can deal with its constitutive processes—language, for instance? Culturalists, on the other hand, saw structuralism as too abstract, rigid, and mechanical to accommodate the lived complexities of cultural processes. Structuralists saw culturalists as lacking theory; culturalists saw structuralists as theoreticist. Culturalism was a homegrown movement, while structuralism was foreign. In the discipline of history, the controversy became quite specific: historians claimed, with some justice, that structuralism was ahistorical and thus denied the very processes historians examined; conversely, structuralists saw culturalist historians as theoretically naive in their understanding of cultural processes.

We can see this controversy displayed in the pages of the *History Workshop*, a journal that began in 1976, developing from a series of seminars and meetings that had been held under that title in Ruskin College, Oxford, since 1967. Explicitly socialist, its first issue carried not one but three editorials-cum-manifestos: the first proclaimed the journal's task as that of bringing "the boundaries of history closer to people's lives" and counteracting the control of the academy over history; the second argued for the importance of feminist histories; and the third announced the end of an informal theoretical treaty by thanking sociology for its assistance in the past and claiming history would provide its own theoretical support in the future. The state of "theory" within the study of history was thus constructed as an issue and a problem for the journal and the discipline.

By the late 1970s, some structuralist work was going on within history: on nineteenth-century popular culture, oral history, and some aspects of ethnographic research. But there were still limits to the acceptability, in particular, of Althusserian notions of ideology. In 1978, Richard Johnson, by then at the CCCS, published an article in *History Workshop* proposing the benefits of structuralism to historians and, among other things, accusing Thompson of "preferring experience to theory." The journal was deluged with letters. Johnson was accused of historical illiteracy, a slavish Althusserianism, a barren and empty theoreticism, and an excessive antihumanism. One of the journal's editors contributed a letter saying he never wanted the article published anyway, while another (affiliated with the Birmingham Centre's work) expressed disgust at the shrillness of the response. While

Johnson might have been seen as a champion of history *within* cultural studies, clearly he was still seen as something of a heretic by historians (see *History Workshop*, Vol. 7, 1979). There was a rematch between Thompson and Johnson at the notorious *History Workshop* conference in 1979, and again the arguments merely exposed the depth of the division between culturalism and structuralism.

A possible effect of this fissure may have been historians' subsequent tendency to avoid analyses of contemporary popular culture and anything that might look like textual analysis. Other consequences have been more worthwhile; the culturalist emphasis on individual experience, the "making" of culture, fed into ethnographic work on subcultures within the mainstream of cultural studies (examples of this work can be seen in Bennett et al. 1981; Hall and Jefferson 1976). As Hall, Johnson, and Bennett have all indicated, however, and as we saw in our account of Williams's theoretical development, Gramsci's theory of hegemony has resolved many of the points at issue between structuralists and culturalists, particularly the sticking points of determination and social change. There is now greater interchange among the various approaches, and with what Bennett calls "the turn to Gramsci" we can consign the culturalism-structuralist split to the past (see Bennett et al. 1986, introduction).

Stuart Hall

An index of Stuart Hall's importance to contemporary formations of British cultural studies is that the detailed discussion of his work since the mid-1970s occurs within subsequent chapters rather than within this survey. But some account of Hall's earlier work should be given here, if only because his theoretical history closely parallels that of British cultural studies itself. An early editor of *New Left Review*, and a secondary school teacher before he became an academic, Hall was among the speakers at the 1960 NUT conference on popular culture and the media. His first book, *The Popular Arts* (Hall and Whannel 1967; first published in Britain in 1964), was deeply indebted to Hoggart and Williams; he joined the

CCCS as Hoggart's deputy in 1966 and replaced Hoggart as director in 1969. During his decade as director, Hall oversaw a tremendous expansion in the theoretical base and intellectual influence of the CCCS. The structuralist enterprise could be said to find its focus there, and the development of both the ethnographic and the media studies strands in cultural studies is clearest there. Cultural studies' development of its distinctive combination of Althusserian and Gramscian theories of ideology and hegemony owes a significant debt to the CCCS and Hall's own work. Hall is now professor of sociology at the Open University and continues to be an influential figure within cultural studies—especially in the new American constructions of the field—and a consistent critic of the ideologies and public policies of Thatcher's Britain. His most recent work, in fact, has become even more engaged with contemporary politics, playing an important role in the current debates on the reorientation of the Left in Europe.

Hall has been on quite a theoretical journey, then. His first book, coauthored with Paddy Whannel, stands in clearest relation to the culture and civilization tradition. There are some key differences, however. *The Popular Arts* is relatively free of the nostalgia and organicism of Leavisite texts, even of the diluted variants found in *The Uses of Literacy* and *Culture and Society*. In fact, Hall and Whannel (1967) explicitly reject the conventional contrast between the "organic culture of pre-industrial England with the mass-produced culture of today":

> This is a perspective that has produced a penetrating critique of industrial society but as a guide to action it is restrictive. The old culture has gone because the way of life that produced it has gone. The rhythms of work have been permanently altered and the enclosed small-scale communities are vanishing. It may be important to resist unnecessary increases in scale and to re-establish local initiatives where we can; but if we wish to re-create a genuine popular culture we must seek out the points of growth within the society that now exists. (p. 38)

As a result of this position, Hall and Whannel are much more interested in dealing with popular cultural forms on their own terms than are any of their predecessors. *The Popular Arts* strikes the note taken up 13 years later by Fiske and Hartley in *Reading Television* (1978) that "the kind of attention we must pay to [in this case, film's] visual qualities is the equivalent of the attention we give to verbal images, rhythms and so on, in our reading" (p. 44). This kind of attention alerts Hall and Whannel to properties of popular forms missed by earlier commentators; their analysis of the signifying function of film stars, for instance, predates Dyer's work by many years but comes to very similar conclusions about the contradiction between a star's typicality and individuality (p. 213). (Dyer's work is dealt with in Chapter 3.)

The Popular Arts is still aimed at developing strategies of discrimination, however. Its advance on Hoggart is that it rejects the idea that the media necessarily and inevitably produce rubbish; as a result, Hall and Whannel's aim is to discriminate *among* the products of the media, not *against* them (p. 15). In order to theorize the artistic possibilities provided within various popular forms, Hall and Whannel develop the influential distinction between popular art (which derives from folk cultures) and mass art (which does not): "The typical 'art' of the mass media today is not a continuity from, but *a corruption of*, popular art," they say. "Mass art has no personal quality but, instead, a high degree of personalisation" (p. 68). Although *The Popular Arts* means well, and intends to legitimate "good" popular art by proposing a historic relation between the form and the culture, it does have problems. As frameworks for aesthetic judgment, its formulations are doomed to expose many contradictions and inevitably to discount the specific pleasures offered by popular cultural forms (familiarity and repetition in popular fiction or television, for instance) no matter how good the intentions. Finally, and once again, the book is limited by the lack of more appropriate analytical tools than those provided by Leavisite literary analysis.

Hall spent the next few years revising his position. Evidence of the comprehensiveness of this revision can be found in "Television as a Medium and Its Relation to Culture." This article was published as a CCCS stenciled paper in 1973, but it was originally prepared as part of a report on TV for UNESCO in 1971. One has to deduce UNESCO's brief from the discussion, but it seems to have required the consideration of how television might be enlisted to support the popularization or dissemination of high art—"Culture." The article makes skilled, confident, and early use of semiotics and its various formulations in the work of Barthes, Wollen, and Pierce. It also radically rewrites Hall's position from *The Popular Arts*. Rather than arguing for "better" television through the adaptation of high art, for instance, Hall argues that the UNESCO brief misunderstands the relation between the medium and the culture. *Popular* television is the center of this relation and to persist in attempting to integrate the domains of art and popular television is "anachronistic." He concludes: "Television invites us, not to serve up the traditional dishes of culture more effectively, but to make real the utopian slogan which appeared in May 1968, adorning the walls of the Sorbonne, 'Art is dead. Let us create everyday life'" (p. 113). This flamboyant final flourish is perhaps a little of its time, but the deployment of the phrase "everyday life" is strategic, invoking the enterprise of cultural studies.

In the same year, 1971, a paper Hall delivered to the British Sociological Association, "Deviancy, Politics and the Media," displays the influence of structuralism and semiotics. To support his attack on American media research, Hall uses the work of Lévi-Strauss, Barthes, Althusser, and Gramsci. These two papers provide evidence of Hall's early interest in European theory, much of it unavailable in English translation, and certainly not widely deployed within the disciplines from which cultural studies was emerging. Indeed, part of Hall's role within cultural studies has been as a conduit through which European structuralist theory reached British researchers and theorists; in the United States, now, he seems to be serving that role for British transformations of that theory.

A substantial proportion of Hall's writings are available as chapters within readers published through the CCCS, or as individual journal articles. He is an editor and coauthor of many of these readers, and is the coauthor of probably the most thorough and magisterial application of cultural studies theory so far, *Policing the Crisis: Mugging, the State, and Law and Order* (Hall et al. 1978). In this book, Hall's own background (West Indian) must have played a part in recovering the issue of race as one of concern to cultural studies: surprisingly, perhaps, issues of race and empire have not been at the forefront of his published work over the years. The analysis of the media, the investigation of practices of resistance within subcultures, and the public construction of political power in Britain have been his overriding concerns. It is difficult for students to form a sense of the body of Hall's work, however; so far he has not been the sole author of a book-length project. A collection of his key articles has recently been advertised (but not yet supplied) by Macmillan under the title *Reproducing Ideologies*, and this may provide a more manageable means of access to this important work. His key articles will be discussed in later chapters: in particular, his theories of textual and ideological analysis of the media, his theorizing of the category of ideology, and his contributions to analysis of institutions and their cultural/political effects.

The Birmingham Centre for Contemporary Cultural Studies

This is a history not only of individual contributors but also of institutions. While there are now numerous institutions around the world participating in and reshaping the field of cultural studies, the Birmingham Centre for Contemporary Cultural Studies can justifiably claim to be the key institution in the history of the field. The Centre's publications have made strategic contributions to academic and public awareness, and in sheer volume dominate the field. A high proportion of the authors listed in the bibliography at the end of this book have worked at, studied within, or are in some way affiliated with the Centre and its work; examples of such individuals include Dick Hebdige, Dorothy Hobson, David Morley, Phil Cohen, Chas Critcher, Charlotte Brunsdon, Iain Chambers, Janice Winship, Paul Willis, Angela McRobbie, Richard Hoggart, Richard Johnson, Stuart Laing, and Stuart Hall. While the specifics of its definitions of cultural studies might well be (and are) contested, the Centre's claim to a special influence on the field's development is beyond argument.

The CCCS was established at the University of Birmingham in 1964. Hoggart was its first director, and clearly his work was seen as the major focus of its attention. The CCCS was to direct itself to cultural forms, practices, and institutions, and "their relation to society and social change" (Hall et al. 1980) (see photo 2.1). Its principal objective was to provide postgraduate research, and until relatively recently it offered no undergraduate degree program in cultural studies.

As the above discussions of the work of Hoggart, Williams, and Hall during the 1960s make clear, Hoggart's project of understanding the everyday, "lived" cultures of particular classes was overtaken by interest in the mass media, which quickly came to dominate the Centre's research and has provided it with its longest-running focus. Initially, this work was heavily influenced by American communication research; as with Williams's *Communications*, the existence of a well-developed body of work in the United States encouraged its adaptation to British topics. While this tradition continued to influence another key center, Leicester's Centre for Mass Communication Research, the CCCS (like Williams) broke with the American influence, with the culture and civilization tradition, and with the empirical aspects of social science research. It moved toward the analysis of the ideological function of the media; within such analysis, the media were defined as a "major cultural and ideological force," "standing in a dominant position with respect to the way in which social relations and political problems were defined and the production and transformations of popular ideologies in the audience addressed" (Hall 1980d, 117). The result was a concentration on the ideological "effectivity" of the media (a more general and indirect idea of the process of determination) rather than on their behavioral "effects." This was an inquiry into structures of power, the "politics" of the media.

Stuart Hall's replacement of Richard Hoggart as director centrally influenced this shift of emphasis. Under Hall's leadership, the relations between media and ideology were

Photo 2.1. Cover of the first issue of the CCCS journal, *Working Papers in Cultural Studies* (*Used with permission.*)

investigated through the analysis of signifying systems in texts. Other kinds of work also prospered. Histories of "everyday life" drew on Thompson's work, but also appropriated ethnographic approaches from sociology and anthropology. For some years such interests were focused on subcultures, examining their construction, their relation to their parent and dominant cultures, and their histories of resistance and incorporation. Much of this work examined the rituals and practices that generated meaning and pleasure within, precisely, that fragment of the cultural field Hoggart had dismissed in *The Uses of Literacy*: urban youth subcultures. Feminist research also benefited from this subcultural approach, using it to examine aspects of women's cultural subordination. Interaction between research on feminine subcultures and on the ways audiences negotiated their own meanings and pleasures from popular television has provided a platform for revisions of our understanding of "the feminine" and of television. And concurrent with all this, work on class histories, histories of popular culture, and popular memory also continued.

Hall was succeeded by Richard Johnson in 1979. Johnson (1983) has noted some discontinuities between the principles followed under Hall and under his own directorship. Textual analysis gave way to a sharper focus on history as the centrality of the need to examine everyday life was reaffirmed. Johnson's own interests were focused on the historical construction of subjectivities rather than on media texts. Somewhat paradoxically, Johnson has expressed skepticism about the rich tradition of ethnographic work within the CCCS. While the work of certain individuals (Hebdige and Willis, for two) is exempted from this skepticism, Johnson (1983, 46–48) has represented ethnography as relatively untheorized, while noting its tendencies toward an elitist paternalism. This latter point derives from what is seen as the arrogance implicit in wandering into someone else's culture and assuming its transparency before one's own methods of analysis. It is a criticism ethnographers themselves have raised.

Johnson has now passed the directorship on to Jorge Lorrain. The nature of the CCCS has changed substantially in the last few years. Under university pressure to be reabsorbed into the Department of English, the CCCS embarked on an international campaign to generate support for its survival. It won the battle but it may not have won the war. The Centre is now a Department of Cultural Studies, offering undergraduate programs in the field. The staff has been augmented by the collapse and dispersal of the University of Birmingham's Sociology Department; two members joined the Department of Cultural Studies. While this almost doubles the staff, now the Centre's staff must divide its time between undergraduate and postgraduate teaching and research.

The CCCS has exerted an influence far beyond what anyone could have expected. At any one time it has had only a handful of staff—never more than three until these most recent additions. But it adopted a policy of encouraging its students to publish their work rather than produce assignments—or even finish their degrees! While this did little for the Centre's "academic throughput figures," it did make the work visible, disseminating the fruits of its research and establishing the reputations of its students. The CCCS also operated through reading and research groups rather than through formal courses.[7] Most of its publications bear the marks of this collectivist practice, a practice that clearly served the research function exceptionally well, while presumably making the teaching and assessment of student work something of a problem. It remains to be seen how the introduction of undergraduate teaching, with defined and programmed course units, will affect the Centre's work, but it seems likely to reduce its output, and possibly its influence, considerably.

Other "Centers"

Birmingham is not the only research center devoted to cultural studies, of course. At the time it was established, a number of other developments also institutionalized an interest in media and popular culture. The Centre for Television Research was set up at Leeds in 1966, and the first chair in film studies in Britain was founded at the University of London in 1967. Possibly of greatest importance was the

Centre for Mass Communication Research at the University of Leicester, established in 1966. Halloran et al.'s (1970) analysis of the media treatment of the 1968 demonstrations (*Demonstrations and Communication*) was a ground-breaking work, and influenced subsequent connections between politics and the media at Birmingham (see Hall et al. 1980, 119). The Leicester center was initially heavily influenced by empiricist communication theory, and then by media sociology and political economy, so its relation to cultural studies has been occasional rather than systematic.

Work within the Leicester center and the CCCS helped to revive a strand of British media sociology that dealt with the media institutions. Institutional studies of media production such as Schlesinger's *Putting Reality Together* (1978) appeared during the 1970's, investigating how the industrial production of news is ideologically constrained. Such work was generated by a particular interest in the way politics was represented in the media. Between 1974 and 1982 the Glasgow Media Group, a collective at the University of Glasgow, applied both empirical and interpretative methods to news reports on such topics as the economy, unions, and the Labour party; their analyses appear in *Bad News* (1976), *More Bad News* (1980), and *Really Bad News* (1982). The collective no longer exists, but it exerted considerable pressure on the BBC and gained widespread attention within the media in the latter half of the 1970s.

A significant institutionalization of the study of the media in Britain was the Open University's Mass Communication and Society course, which began in 1977. Here a great deal of the work being done in the various British research traditions was published, collected, or disseminated. Of even greater importance for cultural studies was the establishment of the Open University's degree program in popular culture. This course drew on history, sociology, and literary studies as well as cultural studies. It was first offered in 1982 to over a thousand students, and its course "readers" have, like the CCCS publications, assisted in the definition of the field by providing students with access to materials otherwise widely dispersed and difficult to find. The work of Tony Bennett, Stuart Hall, Colin Mercer, Janet Woollacott, James Curran,

Michael Gurevitch, and many others went into the Open University courses and into the collections that defined and exported the enterprise. For many outside Britain, the Open University course readers have provided the most accessible and coherent account of the work going on in British cultural studies.

As we have already seen in the case of the *History Workshop* and *Working Papers in Cultural Studies*, journals have played a significant role in this history. The film journal, *Screen*, for example (formerly *Screen Education*), made substantial theoretical contributions to the textual analysis of film and television. It has maintained close links with European semiotic and structuralist theory, but its avant-garde privileging of the "progressive" text recalled elite interpretations of popular culture and exposed it to extended controversies with members of the CCCS—particularly David Morley (1980b).

No intellectual movement is monolithic, no attempt to describe its essential features uncontested. There are certainly more contributing streams to the field of cultural studies than I have listed above. In later chapters, I will be adopting further, complicating, and perhaps even contradictory, perspectives on this history. For the moment, however, and rather than continue this list until all interests are satisfied, I want to close by acknowledging some of the more marginalized, but significant, contributions. Feminist work on media audiences has developed, almost single-handedly, a critique of conventional accounts of the function of TV soap operas for female viewers. Dorothy Hobson, Charlotte Brunsdon, and (from Holland) Ien Ang's work has been incorporated into the mainstream of media studies now, convincingly challenging the orthodoxies on the pleasures offered by popular television. Angela McRobbie has mounted a most effective critique of subcultural studies, including her own early work, as discounting the feminine. Some feminist writers have appealed directly to a general audience, through columns in magazines and newspapers, in order to articulate their critique of masculinist representations. Judith Williamson and Ros Coward, for instance, enjoy little institutional support but wage an extremely effective guerrilla war on the media industries as free-lance writers.[8]

Another margin, for some time, seems to have had a physical location, in Cardiff, where Terence Hawkes, John Fiske, Christopher Norris, and John Hartley all worked. Neither Fiske nor Hartley make much of an appearance in British cultural studies' bibliographies until 1978, when their *Reading Television* appears as a member of Methuen's New Accents series. The series is edited by Terence Hawkes and has continued to feature writers from Cardiff; Catherine Belsey's *Critical Practice,* for example. Fiske and Hartley's book was subjected to some very negative reviews and ignored by much subsequent work coming from the CCCS or from Milton Keynes (the home of the Open University). Fiske, nevertheless, was taken up by Methuen as editor of its Studies in Communication series, which has published Hartley and other Cardiff alumni Tim O'Sullivan and Danny Saunders. (My own contribution to this series, *Film as Social Practice,* was implicated in this network; John Fiske and I were colleagues for a number of years at the Western Australian Institute of Technology.) Both *Reading Television* and the series have been influential teaching texts in colleges and universities, but Fiske and Hartley enjoy much higher profiles in the United States and Australia than they do in the United Kingdom. It seems possible that the field of study has been subject to a degree of metropolitan control and that there are geographical margins as well as theoretical or ideological ones. It may be significant that Fiske and Hartley both extended their marginality by moving to Australia; there is a comforting symmetry in the fact that the journal they helped develop in Australia, the *Australian Journal of Cultural Studies,* has itself been returned to "the center" as the international journal, *Cultural Studies*.

The importance of Methuen's in rescuing this group from the margins and placing them in their preferred export bag is not to be underestimated. Publishing firms are institutions, too, and Methuen's (now Routledge) move into cultural studies and literary theory in the mid-1970s provided an outlet for the work of many who are now key figures in cultural studies theory and practice, while the establishment of the two series (Studies in Communication and New Accents) helped to stake out a market. For those who developed their understanding of cultural studies through publishers' leaflets and bookshop bulletins, the accumulation of titles on the Methuen list constituted a map of the field. It is an indication of Methuen's success that this is no longer the case; competitors have entered the field and the opportunities to publish have expanded in consequence. Being marginal is not quite as easy as it used to be.

Notes

1 Both books were first published in 1964. The latest editions are cited here.
2 Critcher's (1979, 18) critique of the book attacks this sentimental inversion of class history and points out key absences in the book, particularly, the lack of any consideration of the experience of work or the function of the trade union.
3 It is instructive to compare this kind of analysis with later work on urban and youth subcultures, which, paradoxically, grew from this foundation, and a discussion of which will be presented in Chapter 4.
4 Eagleton (1978, 33) makes this point in his otherwise quite hostile review of Williams's career.
5 The latest edition, 1975, is the version cited throughout this book.
6 I am indebted to Patrick Buckridge for bringing this article to my attention.
7 Michael Green (1982) presents a detailed outline of these matters. Some of this information was reinforced and elaborated in a conversation with Richard Johnson during a brief visit to CCCS in 1988. I am grateful for his time and assistance.
8 Hobson, Brunsdon, and Ang's work will be dealt with in Chapter 4. An example of Williamson's journalistic work is available in the collection *Consuming Passions* (1987) and of Coward's in *Female Desire* (1984).

PART II

Central Categories

3

Texts and Contexts

The most recognizable and possibly the most important theoretical strategy cultural studies has developed is that of "reading" cultural products, social practices, even institutions, as "texts." Initially borrowed from literary studies, its subsequent wide deployment owing significant debts to the semiotics of Barthes and Eco, textual analysis has become an extremely sophisticated set of methods—particularly for reading the products of the mass media. This chapter, consequently, will concentrate on textual approaches to the mass media.

Chapter 2 has already described how British literary studies attempted to extend its territory by dealing with media products and popular cultural forms; Hoggart, Williams, and Hall and Whannel all accomplished this extension. In general, however, the success of such attempts was limited by a reluctance to modify literary studies' methods and the ideological/aesthetic assumptions upon which these methods were based. For most, this reluctance took some time to overcome; it was not until the late 1960s and early 1970s that the necessary modifications began to occur, and this was largely due to the importation of semiotics. European explorations of semiotics began to appear in English in the late 1960s; Barthes's *Elements of Semiology* was published in England in 1968, *Mythologies* in 1972, and Eco's "Towards a Structural Enquiry into the Television Message" also in 1972. Within literary theory, local variants appeared quite quickly; Stephen Heath and Colin McCabe published their collection on semiotics, *Signs of the Times: Introductory*

Readings in Textual Semiotics, in 1971. Hall, in particular, appears to have assimilated these ideas very early on; his "The Determination of News Photographs" (1980b), first published in 1972, applies Barthesian semiotics to a series of news photographs in the British press.

If the first wave of media analysis derived from literary studies, this next wave found its initial stimulus elsewhere—in sociology, in particular, in sociology's interest in the mass media's role in the construction of social and political consensus. The part the media played in determining definitions of the normal, the acceptable, and the deviant had become an explicit public concern during the political demonstrations of 1968. Sociologies of deviance focused on how such categories were constructed and defined through their representation in the media, especially in the news. Possibly the earliest "standard" critical work on the media's construction of reality, Cohen and Young's *The Manufacture of News* (1973), was explicitly situated within the sociology of deviance. As their preface to the 1980 revised edition says, Cohen and Young's "search for the overall models of society implied in the media's selection and presentation of stories about crime, deviance and social problems" may have been novel in 1973 but by 1980 it had become much less so (p. 10). With the wider acceptance of the subject matter came the adoption of new methods of analysis from outside sociology. Cohen and Young's revision of the contents for the 1980 edition is significant; while the sociological framework remained, a number of strategic changes were made: several American mass communication studies were deleted, and new pieces from the Birmingham Centre for Contemporary Cultural Studies were included. The new pieces deployed semiotic/structuralist methods of textual analysis and Althusserian theories of ideology—the markers of British cultural studies.

It does seem as if the late 1960s/early 1970s is the point at which aesthetic/moral analyses of the media give way before the more sociological accounts. The result is an increased focus on social meanings and on the political implications of media messages. When semiotic analytical methods are incorporated into such interests, both the power of "texts" and the importance of the social and political contexts of their production and reception are acknowledged. This combination—a legacy of the mixed parentage of literary studies and sociology—gave the cultural studies tradition of textual analysis its distinctive character, in theory and in practice.

Encoding/Decoding

While it is difficult to specify any precise moment as *the* seminal one when the practices of "left-Leavisism" became semiotic/structuralist, it is customary to see Stuart Hall's important article "Encoding and Decoding in Television Discourse" as a turning point.[1] In it, Hall makes a conclusive break with the hitherto dominant American communication models, with aesthetics, and with the notion of the audience as passive consumers of mass culture. In their place, Hall installs a new vocabulary of analysis and a new theory of cultural production and reception.

The article opens with a ritual attack on American empiricist and behavioral explanations of the processes of communication. Hall (1980c) argues with those explanations that see communication as a "loop," or as a direct line from sender to receiver. He points out that just because a message has been sent, this is no guarantee that it will arrive; every moment in the process of communication, from the original composition of the message (encoding) to the point at which it is read and understood (decoding), has its own determinants and "conditions of existence" (p. 129). What Hall emphasizes is that the production and the consumption of the message are overdetermined by a range of influences, including the discourses of the medium used (the use of the image in TV, for instance), the discursive context in which the composition takes place (such as the visual conventions of TV news), and the technologies used to carry the message (the different signifying function of "live" or taped coverage, say, of a TV news story).

Hall insists that there is nothing *natural* about any kind of communication; messages have to be constructed before they can be sent. And just as the construction of the message is an active, interpretive, and social event, so is the moment of its reception. Society is not homogeneous, but is made up of many different groups and interests. The television audience cannot be seen as a single undifferentiated mass; it is composed of a mixture of social groups, all related in different ways to dominant ideological forms and meanings. So, there is bound to be a lack of fit between aspects of the production and reception processes—between the producer's and the audience's interpretation of the message—that will produce misunderstandings or "distortions."

This potential for misunderstanding is limited, Hall points out, by the fact that our communication systems—both the linguistic and the nonlinguistic—work to "encode" our languages for us in advance. We do not have to interpret the television discourse from square one because we have already learned the codes from which it is constructed. When we receive a message about the world that minimizes the use of verbs, pronouns, and articles (as in "French Aircrash Disaster Inquiry Shock") we immediately recognize the codes of news. Some codes are so thoroughly learned that they appear not to be codes at all, but to be "natural":

> Certain codes may, of course, be so widely distributed in a specific language community or culture, and be learned at so early an age, that they appear not to be constructed—the effect of an articulation between sign and referent—but to be "naturally" given. Simple visual signs appear to have achieved a "near-universality" in this sense: though evidence remains that even apparently "natural" visual codes are culture-specific. However, this does not mean that no codes have intervened; rather, that the codes have been profoundly *naturalised*. (p. 132)

As Hall goes on to explain, the more "natural" a code appears to be, the more comprehensively the practice of coding has been disguised.

Visual communication (the photo and the television image, in particular) appears not to be composed of discourses at all, since its signs appear to be natural images of the real world (after all, a picture of something is just that—a picture of something). It is necessary to emphasize the fact that the visual sign in the television message has to be encoded too. Indeed, visual "languages" work like any other languages. To the extent that visual languages may fool us by appearing to be natural, it is crucial to crack the codes, interpret them, and release their social meanings.

All of this provides us with a slightly contradictory model: of a television message that is open to various readings by various readers, but that is composed through a set of highly conventionalized codes that we apprehend as natural and that we are therefore unlikely to decode in ways that differ markedly from the intentions of the encoder. Hall deals with this contradiction by arguing that the television message may be polysemic, but it is not totally pluralistic; that is, while there is a degree of openness about its meanings, there are also limits. If meanings are not entirely *predetermined* by cultural codes, they are composed within a system that is *dominated* by accepted codes:

> Connotative codes are *not* equal among themselves. Any society's culture tends, with varying degrees of closure, to impose its classification of the social and cultural and political world. These constitute a *dominant cultural order*, though it is neither univocal nor uncontested. . . . The different areas of social life appear to be mapped out into discursive domains, hierarchically organized into *dominant* or *preferred* meanings. (p. 134)

This notion is important because it emphasizes the fact that dominant meanings are not irresistibly imposed, they are only "preferred." Readers from social groups who find themselves at odds with these dominant meanings—subcultural groups, workers on strike, single mothers, blacks—may well resist them in their own interpretations of the television message.

The process of constructing, as well as the process of reading, the message is similarly complex. To look at it from the "encoder's" side of the process, although there are rules and conventions that facilitate the reproduction of the dominant way of seeing and representing the world, actual signifying practices involve a kind of performance, a calling up and deployment of what one considers to be the appropriate codes and discourses. From the point of view of the television program producer, the problem is not so much one of breaking out of a restrictive straitjacket of codes, but of convincing the viewer to construct the same reading of the program as the producer. So, TV drama producers will use ominous music to warn us of a threat, and to fix its meaning *as* a threat. Or the use of specific representational codes tells us immediately how to view a character; there is little point in arguing about whether or not Cybill Shepherd's character in *Moonlighting* is attractive or not—the halo of diffused light that surrounds her image in many shots defines her as an object of desire, whether we, as individual viewers, desire her or not. Representational codes are made to "work" toward the preferred meaning. As Hall (1980c) puts it:

> In speaking of *dominant meanings*, then, we are not talking about a one-sided process which governs how all events will be signified. It consists of the "work" required to enforce, win plausibility for and command as legitimate a *decoding* of the event within the limit of dominant definitions in which it has been connotatively signified. (p. 135)

"Encoding" television discourse is the process of setting "some of the limits and parameters within which decodings will operate. If there were no limits, audiences could simply read whatever they liked into the message" (p. 135).

Hall next considers how the audience's relation to these limits might be better understood. And it is here he makes his most influential formulations. Drawing on the work of the sociologist Frank Parkin, Hall argues that we can identify three "hypothetical" positions from which the decoding of a television message may be constructed: he calls these the dominant-hegemonic position, or (as it is more widely described now) the "preferred" reading, the "negotiated" position, and the "oppositional" position. To read the message from the dominant or preferred position, the viewer "takes the connoted meaning from, say, a television newscast or current affairs program full and straight, and decodes the message in terms of the reference code in which it has been encoded" (p. 136). It has become clear that while such a position might exist theoretically, it rarely occurs in practice. The majority of us read television by producing what Hall calls "negotiated" readings, which "accord the privileged position to the dominant definitions of events while reserving the right to make a more negotiated application to local conditions." As he goes on to say, this negotiated reading will be "shot through with contradictions" (p. 137). A worker on strike may agree with a current affairs report arguing that it is in the national interest for wage increases to lag behind inflation, while still maintaining his claim for better pay or working conditions in his particular place of employment. The negotiated reading will acknowledge the dominant definitions of the world but may still claim exceptions to the rule in specific cases.

The final position is the oppositional. Here the viewer understands the preferred reading being constructed, but "retotalizes the message within some alternative framework of reference": "This is the case of the viewer who listens to a debate on the need to limit wages but 'reads' every mention of the 'national interest' as 'class interest'" (p. 138). We occupy this position every time we witness a political broadcast or advertisement for the political party we usually vote *against*. Instead of reading sympathetically or compliantly, we adopt an opposing position to that from which the message is produced. The result is a reading that is the opposite of what seems intended, possibly confirming our decision to vote for the opponent.

Hall sees these three positions as anything but discrete. He talks of the "most significant political moments" being the point "when events which are normally signified and decoded in a negotiated way begin to be given an oppositional reading" (p. 138). Texts can change their meaning and can be worked on by their audiences. Sexist advertising, for instance, is a dominant practice that nevertheless offends many and provokes opposition. To read such ads as offensive or degrading is to hijack their meaning, turning the dominant into the oppositional. Over such representations, Hall says, the "struggle in discourse" is joined (p. 138). The "structured polysemy" of messages makes their specific reading at any one time a political struggle between dominant and subordinated meanings.

To talk of the battle for the control of the message is not merely hyperbolic. As I write, the Chinese government is engaged in just such a struggle, reconstituting film of the massacre in Tiananmen Square so that its dominant meaning is reversed; the students' demonstration is reframed as an attack upon the soldiers, its participants criminalized in order to legitimate their punishment and the resultant program of repression. Here the struggle over the meaning of one set of television messages has literally become a struggle of life and death.

The importance of the "Encoding/Decoding" article lies in its demonstration that although the moments of constructing and reading a television message may be determinate moments, there is still a range of possible outcomes in both cases. Now that textual analysis is well established, this may not seem such a radical advance. But when one considers the preeminence of American communication theory at the time, it was a significant break with conventional assumptions. Not only does Hall insist on the possibility of a lack of fit between the codes used by the encoder and those used by the decoder (this does occur in American traditions too), but he also insists on explaining this disjunction in ideological, political terms. Hall suggests that such moments are not accidents, but are the signs of structural differences produced and determined by other social/economic/cultural forces and made available for analysis in the reading of the television message. This message then becomes a new kind of research resource for inquiries into culture and society. Where the earlier notion of the "effects" of the media localized the meaning (and the effect) of the message in the individual reader, the encoding/decoding model defined media texts as moments when the larger social and political structures within the culture are exposed for analysis.

The Establishment of Textual Analysis

Reading Hall's article now, one can see how strongly it asserts the polysemic nature of the message and how presciently it alludes to new conceptualizations of the television audience—conceptualizations that have only in the last five or six years been further developed. Yet, the primary use made of this article during the 1970s was to describe the ideological forces that shape television messages. Most British cultural studies analyses of television during these years examined the ideological and discursive "work" Hall mentions from a particular perspective, concentrating on the ways in which the contradictions and divisions within society are smoothed over or naturalized within specific television programs and genres. Cultural studies analysis of the media generally emphasized the construction of consensus, the reproduction of the status quo, the irresistibility of dominant meanings. So, although the idea of the passivity of the audience was dismantled in favor of the "preferred," "negotiated," and "oppositional" reading models, the application of these models tended to construct an audience that was, nevertheless, still helpless before the ideological unity of the television message. Although the theoretical possibility of aberrant readings was always admitted, the primary effort was put into establishing just how difficult, *how* aberrant, such readings in practice would be. The power of the text over the reader dominated this stage of media analysis.

Nevertheless, the period produced extremely useful, pioneering studies. Charlotte Brunsdon and David Morley's (1978) analysis of the BBC magazine program *Nationwide* is a case in point. (*Nationwide* was an early evening magazine program, closer in format to American or Australian breakfast television than to the conventional current affairs program. It was outstandingly successful, a TV institution in Britain for some years.) In the first of a number of studies of this program, Brunsdon and Morley present a textual analysis of the codes and conventions that define *Nationwide* for its viewers, supported by some quantitative analysis of its patterns of selection—what kind of stories appear most frequently, for instance. They stress how actively *Nationwide* works to present itself as a simple reflection of the way its viewers see the world:

> It [*Nationwide*] presents itself as catching in its varied and comprehensive gaze "everything" which could possibly be of interest to us, and simply "mirrors" or reflects it back to us. What is more, it "sees" these events in exactly the same perspective, and speaks of them in exactly the same "voice", as that of its audience. Everything in *Nationwide* works so as to support this mirror-structure of reflections and recognitions. The ideology of television as a transparent medium—simply showing us "what is happening"—is raised here to a high pitch of self-reflexivity. The whole of the complex work of the production of *Nationwide*'s version of "reality", sustained by the practices of recording, selecting, editing, framing and linking, and the identificatory strategies of producing "the scene, *Nationwide*", is repressed in the program's presentation of itself as an unproblematic reflection of "us" and "our world" in "our" program. *Nationwide* thus naturalises its own practice. (p. 9)

Analyzing the ways in which this is done, Brunsdon and Morley highlight a variety of discursive (or "encoding") conventions and expose their effects. For example, we may recognize their description of the inclusiveness of television anchorpersons' cozy address to their audience:

> The audience is constantly implicated through the link-person's discourse, by the use of personal pronouns: "tonight we meet . . .", "we all of us know that . . .", ". . . can happen to any of us", "so we asked . . .". The audience is also implicated by reference to past or coming items, which we have all seen/will see, and (by implication) all interpret in the same way. There is a reiterated assertion of a co-temporality ("nowadays", "in these times of . . .") which through its continuous present/immediacy transcends the differences between

us: "of course . . ." *Nationwide* assumes we all live in the same social world. (pp. 18–19)

Brunsdon and Morley explore this mode of address in their examination of the links created between segments within the program:

> This [the elision of the distinction between presenters and audience] can be most clearly seen in the use of . . . "Let's . . .". Tom Coyne: "Let's take a look at our weather picture"; "Let's go to Norwich"; Michael Barratt: "Let's hear from another part of East Anglia". Here, the audience's real separation from the team is represented in the form of a unity or community of interests between team and audience; the construction of this imaginary community appears as a proposition we can't refuse—we are made equal partners in the *Nationwide* venture, while simultaneously our autonomy is denied. This, with its attendant, possessive, "*our* weather picture", is the least ambiguous form of the "co-optive we", which is a major

Photo 3.1. Hugh Scully and Frank Bough—two of the presenters of BBC-1's *Nationwide* (*Used with kind permission from the BBC.*)

feature of the discourse and linking strategies in *Nationwide*. (p. 19)

Even though the picture of British life transmitted through *Nationwide* is extremely selective, Brunsdon and Morley demonstrate how actively and successfully its constitutive codes and discourses construct a consensual, "preferred" view—not only of the meaning of the program but of its definition of the society.

Hall et al. (1981), in "The Unity of Current Affairs Television," draw similar conclusions from their analysis of the serious BBC current affairs program, *Panorama*.[2] Their argument is constructed a little differently, however. Starting from an investigation of the notion of bias—television journalists' lack of objectivity—the authors discovered how evenhanded, in fact, treatment of a specific political issue had been: both in the time allowed contending parties and in the way in which they had been treated. This did not end the inquiry, however. Rather, by interrogating how the notions of "objectivity," "neutrality," "impartiality," and "balance" were understood by the journalists and their audience, the authors formed the view that these very principles supported the status quo and militated against the consideration of alternative points of view.

The Glasgow Media Group's (1976, 1980, 1982) work has shown how the media will always seek out opinion from those persons or groups already, almost automatically, authorized to speak: parliamentary political parties, employers' groups, trades unions, and so on. On any one topic, the range of interests canvassed and explanations sought will in practice be limited to those already recognized and legitimated by previous media representations. Occasionally, even this narrow range can be further restricted. The Glasgow group's research revealed that in at least one case no union or workers' explanation of the purpose of a crippling strike in Scotland was ever broadcast on the television news to counter government and employers' groups' accusations. Professional news-gathering practice must take some of the blame for this, as well as the news producer's need to construct a sense of unity with the program's audience. But Hall et al. (1981) take the Glasgow research a little further; not only are certain groups recognized as having a voice and others not, but the system of recognition is dramatically skewed in favor of parliamentary definitions of politics:

> Television *reproduces selectively* not the "unity" of any one Party, but *the unity of the Parliamentary political system as a whole. Panorama,* above other Current Affairs programs, routinely takes the part of guardian of unity in this *second* sense. . . . As a consequence, the agenda of problems and "prescriptions" which such a program handles is limited to those which have registered with, or are offered up by, the established Parliamentary parties. (p. 115)

This may not seem much of a worry until one realizes how often parliamentary agendas exclude issues nonparliamentary groups consider to be of national importance. "Green" or environmental politics, for instance, has only recently achieved legitimacy (that is, elected representatives) in some countries, and has still to achieve it in others. Yet, conservationists have been trying to secure recognition of their agenda for years. One can see how this agenda might challenge the interests of business, economic growth, and "progress"—all firmly established within the ideologies of the major political parties. It is not hard to imagine in whose interests the marginalization of green politics may have been. Despite its persistence and resourcefulness, it is only where green politics has been accepted within mainstream, electoral or parliamentary, politics that the media represent its definition of issues as legitimate. As a result of green candidates winning elections in Europe and Australia (to use two examples I am aware of personally), media representations of conservationist policies have changed, gradually, to the point where they are authorized as "experts" or consulted as "concerned citizens" rather than as members of the lunatic fringe. Hall et al. help explain how such exclusions occur, and how they can be reversed:

> The media remains a "leaky system", where ideological reproduction is sustained by "media work" and where

> contradictory ideologies do in fact appear; it reproduces the existing field of the political class struggle in its contradictory state. This does not obscure the fact, however, that the closure towards which this "sometimes teeth-gritting harmony" tends, overall, is one which, without favouring particular positions in the field of the political class struggle, *favours the way the field of political struggle is itself structured*. (p. 116)

Given such an account, one might understand why the authors focus so strongly on the reproduction of dominant ideologies through the media; for them, the possibilities of change are extremely limited.

Hall et al.'s discussion had explicit political objectives; similarly, in the case of the Glasgow Media Group the political objectives injected a lively note of polemic. Nevertheless, the political basis of cultural studies analyses of the media during the 1970s was significantly and, in general, overshadowed by the novelty and productiveness of the analytical methods employed. The most notable effect of such interventions as those outlined above was an explosion of interest in the "reading" of cultural texts—for their own sake as much as for their cultural significance as "maps of meaning." The most widespread development of teaching and publication in cultural studies has occurred in this form. The Methuen New Accents series published Hawkes's *Structuralism and Semiotics* (1977) and Fiske and Hartley's *Reading Television* (1978). Shortly after this, Methuen's Studies in Communication series published a set of books aimed at applying these analytical methods to each of the mass media in turn: John Hartley's *Understanding News* (1982), Gillian Dyer's *Advertising as Communication* (1982), and Andrew Crisell's *Understanding Radio* (1986), with later additions from Roy Armes, *On Video* (1989), and myself, *Film as Social Practice* (1988). Supporting these specific applications came an introductory text, Fiske's *Introduction to Communication Studies* (1982), and a useful glossary of terms, O'Sullivan et al.'s *Key Concepts in Communication* (1983). Other publishers entered the field, too; one particularly successful venture was Boyars's publication of Judith Williamson's *Decoding Advertisements*

(1978). While it was distinctive for its explicit feminist and post-Freudian influences, *Decoding Advertisements*, like the others, introduced readers to the principles of, largely, semiotic analysis and then applied them to the particular media forms with which it was concerned.

During the late 1970s and early 1980s, the semiotic/structuralist tradition of textual analysis became institutionalized in media studies and communications courses in secondary and university education in Britain. The existence of a similar practice—the close analysis of literary texts—in traditional English courses in higher education probably contributed to the readiness with which this new field of study was taken up. It may also explain why Fiske and Hartley's *Reading Television* (1978) spends so much of its time, on the one hand, drawing analogies between the need to analyze the literary text and the need to analyze television while, on the other hand, explicitly excluding literary modes of analysis and literary assumptions of value. Most of the work produced at this time by, for instance, the CCCS had long forsaken literary models, and so these admonitions were clearly addressed to a new, noncultural studies audience. *Reading Television* was significant because it took these new methods to new audiences and to new classes of students.

As was Raymond Williams around this time, Fiske and Hartley were keen to differentiate themselves from the dominant American traditions of communication study. Their account of content analysis, and of traditional explanations of the function of television (largely, its socializing effects), is used to justify the proposition of alternative approaches: semiotic analysis and Fiske and Hartley's idea of television as the equivalent of "the bard" in modern society.

Fiske and Hartley (1978) approach television as an oral, rather than a literate, medium, and resist its incorporation into literary studies:

> Every medium has its own unique set of characteristics, but the codes which structure "the language" of television are much more like those of speech than of writing. Any attempt to decode a television "text" as if it were a literary text is thus not only doomed to failure but it is also likely to

> result in a negative evaluation of the medium based on its inability to do a job for which it is in fact fundamentally unsuited. (p. 15).

Their description of the function of television draws on Hall's encoding/decoding model:

> The internal psychological state of the individual is not the prime determinant in the communication of television messages. These are decoded according to individually learnt but culturally generated codes and conventions, which of course impose similar constraints of perception on the encoders of the messages. It seems, then, that television functions as a social ritual, overriding individual distinctions, in which our culture engages in order to communicate with its collective self. (p. 85)

Television, they suggest, performs a "bardic function" for the culture. Just as the bard translated the central concerns of his day into verse, television renders "our own everyday perceptions" into its specialized language system. It serves the needs of the culture in particular ways: it addresses collective audiences rather than the individual; it is oral rather than literate; it operates as a centering discourse, appearing as the voice of the culture with which individuals can identify; and it takes its place in the cycle of production and reproduction of the culture's dominant myths and ideologies. Fiske and Hartley divide television's bardic function into categories that include the articulation of a consensus about reality; the implication of individuals into membership of the culture; the celebration, explanation, interpretation, and justification of the doings of individuals within the society; the demonstration of the practical adequacy of the culture's ideologies and mythologies, and, conversely, the exposure of any practical inadequacy resulting from changed social conditions; and the guarantee of audience members' status and identity. There is some overlap in these categories, but the general notion of the bardic function continues to be useful. Of particular importance is its explicit refutation of enduring popular demonologies of television: accounts of the medium's function that assume it serves purposes never previously conceived of or needed, and therefore to be deplored.

The second half of *Reading Television* consists of textual readings of individual television programs: dancing competitions, game shows, news, sport, and drama. In most cases, the mode is explanatory, outlining the construction of the dominant or preferred meaning. Since the readings function as demonstrations of the semiotic methods outlined earlier in the book, there are few occasions to interrogate current theoretical models. However, in the most interesting reading, that of the popular BBC game show *The Generation Game*, Fiske and Hartley develop a critique of the notion of the "preferred reading."

The analysis is enclosed within a chapter dealing with rituals of competition in game shows and in sport on television. Fiske and Hartley note *The Generation Game*'s difference from other kinds of quiz shows—*Let's Make a Deal*, for instance. *The Generation Game* was an evening

Photo 3.2. Bruce Forsyth and a contestant on *The Generation Game* (*Used with kind permission from the BBC and Bruce Forsyth.*)

game show, hosted by ex-vaudeville comic Bruce Forsyth, in which competing family groups were given a range of comical tasks to perform in order to earn points toward a prize at the end. *The Generation Game*, however, despite its use of prizes, was markedly noncompetitive, exploiting the spectacles of embarrassment provided by its competitors' attempts to do things they were no good at: "throwing" a pot, decorating a cake, performing amateur theatricals, and so on. (See photo 3.2.) Participation held its own rewards:

> This loss of substance of the competitiveness may well signify the irrelevance of the values of a free-enterprise, competitive society to the norms of family or community life. *The Generation Game*, in its final effect, asserts the validity of non-competitive communal values within the structure of a competitive society, and is thus working within an area of cultural tension for which our society has not found a comfortable point of equilibrium. (p. 157)

Fiske and Hartley move from this perception to a suggestion of dissatisfaction with the notions of domination that have underpinned their analyses throughout the book:

> So while the simple binary model of dominant/dominated may indicate the basis of our class structure, we must be chary of applying it too directly to the texts. A cultural text is always to a certain extent ambivalent. It never merely celebrates or reinforces a univalent set of culturally located attitudes, but rather reflects the tensions caused by the many contradictory factors that any culture is continually having to reconcile in a working equilibrium. (p. 157)

To move further into the analysis of these tensions within particular historical moments, or of the specific sociocultural reasons for the difference of *The Generation Game*, is something the book is prevented from doing by its concentration on textual analysis and by its introductory nature. Also, within the field of study itself, while the relation between texts and culture was well outlined, the theoretical orthodoxies that might account for the relation between texts and history still remained to be developed.

If Fiske and Hartley are ultimately limited by their textual focus, Richard Dyer's work shows at least one way out of that difficulty. First of all, while Dyer subjects texts to analysis, he avoids any suggestion that he is examining the "text in itself"—the text as an independent, discrete object of analysis. Dyer is interested in the discourses used to construct texts and the social histories of these constitutive discourses. Second, he broadens the idea of the text by acknowledging the importance of extratextual material in the construction of any particular text's meanings. Consequently, his analyses draw on representations not normally considered (fan magazines, for instance). Dyer's analytical procedure is strenuously intertextual and also, as he puts it, "dialectical, involving a constant movement between the sociological and the semiotic" (Dyer 1982, 2). The result is the mobilization of textual analysis in the service of the social analysis of discourse.

His subject, in the books I refer to here, is the meaning of film stars: the social meaning of the images of a Jane Fonda, a Marilyn Monroe, or a Marlene Dietrich. Dyer's first book dealing with this topic, *Stars* (1982), asks specific questions about just what kind of "social reality" film stars might construct, what they might signify, and how they might function within film texts. Dyer examines the social construction of the image of the star through the full range of its representations—fan magazines, interviews, pinups, news stories, publicity and promotional material, and so on—and how this is inscribed into specific film narratives. He reveals how stars accrue meanings that are relatively independent of the characters they play but that contribute to their characterizations on the screen; this is why it is unsurprising for us to find that James Stewart plays the naive liberal lawyer and John Wayne the retired gunslinger (rather than the other way around) in *The Man Who Shot Liberty Valance*. In his analysis of Jane Fonda's career, Dyer outlines how "her" meanings changed *between* texts, as it were, over time. And, finally, he examines the ideological function of stars for society: how they manage to represent both the type and the ideal of the individual in society. Dyer explores the central contradiction in the signification of stars: they are simultaneously representative of society and uniquely individual, both typical and extraordinary. In *Stars* and in his second study, *Heavenly Bodies* (1986), Dyer insists on the social content of cinema texts, on the historically produced competencies and expectations brought to the cinema by the audience, and on the already coded meanings that enter the sound stage with the performers. *Heavenly Bodies,* too, provides accounts of the ways in which subgroups within the mass audience can appropriate a star's image and insert it into new contexts, giving it new meanings: his discussion of Judy Garland's particular meaning for gay subcultures is an example of this.

Dyer's work does not belong to the same tradition as that of the Birmingham CCCS. While not typical of it, his interests in cinema are part of that branch of screen studies most closely identified with the British Film Institute (BFI) in London, and the major film journal in Britain, *Screen.* *Screen* has been influential and controversial, identified with a particular theoretical/critical "line," a particular aesthetics, and a particular political stance. Influenced by the semiotic/psychoanalytic cinema theory of Christian Metz and by Althusserian theories of ideology, and focused on the problem of the construction of subjectivities particularly as defined in post-Freudian and feminist appropriations of psychoanalysis, *Screen* marked out a position that opposed much of the cultural studies work done in Britain in the 1970s. While articles published in *Screen* made important contributions to the development of textual analysis, the journal's prevailing theoretical position involved an extreme textual determinism. At one point, the CCCS set up a special research group to consider what became known as "*Screen* theory"; Stuart Hall's (1980e) and David Morley's (1980b) critiques are among the products of that research group.

It would be wrong to see *Screen* as speaking with one voice over its career, but certain concerns and preferred theoretical protocols do pervade its pages. *Screen*'s concern with semiotic explanations of the relation between language and the subject, and its interest in Lacan's view of subjectivity as an empty space to be filled through language, lead it to foreground vigorously the role of representation and thus of the text, in constructing the subject. *Screen* theory saw the processes of *interpellation*, the way the individual subject is "written into" the ideologies of his or her society through acquisition of its language systems, as central and comprehensive processes, particularly in film and television. Texts are discussed in terms of their capacity to place or "position" the viewer, inserting or "suturing" him or her into a particular relationship to the narrative and into an uncomplicated relationship to dominant ideologies. There is little the viewer can do about this ideological positioning other than to accept it; in *Screen* theory, texts always and irresistibly tell us how to understand them.

Understandably, this textual determinism provoked some argument. Among the most controversial aspects of the position was its apparently categoric character; could we really say that *all* texts worked like this for *all* readers? On British TV at the time (mid-1970s), a subgenre of critical dramatized documentaries was in vogue, producing texts whose narratives appeared to undermine dominant ideologies. The British docudrama *Days of Hope*, which dealt with aspects of British working-class history from the Great War to the beginnings of the Depression, was widely seen as a genuinely political critique of both Labour and Conservative party politics over that period that established unmistakable parallels between the Britain of the 1920s and a contemporary Britain torn by inflation, unemployment, and battles between unions and government. It was a particularly realistic piece of television, and it provoked outcry from the Conservatives, who pilloried the BBC and its writer, Jim Allen, for their (supposed, in the BBC's case) Marxist leanings.

The debate over this text reached epic proportions.[3] *Screen* theory replied through Colin McCabe, arguing that the generic form of the program, its realism, far from enhancing its progressive effect, actually rendered it unable to criticize society.[4] Realism, McCabe (1981) argues, is a set of representational codes that offers the viewer a comfortable position from which to see even bitter political struggles as natural or inevitable. Setting such struggles in the past inevitably implies their resolution in the present, while the narrative's construction of a superior, knowledgeable position for viewers protects them from responding critically or "progressively" to the events depicted. Realism, the argument goes, precodes the reality it represents within commonsense understandings of the world; so even when it depicts terrible happenings, we leave the text, sighing acceptingly, "Oh well, that's the way it is (or was), there is little we can do about it." Realistic fictions in all media inscribe the reader into a controlling discourse—a set of values, a narrator's voice, or the control of the perspectives of the camera—that takes on the role of an authoritative narrator. McCabe argues that this authoritative narrator tells the reader what to think, closes off questions, and rewards them by delivering them to the end of the fiction. The realist text cannot question reality or its constituent conditions without destroying the authority of this narrator. And since the realist text depends on the reader seeing *it* as reality, it cannot question itself without losing its authenticity. The progressive alternative would be a text that challenges viewers by questioning their commonsense views of the world, and, *Screen* theory argues, this can be done only by breaking the conventional patterns of representation—by breaking with the dominant conventions of realism.

The "realism debate" has been influential and lasting. The celebrated BBC TV drama, *The Boys from the Blackstuff*, screened in the early 1980s, provoked a rematch between the *Screen* theorists and those who felt that TV realism *did* have the potential to produce an "oppositional" reading despite its dominant generic form. Stephen Heath (1985) and others have argued that it is impossible to "read off" a set of ideological positions automatically from the generic form of a text, and I have argued elsewhere that the realist form used in some Australian cinema has offered clearly progressive readings as dominant positions (Turner 1988). Ultimately, such protests prevailed. The idea that the realist text is "not so much 'read' as simply 'consumed/appropriated' straight, via the only possible positions available to the reader—those reinscribed by the text" (Morley 1980b, 166–67) is usually presented in a much less categoric fashion now—even in *Screen*.

The position taken on this issue, however, is typical of

Screen theory. It presented a consistent critique of conventional, popular film and television texts, proposing a renovatory, avant-garde aesthetic that questioned dominant representational conventions. The search for the "progressive text," which was both textually unconventional (nonrealist) and politically antibourgeois, dominated much of the work published in *Screen* in the late 1970s and early 1980s. Indeed, for some time it became a reflex to deal with new television and film texts in terms of their perceived progressiveness or their lack of it, and this led *Screen* into an elitist political cul-de-sac from which it was difficult to say anything useful about any popular text. One reason for *Screen* theory's insistence on challenging conventional textual forms was the conviction that the text itself, rather than forces outside of and prior to the text, constructed the subject position from which the viewer made sense of it. The avant-garde offered a way out of this; a more interrogative set of representational conventions might produce a more critical and questioning audience/subject. While there has been widespread acceptance of this last proposition, *Screen* theory in general has been contentious. Representatives of the CCCS vigorously resisted *Screen*'s textual determinism as denying history, the polysemic nature of signs and discourses, and the "interrogative/expansive nature of all readings" (Morley 1980b, 167). Subsequent revisions of the position seem to acknowledge the fact that *Screen* theory tended to isolate "the encounter of text and reader from all social and historical structures *and* from other texts . . . which *also* position the subject" (Morley 1980b, 163).

One stream within this body of theory, however, that clearly does *not* ignore the formation of the subject within other texts or social structures is the feminist critique of popular film narrative. Laura Mulvey's 1975 *Screen* article "Visual Pleasure and Narrative Cinema" is almost invariably cited as the key text, but the critique is more widespread and diverse than this would suggest. In general, feminist criticisms of mainstream film and television argue that the way in which these media represent the world replicates other representational structures' subordination of women. Crudely, the argument is that if popular texts establish a position from which we find it comfortable to view and identify with them, it should not surprise us to discover that the viewing position constructed within the conventional discourses of (say) Hollywood cinema is that of the male, not the female, viewer. While the female body is, conventionally, traversed by the camera—lit, framed, and explored as an object of male desire—the male body is not subjected to the same regime of inspection for the pleasure of the female viewer. This, despite the fact that half the audience, on balance, will be female. Mulvey and others argue that even the pleasures offered by film are colonized, offered to women as experiences that involve the denial of their own female subjectivity if they are to be enjoyed. The pleasures of looking, of voyeurism and narcissism, proffered by Hollywood cinema, Mulvey argues, are masculinist and, in some genres (e.g., horror films, certain kinds of thrillers), actively misogynist. While Mulvey's original formulations have been revised by herself and others, and while it is possible to argue with her assessment, say, of the work of Hitchcock, as Tania Modleski (1988) has recently done, they alert us to the way that texts can provide a very limited number of viewing positions for an audience to occupy, and to the fact that these correspond to a narrow range of ideological effects. Despite the formation of each member of the audience as a separate subjectivity, and despite the polysemy of the text, we are not granted a temporary exemption from the ideological frames of our social existence when we enter a movie theater. Feminist critiques demonstrate that the vastly dominant discourses in the media naturalize masculine pleasures; we need to be shown how to notice this effect.

Dethroning the Text

David Morley was among the foremost critics of *Screen* theory and its privileging of the power of the text, and his work has provided one of the most important countervailing strands of thought. It will be addressed in more detail in the following chapter, but for the moment it is important to note how

Morley's attempt to develop Hall's encoding/decoding model came to demonstrate, instead, that individual readings of television are much more complex and unpredictable than Hall's model would allow. As a continuation of the Brunsdon and Morley (1978) textual analysis of *Nationwide*, Morley (1980a) played an episode of the program to 26 groups of varied class, social, and occupational backgrounds and then studied their decodings of the text. The results conclusively undermine the linkage of particular readings with particular class positions (as if the working classes all read one way, and the middle classes all read another); they also reveal that making sense of television is an intensely social and interactive activity. Given the diversity of response Morley collected in the *Nationwide* study, it was difficult to see how the text *could* produce a subject position that overrode those produced by other social forces such as gender, ethnicity, occupation, and so on. It was also clear, however, that the subject positions produced by these other social forces were also unpredictable, disunited, and even internally contradictory. Thus, Morley—and others who developed this area of audience studies—reestablished the importance of the context in which texts are consumed and of the social content brought to them by specific audiences.

Other work proceeding within Birmingham and elsewhere at the time proved complementary. The so-called subcultures group at the CCCS established approaches that emphasized the minority rather than the majority, the subordinate rather than the dominant, the subculture rather than the culture. Studies of urban youth in Britain that drew on history, sociology, and anthropology had emphasized the strategies subordinate groups used to make their *own* meanings in resistance to those of the dominant culture. Not only did they negotiate with or oppose the dominant, but in many cases they actively appropriated and transformed (and thus subverted) dominant meanings. (Examples of this tradition of research can be found in Hall and Jefferson 1976; further discussion of this tradition will be presented in Chapter 5.)

The introduction to *Resistance Through Rituals* (Hall and Jefferson 1976) argues that culture is made up of contributing smaller groups or class fragments, social groups that develop their own "distinct patterns of life," giving "expressive form to their social and material life-experience." Culture is not monolithic, as in a sense is implied by the encoding/decoding models, but is made up of many competing, overlapping, and conflicting groups. Each of these groups defines itself through its distinctive way of life, embodied in its institutions (a motorbike club, for instance), its social relations (their specific place within the domain of work, or the family), its beliefs and customs, and its "uses of objects and material life." All these "maps of meaning" constitute the subculture and make it intelligible to its members (p. 10). Within a subculture, then, the most mundane object can take on specific meanings; within punk culture, the humble safety pin was appropriated as an offensive decoration and worn openly on ripped clothing or in some cases inserted into the skin.

Many subcultural studies examined the way in which these maps of meaning were composed, and what meanings were attributed to the practices, institutions, and objects within the subcultural group. As Hall and Jefferson (1976) point out, the study of subculture is more than an essentially sociological study of the structure and shape of social relations; it becomes interested in "the way [these structures and shapes] are experienced, understood and interpreted" (p. 11). The effect—at least in that part of the tradition I am going to consider here—is to turn the subculture into a text, its examination into a variant of textual analysis, and the interpretation of its meanings into a highly contingent activity.

As a result, the definition of what constitutes a text broadened dramatically; the new definition included cultural practices, rituals, dress, and behavior as well as the more fixed and "produced" texts such as television programs or advertisements. The emphasis shifted toward the generation of meanings through social practices and, even more significant, toward the location of these meanings in those who participated in the practice rather than the practice itself. This reinforced the importance of the audience/participants in the production of meaning and highlighted how often texts are in fact read "against the grain," through oppositional socially produced positions that "make over" their dominant meanings. The "meaning" of a text was allowed to be more provisional, perhaps contradictory, and subculturally specific. As a consequence, it became debatable whether or not the primary source of meaning was the set of social relations into which the text was inserted or the specific forms of the texts themselves. The text was "dethroned"; it lost its determining authority, its ability to determine how it would be understood by its readers.

Possibly the most influential deployment of subculture studies within the mainstream of cultural studies was Dick Hebdige's *Subculture: The Meaning of Style*, published in Methuen's New Accents series in 1979. In this book, Hall's textual struggle for meaning takes on a material form in subcultural style: the dress codes of punks, the musical codes of reggae, the retrospective dandyism of the teddy boys. Hebdige's is one of the livelier and more accessible of the books to come out of this tradition, and his account of the representational codes of specific urban subcultures in 1970s Britain still makes stimulating reading.

In *Subculture*, Hebdige uses semiotics to interpret the meanings—ambiguous and contradictory—produced by subcultural dress, music, and behavioral styles. One influence on Hebdige's approach is literary criticism (specifically the work of the *Tel Quel* group in France); another influence comes from cultural studies' appropriations of ethnographic techniques, particularly the work of Phil Cohen.

Hebdige singles out Cohen's work for its linkage of class experience and leisure styles, and for his explanation of the relation between youth subcultures and their parent cultures. Cohen exerted a profound influence on the CCCS's research on subcultures; this is evident in *Resistance Through Rituals*, as Hebdige notes, in the various authors' interpretations of "the succession of youth cultural styles as symbolic forms of resistance" (p. 80). Most important, Cohen's explanation of the basic or "latent" function of subcultures provides the rationale for Hebdige's own reading of specific subcultures as texts. For Cohen, the function of subculture was to "express and resolve, albeit magically, the contradictions which remain hidden or unresolved in the parent culture"

(p. 77). The skinheads' fundamentalist caricature of working-class dress is thus read as a challenge, confronting the gradual embourgeoisement of working-class culture. Cohen

Photo 3.3. Cover of Dick Hebdige's *Subculture: The Meaning of Style* (*Used with kind permission of Methuen and Co.*). Appropriately enough, this is the only one of the New Accents series to feature a genuinely stylish cover.

relates the specifics of style to the more general "ideological, economic and cultural factors which bear upon subculture" (p. 78) through a close reading of leisure styles that Hebdige regards as exemplary:

> Rather than presenting class as an abstract set of external determinations, [Cohen] showed it working out in practice as a material force, dressed up, as it were, in experience and exhibited in style. The raw material of history could be seen refracted, held and "handled" in the line of a mod's jacket, in the soles on a teddy boy's shoes. (p. 78)

Subculture: The Meaning of Style offers readings and case studies that reflect changes in the way texts were being defined and that exerts an influence on the studies of popular culture that follow it; one can see the continuities between Hebdige's work and that of Iain Chambers, for instance. But Hebdige's assessment of the political function of subcultural style was probably his most significant contribution. The meaning of subculture, he says, is like any other ideological territory—open to contestation: "and style is the area in which the opposing definitions clash with most dramatic force" (p. 3). Further, subcultures are enclosed within the larger processes of hegemony, against which their signifying practices need to be set:

> Individual subcultures can be more or less "conservative" or "progressive", integrated *into* the community, continuous with the values of that community, or extrapolated *from* it, defining themselves *against* the parent culture. Finally, these differences are reflected not only in the objects of subcultural style, but in the signifying practices which represent those objects and render them meaningful. (p. 127)

Hebdige is most interested, however, in those subcultural styles that seem to challenge hegemony, that offer an "oblique gesture of Refusal"; there, "the objections are lodged, the contradictions displayed . . . at the profoundly superficial level of appearance: that is, at the level of signs" (p. 17).

The book largely engages with subcultures at the level of signs, too: an example is this account of the mode of dancing associated with British punks, the "pogo":

> Dancing, usually an involving and expressive medium in British rock and mainstream pop cultures, was turned into a dumbshow of blank robotics. . . . the pogo was a caricature—a *reductio ad absurdum* of all the solo dance styles associated with rock music. It resembled the "anti-dancing" of the "Leapniks" which Melly describes in connection with the trad boom. . . . The same abbreviated gestures—leaping into the air, hands clenched to the sides, to head an imaginary ball—were repeated without variation in time to the strict mechanical rhythms of the music. . . . the pogo made improvisation redundant: the only variations were imposed by changes in the tempo of the music—fast numbers being "interpreted" with manic abandon in the form of frantic on-the-spots, while the slower ones were pogoed with a detachment bordering on the catatonic. (pp. 108–9)

Hebdige lays out his texts for us to examine, but always insists on their subversive, resistant potential:

> Style in subculture is, then, pregnant with significance. Its transformations go "against nature", interrupting the process of "normalisation". As such, they are gestures, movements towards a speech which offends the "silent majority", which challenges the principle of unity and cohesion, which contradicts the myth of consensus. Our task becomes, like Barthes', to discern the hidden messages inscribed in code on the glossy surfaces of style, to trace them out as "maps of meaning" which obscurely re-present the very contradictions they are designed to resolve or conceal. (p.18)

Interestingly, in Hebdige's latest book, *Hiding in the Light* (1988), he bids "farewell" to the study of youth subcultures by denying the connection between youth subcultures and the signification of negation or resistance. Admitting that his argument was reinforced by punk's explicit political agenda, and that subsequent youth movements no longer seem to articulate such a strong political resistance, Hebdige draws the useful theoretical lesson that "theoretical models are as tied to their own times as the human bodies that produce them." While Hebdige may overstate the case to maintain that "the idea of subculture-as-negation grew up alongside punk, remained inextricably linked to it, and died when it died" (p. 8), it is true that this formulation did run the risk of merely inverting the politics of consensus, simply equating the subordinate with the resistant.

Polysemy, Ambiguity, and Reading Texts

Aspects of the work described in the preceding section—the focus on the audience and on strategies of resistance within subcultural fragments of the "mass" audience—have been mobilized in other ways. Currently, and as something of a reaction against the dethroning of the text, some are arguing that, especially in the case of television or popular texts, this potential for resistant readings is in fact a property of texts themselves, and not merely of the audience members' socially produced methods of reading them. Where once the endeavor was to alert us to the construction of a consensual reading, a considerable number of studies have now begun to describe strategies of resistance within the text; networks of ambiguity and contradiction that invite and accommodate the reader's adoption of different, even ideologically contradictory, subject positions. Texts are seen to be loaded with an excess of meaning, leaking through the boundaries of any "preferred" readings into the social formations of the readers, and thus producing a range of meanings and pleasures. In this section, I will note some aspects of the development of this conceptualization of the relationship between text and reader.

In "Dance and Social Fantasy," Angela McRobbie (1984) resists the emphasis on social rather than textual influences on readers and audiences, and attacks the kind of subcultural and ethnographic research on youth discussed in the preceding section:

> One of the marked characteristics of most academic writing on youth has been its tendency to conceive of youth almost entirely in terms of action and of direct experience. Attention has been paid to young people in school, on the dole, and on the street, all sites where they are immediately visible to the social observer. This has had the effect of reducing the entire spectrum of young people's experience implicitly to these moments, neglecting almost totally those many times where they become viewers, readers, part of an audience, or simply silent, caught up in their own daydreams. To ignore these is to miss an absolutely central strand in their social and personal experience. It means that in all these subcultural accounts we are left with little knowledge of any one of their reading or viewing experiences, and therefore with how they find themselves represented in these texts, and with how in turn they appropriate from some of these and discard others. This absence has also produced a real blindness to the debt much of those youth cultural expressions owe to literary texts, to the cinema, to art and to older musical forms. (p. 141)

Texts are social formations, too, not simply raw material to be processed through other social determinants like gender and class. Furthermore, McRobbie suggests that the varying social uses to which texts may be put are available to us through close analysis. She cites as an example the way in which discussion of a film may become a social activity or event; her point is that this is possible only because even popular texts like Hollywood films inscribe into their forms an awareness of their varied usage: "The polysemy (or multiple meanings) of the text rises to the surface provoking and pandering to *different* pleasures, *different* expectations and *different* interpretations" (p. 150).

McRobbie concludes her argument by criticizing an earlier piece of her own, on the magazine *Jackie*, which attacked the fantastic, nonrealist properties of *Jackie*'s view of the world. In the more recent piece, McRobbie admits that her earlier account misunderstood and undervalued the pleasures the magazine offered, and attempted instead to impose an idealized notion of her own in their place. Her misunderstanding of the pleasures of the text, she argues, led to a devaluing of the readers' experience of it.

The notion of pleasure has increasingly been placed in opposition to that of ideology. There are varieties of pleasure that are located within the body, their production having physical sources. Whereas the meanings we give to the world we live in are socially produced, there is an argument that suggests our physical pleasures are our own. Such a theory implies a limited degree of individual freedom from the forces of ideology. As is so often the case, Barthes provides a starting point here with his discussion of the pleasures produced by certain kinds of literary texts in *The Pleasure of the Text* (1975). While the complexities of this position are not relevant here (I will talk a little more about them in Chapter 6), the effect of theories of pleasure is to raise the possibility that communication may have more consequences than the generation of meaning. Further, and more centrally for our purposes here, where texts are seen to produce both pleasures *and* meanings, the two may well contradict or counteract each other. Male audiences may find it hard to resist the voyeuristic pleasures offered in the Robert Palmer music video, "Simply Irresistible," no matter how ideologically alert they may be to its chic sexism. As Colin Mercer (1986) says, analysts of popular culture may need to "look over [their] shoulders and try to explain a certain 'guilt' of enjoyment of such and such *in spite of* its known ideologies and political provenance" (p. 54). Alternatively, some marginalized individual pleasures may contradict and resist dominant ideological positions.

John Fiske's current work represents perhaps the most unequivocal development of this last possibility; he identifies the category of "the popular" with those pleasures he believes resist and stand outside the forces of ideology. Fiske characterizes popular culture in general, and popular television in particular, by its ability to generate "illicit" pleasures and therefore subversive meanings.

One can chart the development of this position over the last few years. In his contribution to Robert Allen's collection, *Channels of Discourse,* Fiske (1987a) describes the complexity of the relations among texts, readers, and culture in an impeccably evenhanded manner, acknowledging the dialectics of resistance and determination, textual openness and ideological closure, in the production of textual meaning:

> A close reading of the signifiers of the text—that is, its physical presence— . . . recognizes that the signifieds exist not in the text itself, but extratextually, in the myths, counter-myths, and ideology of their culture. It recognizes that the distribution of power in society is paralleled by semiotic struggles for meanings. Every text and every reading has a social and therefore political dimension, which is to be found partly in the structure of the text itself and partly in the relation of the reading subject to that text. (p. 273)

The picture here is one of balance, but nevertheless one that depicts ideological systems maintaining their purchase against significant competition. The evenhandedness works to produce a consensual model of cultural production that recalls Hall's encoding/decoding explanations.

Fiske ultimately distances himself from such a position in order to explain why there is, in practice, no direct or necessary equation between popularity and ideological unity. To do this, Fiske draws on, among others, John Hartley's "Encouraging Signs: Television and the Power of Dirt, Speech and Scandalous Categories" (1983), in which Hartley discusses television as a "dirty" (socially unsanctioned) category that thrives on ambiguity and contradictions. Television's special quality, he says, is its ability to "produce more meaning than can be policed" (p. 76), a quality television producers deal with by attempting to limit their programs' potential for meaning. This, Hartley argues, inevitably fails, as ambiguity "leaks" into and out of the text. An "encouraging sign" of the weakness of the tenure of any hegemonic meaning, this leakage is the result of "semiotic excess," a proliferation of possible readings, an excess of meaning. Fiske (1986) suggests that this semiotic excess—not ideological unity—is intrinsic to popular cultural forms, explaining both their popularity and the apparent unpredictability of reactions to them:

> I suggest that it is more productive to study television not in order to identify the means by which it constructs subjects within the dominant ideology (though it undoubtedly and unsurprisingly works to achieve precisely this end), but rather how its semiotic excess allows readers to construct subject positions that are theirs (at least in part), how it allows them to make meanings that embody strategies of resistance to the dominant, or negotiate locally relevant inflections of it. (p. 213)

Fiske's enterprise can here be understood as an attempt to explain how popular culture seems, on the one hand, to be at the mercy of the culture industries and, on the other hand, to exercise a stout resistance and even subversiveness at times in its response to specific texts and their proposed meanings. The attribution of ambiguity to the text explains how texts might determine their preferred readings while still containing the potential for subversive or resistant "misreadings."

In *Television Culture*, Fiske (1987b) mobilizes developments in audience studies, the dethroning of the text, and his sense of the subversiveness of pleasure to present a view of popular culture audiences that is many miles from the manipulated masses of "effects" studies. Drawing on de Certeau's theorizing of the creativity of popular culture, Fiske sees "the popular" in rather a Brechtian way—as a relatively autonomous, if subordinated, voice competing with the dominant for representation. The making over of the dominant meanings in popular culture is seen as a successful political strategy that "empowers" otherwise subordinated groups and individuals.[5] The textual analysis this motivates is most interested in the production of politically progressive readings. The majority of *Television Culture* deals with what Fiske calls "activated texts," those produced largely through appropriation by their audience rather than, say, successful positioning by their producers. These activated texts do not constitute an aberration, at the fringe of television's cultural function, but are among its defining characteristics:

> Television's open-ness, its textual contradictions and instability, enable it to be readily incorporated into the oral

> culture of many and diverse groups in many and diverse ways so that, while it may not in its broadcast mode be a form of folklore, it is at least able to serve folkloric functions for some of its audiences. Its popularity among its diversity of audiences depends upon its ability to be easily and differently incorporated into a variety of subcultures: popularity, audience activity, and polysemy are mutually entailed and interdependent concepts. (p. 107)

Fiske is aware of the implications of announcing that capitalism's determining structures do not work, however; and so he is careful to acknowledge that the "plurality of meanings" within television texts is not "of course, a structureless pluralism," but is "tightly organized around textual and social power." The emphasis is nevertheless on the alternatives to the preferred meanings and the politics of their construction:

> The preferred meanings in television are generally those that serve the interests of the dominant classes: other meanings are structured in relations of dominance-subordination to those preferred ones as the social groups that activate them are structured in a power relationship within the social system. The textual attempt to contain meaning is the semiotic equivalent of the exercise of social power over the diversity of subordinate social groups, and the semiotic power of the subordinate to make their own meanings is the equivalent of their ability to evade, oppose, negotiate with this social power. Not only is the text polysemic in itself, but its multitude of intertextual relations increases its polysemic potential. (p. 127)

The obvious limitation to the progressive effect of this multitude of textual possibilities is that the textual system may well be more porous than the social system; making over the meaning of a television program may be much easier than climbing out of a ghetto, changing the color of one's skin, changing one's gender, or reducing one's dependence on the varied mechanisms of state welfare.

In some of Fiske's (1988) most recent work, the category of the text has itself vanished under the pressure of these competing definitions and forces:

> What excites me are the signs that we may be developing a semiotic ethnography that will help us toward understanding concrete, contextualised moments of semiosis as specific instances of more general cultural processes. In these moments, there are no texts, no audiences. There is only an instance of the process of making and circulating meanings and pleasures. (p. 250)

At this point, it is as if British cultural studies has turned back on itself, expunging the category of the text as if it is an impediment to the analysis of discourse. Yet, as we have seen, textuality is merely a methodological proposition, a strategy to enable analysis, not an attempt to claim privileged status for a range of cultural productions. In cultural studies, no text is independent of the methodology that constructs it as one. So far, the methodologies have not been conservative or rigid structures, inhibiting further development. The trends I have been charting, in fact, reveal how directly changes in method have been produced by shifts in the definition of what constitutes a text.

The category of the text, however, and explanations of the production of textual readings have become increasingly problematic. The difficulty is that, from one point of view, texts are held to contain meanings immanent in them, at least in the form of a set of limits so that one cannot read simply what one wants off them; they are also held to reproduce dominant ideological structures and thus must exercise some degree of dominance or preference toward a reading or group of readings. From the contrary point of view, however, texts contain the possibility of being read against the grain and producing resistant, or subordinated readings, mobilized by specific groups within the culture; they are also held to be historically contingent, subject to shifts in the contexts of their reception that can entirely change their specific meanings and their wider cultural significance. This last factor is one not yet explored here, and to deal with it I cite a book that takes the problems of defining and reading the text very seriously indeed—but without jettisoning the category altogether.

Bennett and Woollacott's (1988) book on the popular fictional hero, James Bond, goes beyond Morley's (1980a) account of different readers producing dominant, negotiated, and oppositional readings of the *Nationwide* text; these authors outline how different social and historical conditions can produce vastly different *dominant* readings of the multitextual figure of James Bond. *Bond and Beyond: The Political Career of a Popular Hero* is in many ways exemplary in its attempt to survey the historical, industrial, and ideological field that produces its texts—the films, novels, and publicity connected to the figure of James Bond. The book contains analyses of the internal structures of individual texts, of the ways in which the meanings of the texts might be historicized, of how Bond's meaning has changed over time, of the relationship between the films and the novels, and of the professional ideologies of the filmmakers and how these might have affected the specific translations of the novels into film. The problem of fully explicating a body of popular texts, however, is apparent in the fact that even this well-designed set of approaches has left gaps for the critic and the fan alike to question.

Bennett and Woollacott frame their project, quite explicitly, within arguments about textual analysis. Their instincts would seem to lie with those audience studies that recognize the social and discursive factors mediating the relations between texts and audiences; they are very critical of an excessive emphasis on the properties of the text:

> The case of Bond throws into high relief the radical insufficiency of those forms of cultural analysis which, in purporting to study texts "in themselves", do radical violence to the real nature of the social existence and functioning of texts in pretending that "the text itself" can be granted an existence, as a hypostatised entity, separated out from the always variable systems of intertextual relations which supply the real conditions of its signifying functioning. (pp. 6–7)

This view aligns Bennett and Woollacott with those who would follow discourse(s) as the object(s) of study, who would see texts as "sites around which a constantly varying and always many faceted range of cultural and ideological transactions are conducted" (p. 8). However, as they reveal later in the book, while their sympathies might lie with the audience studies, they reject at least one of Morley's unspoken assumptions: that the varying readings of the one program are of the "same" text, rather than the production of many, multiple texts.

Having distanced themselves from the two major traditions, Bennett and Woollacott develop a number of terms to help them redefine the connection between texts and society. First, they extend the idea of intertextuality, the system of internal references between texts: they introduce the hyphenated term *inter-textuality*, which refers to "the social organisation of the relations between texts within specific conditions of reading" (p. 45). Bennett and Woollacott insist that texts cannot relate even to each other independently of specific social conditions and the meanings they put into circulation. The term *inter-textuality* forces analysis to move continually between the text and the social conditions that frame its consumption, and limits textual interpretations to specific historical locations. The career of James Bond spans more than three decades, and his meanings have been produced by quite different social and textual determinants at any one point. James Bond, within one set of inter-textual relations, is an aristocratic, traditional British hero who celebrates the imperial virtues of breeding, taste, and authority; and within another set of inter-textual relations, the *same* books are read as producing a figure who is modern, iconoclastic, a living critique of an outmoded class system, and whose politics are those of Western capitalism, not merely of Britain. The inter-textual relations examined and exposed at any specific historical point are seen to exert some force on the reader and on the text, producing what Bennett and Woollacott call "reading formations":

> By "reading formations" here, we have in mind . . . those specific determinations which bear upon, mould

> and configure the relations between texts and readers in determinate conditions of reading. It refers, specifically, to the inter-textual relations which prevail in a particular context, thereby activating a given body of texts by ordering the relations between them in a specific way such that their reading is always already cued in specific directions that are not given by those "texts themselves" as entities separable from such relations. (p. 64)

This is not to suggest that texts are absolutely relative and bear no determining characteristics at all, but to emphasize the fact that texts do not simply contain set meanings they will generate, willy-nilly, no matter what the conditions of their reception. Even relatively stable textual properties, such as genre, can be seen as "cultural and variable" rather than "textual and fixed" (p. 81). The authors demonstrate this by insisting on the temporal variation of dominant readings of the Bond texts, by examining the shifts in the ideological significance James Bond carries at specific points in the figure's history. "Textual shifters" allow us to chart the ways in which certain aspects of the figure are foregrounded in one ideological context and other aspects in another context, as "pieces of play within different regions of ideological contestation, capable of being moved around differently within them" (p. 234). One such "shift," for instance, is the representation of Bond's girlfriends, the varying sexual and power relations constructed between Bond and the girls over time and across texts. Similarly, the shift in the depiction of the villains as, at one time, Cold War fanatics and, at another time, as rapacious criminal masterminds.

This is difficult stuff, so it might be best to quote a brief section of the account of the "textual shifters" and their effect on the ideological significance of Bond. Below, Bennett and Woollacott summarize the ideological effect of the different readings of James Bond outlined in the preceding paragraph's explanation of inter-textuality. They are examining the distinction between the Bond of the late 1950s and that of the mid-1960s; between an earlier Bond who signified traditional, autocratic Britain, nostalgic for its imperial past, and the later Bond who was the epitome of the modern, classless, swinging, "pop" Britain—the version ultimately to be confirmed with Sean Connery's casting in the first generation of Bond films:

> Whilst, initially, Bond had supplied a point of fictional reference in relation to which an imperialist sense of nation and nationhood could be symbolically refurbished, he was now made to point in the opposite direction—towards the future rather than the past. Functioning as a figure of modernisation, he became the very model of the tough, abrasive professional that was allegedly destined to lead Britain into the modern, no illusions, no-holds-barred post-imperialist age, a hero of rupture rather than of tradition. (p. 239)

Such judgments go beyond the demonstration of a simple difference of interpretation in different contexts; the work of the "textual shifters" does not merely produce different readings of the "same text" but, rather, acts "upon the text, shifting its very signifying potential so that it is no longer what it once was, because, in terms of its cultural location, it is no longer where it once was" (p. 248). It is a different text.

Often, even those accounts of audiences that acknowledge the audience's freedom to read texts in their own way still read the text first and then ask the audience for their, possibly variant, readings. The codes of the text are examined first to establish "*what it is* that is variantly decoded" (p. 261). In such cases (and we shall meet some examples in the following chapter), the authority of the text over its readings is implicitly accepted. Bennett and Woollacott argue that this is illogical; a text cannot have an entirely abstract meaning that is independent of what the (a) reader makes of it. Texts and readers generate their meanings in relation to each other and within specific contexts:

> The relations between texts and readers, we have suggested, are always profoundly mediated by the discursive and inter-textual determinations which, operating on both, structure the domain of their encounter so as to produce,

> always in specific and variable forms, texts and readers as the mutual supports of one another. (p. 249)

Bennett and Woollacott argue for a more genuine balance: for the recognition that texts, readers, and readings are culturally produced and that one should examine their formation as a complex set of negotiations and interrelations. The competition between text and context is reformulated, not reducing the text to its context or redefining the idea of context itself, but rather proposing that "neither text nor context are conceivable as entities separable from one another" (p. 262). Currently, and in principle, there seems little to argue with here; as aspects of Bennett and Woollacott's own book demonstrate, the problem remains one of practice, of actually carrying out such a program.

This is a problem because while we might all theoretically accept the contingency of the text, in practice we all tend to see *certain* readings as inextricably bound into specific texts. We might argue for a multitude of possibilities, but this does not mean that, as Bennett and Woollacott say, "all readings have the same cultural weight, or that any old reading can come along, parachute itself into the arena of readings and secure a space for itself." Their view is that there are usually historical (that is, extratextual) reasons the "readings of a text cluster around a set of limited options" (p. 267). However, the nomination of those historical reasons for the Bond texts has occupied a book, and to explore fully the "limits" to the range of options available would take many others. Thus, it is hard to imagine a means of testing this proposition. Further, and for only one example of competing arguments, studies of narrative reveal remarkable structural similarities in texts from a range of periods and cultures. There is at least a suggestion that these structures exert a determinate force on their readers. So, we are still left with the thorny problem of the nature of critical practice. Texts are potentially both open and closed, their readings and their textual forms are produced and determined by wider cultural and ideological factors; yet we can talk, as do Bennett and Woollacott, of the dominant construction of Bond (say) in the 1960s, as if these limits are available and can be specified. We know that as soon as we specify them we can be accused of trying to fix a singular meaning, or we can be challenged on just whose meaning we propose.

One strategic response to this problem is to decenter the text altogether, using it only as a resource through which one might examine other aspects of social life. Richard Johnson (1983) talks of a CCCS study of the media's representation of the first "post-Falklands" Christmas in Britain in 1982. This study was "premised on the belief that context is crucial in the production of meaning," and used texts as a means of examining the construction of a holiday period during a specific historical moment. In this example, texts were not studied for themselves, but "for the subjective or cultural forms" they "realised" and made available (p. 35). In Johnson's case, the subjectivities constructed through such forms are of primary interest. The texts still needed to be "read," however, and dominant meanings proposed. Stuart Laing also offers the representational history of a period through the survey of texts in *Representations of Working Class Life 1959–64* (1986). Here, the analysis of literary, television, stage, and film texts is combined with intellectual and social histories to produce an account of the popular construction of the working class during these years. In many ways a model for a new kind of cultural analysis, Laing's book still has the problem of opting for one dominant reading of the texts he consults.

Notwithstanding these difficulties, such studies adopt an approach to the text that usefully exploits the theoretical shifts we have been describing; they reject the Leavisite notion of the unique, unified text; they acknowledge the historical determinations of texts' meanings for their audiences; and they are skeptical about the authority of the readings produced by the critic/analyst. Importantly, these approaches enable us to move from the text to the audience.

To this latter aspect we turn now. Given the complexity of the history of textual analysis within cultural studies, the distance it has traveled from its roots in literary studies (indeed, the distance it has helped literary studies to travel!), and the genuine theoretical problems, we can imagine how liberating it must have been to turn to the audience and inquire into how *they* read their texts. At a stroke, the presumption of the critic could be displaced, or at least deferred. The sense of security that empiricist reporting, rather than interpretive argument, engenders must have come as a relief, too. Yet, audience studies are more than a scientific cul-de-sac away from the mainstream of cultural studies. In the past five years, they have become the major new influence on the theory and practice of contemporary cultural studies. In the following chapter, I will look at the growth in studies of the audience within cultural studies, focusing in particular on the work of Morley and Hobson.

Notes

1 This was published as a CCCS stenciled paper in 1973, but is more readily available in an edited version, "Encoding/Decoding" (Hall 1980c), published in *Culture, Media, Language*. It is this latter version that is cited throughout this book.

2 This work was originally a CCCS stenciled paper (No. 9, 1976).

3 Bennett et al.'s (1981) *Popular Television and Film* devotes a section to this debate, introducing it and reprinting the key articles, including those by Colin McCabe and Colin MacArthur.

4 The key article here, also reprinted in *Popular Television and Film* (Bennett et al. 1981) is McCabe's "Realism and the Cinema: Notes on Some Brechtian Theses" (1981).

5 "Empowerment," however, is essentially a psychological, individual effect that does not necessarily presume any wider political or structural consequence. It is an idea more widely valued in American cultural studies than in the British tradition.

4

Audiences

Morley and the *Nationwide* Audience

One consequence of cultural studies' concentration on textual analysis from the early 1970s onward was the deflection of attention away from the sites at which textual meaning was generated—people's everyday lives. Paradoxically, the stuff of these lives lay at the heart of the enterprise of cultural studies, and yet the progressive concentration on the text distanced cultural studies from this initial interest. An additional worrying by-product of textual analysis was the elitism implicit in its de facto privileging of the academic reader of texts. It could be argued that the development of its own tradition of audience studies challenged such elitism and reconnected cultural studies research with the lives it most wished to understand.

"Audience studies" within cultural studies are almost exclusively studies of *television* audiences, and that will be the focus of this chapter, too. David Morley's *The "Nationwide" Audience* (1980a) is our starting point. Widely discussed and criticized—even by Morley himself in a subsequent book, *Family Television* (1986)—*The "Nationwide" Audience* has exerted a significant influence over the approach taken to audiences since its publication. This is a testament not so much to the success of its project (testing out the Hall/Parkin encoding/decoding model) as to its categoric demonstration of the complex polysemy of the television text and the importance of *extratextual* determinants of textual meaning.

Morley's book builds on his (and Charlotte Brunsdon's)

earlier analysis of *Nationwide,* referred to in the previous chapter. Brunsdon and Morley (1978) focused on the way the program structured its relationship with the viewer and reproduced a particular version of "common sense" in its account of the world. The authors took for granted the audience's predisposition to accept the dominant or preferred meaning, and concentrated on locating the textual strategies they saw as reinforcing this predisposition (I noted some of these in Chapter 3). While *The "Nationwide" Audience* is informed by similar assumptions, its primary objective is quite different: it tracks down the *variations* in specific audiences' decodings of the same *Nationwide* program.

Morley is clearly aware of the criticisms of Hall's original encoding/decoding model. Its inference that different readings might be the product of audience members' different class positions had proved to be particularly contentious. Nevertheless, *The "Nationwide" Audience* is aimed at examining what Morley characterizes as the "close" relation between the audience members' specific interpretation of the television message and their social (that is, not merely class) position: the ways in which "individual readings will be framed by shared cultural formations and practices pre-existent to the individual" (p. 15). Such a view may resist the idea of a "mass," undifferentiated audience, but it also resists the temptation to individuate each audience member completely. Audiences are not passive consumers of the television message, but their reading positions are at least partially socially determined. This point of balance between autonomy and determination is still the orthodox one, and this may largely be due to Morley's effective demonstration of its validity in this study. Less widely shared is his more particular goal, that of tracing the "shared orientations" of individual readers to specific factors "derived from the objective position of the individual reader in the class structure" (p. 15). It is not surprising that Morley fails to achieve this goal in *The "Nationwide" Audience*; many would hold that the "specific factors" (class, occupation, locality, ethnicity, family structure, educational background, access to varied forms of mass communication, and so on) are so many and so interrelated that even the attempt to make definitive empirical connections is a waste of time.

A more fruitful proposition, advanced in Morley's introductory chapters and more extensively developed in his conclusion, foregrounds the role of discourse in constituting and differentiating individual readings. Morley (1980a) argues that readers decode texts through the available and relevant discourses:

> The meaning of the text will be constructed differently according to the discourses (knowledge, prejudices, resistances etc.) brought to bear upon the text by the reader and the crucial factor in the encounter of audience/subject and text will be the range of discourses at the disposal of the audience. (p. 18)

This raises a question that may in fact be appropriate for empirical research, the unequal distribution of "cultural competencies": that is, the way cultural apparatuses such as the education system regulate people's access to knowledge, to ways of thinking—discourses. An individual's particular mode of access will allow him or her more or less choice, and specific *kinds* of choices. Individuals will be "culturally competent" in a more or less restricted/elaborated range of discourses. The work of Pierre Bourdieu in France has produced important evidence of the workings of such mechanisms there, but it has not yet been replicated in other countries (see, e.g., Bourdieu and Passeron 1977).

This is not a question *The "Nationwide" Audience* follows through, however. For this book, Morley examined the production of textual meaning by showing an episode of *Nationwide* (already "processed" by the researcher) to 26 different groups of viewers. Each group was then asked about its response to the program, initially through relatively "open" questions that became more "focused" and direct as the interviews developed. Groups were used rather than individuals in order "to discover how interpretations were collectively constructed through talk and the interchange between respondents in the group situation" (p. 33). While there were quite significant variations *among* groups, there was little disagreement *within* groups as to their view of the program. The composition of the groups did not constitute a representative cross section of the community; all participants were part- or full-time students. Nevertheless, the range of occupation among these students was wide: they included trade union organizers, university arts students, schoolboys, apprentices to trades, bank managers, teaching training students, and print managers. The racial mix ranged from totally white groups to mixed-race groups to totally black groups. Morley notes each group's dominant party-political orientation, class background, gender, and ethnicity, and then summarizes their responses—occasionally quoting verbatim, occasionally reporting "objectively," and occasionally actively constructing an interpretation of what was being said.

The results are curious. Some groups, particularly the predominantly black ones, found the program utterly irrelevant, would never have watched it voluntarily, and expressed impatience at the whole exercise. Others participated very actively in the experience but produced readings that were internally contradictory and actually rejected what one might have thought were the interests of their own class. One such group of white male union officials with working-class backgrounds and Labour (left of center) political orientations found itself largely in sympathy with the dominant reading position, which was, according to Morley's account, socially conservative and slightly antipathetic to left-wing politics. The group's acceptance of this position was not thoroughgoing, however; at one point in the program's discussion of government economic policy, the group members vigorously rejected what they saw as the dominant position. Morley seizes on this "rejection of a *particular* position within an overall acceptance of the *Nationwide* framework" as "a classic" example of the Hall/Parkin negotiated code (p. 103).

By the end of the exercise, apprentice groups, schoolboys, and bank managers were aligned with each other as those groups that most readily reproduced what Morley had categorized as the dominant decodings. Clearly, there could be no simple correlation between their readings and their occupational groups, or between their readings and their classes. Morley has to concede that social position "in no way correlates" (p. 137) with the readings he has collected, although he does attempt to argue for a formula that links social position *plus* the possession of certain "discourse positions" (p. 134). It is clear, however, that the attempt to tie differential readings to gross social and class determinants, such as the audience's occupation group, was a failure. The polysemy of the message is a product of forces more complex and more subtle than these, and Morley admits this. In his closing sections, Morley presents an exemplary account of the problems of textuality dealt with in Chapter 3 of this volume, which argues that while texts can be appropriated by readers in different ways, and cannot be said to "determine the reader," interpretations are not "arbitrary": they "are subject to constraints contained within the text itself" (pp. 148–49).

Critics have attacked the methods Morley used in this study. First of all, Morley's own admission of the minimal variations *within* each group's reading should make us question these readings. It is likely that a consensualizing process was engendered by the grouping itself, so the experiment may well have been measuring *that* process, not the normal process of the individual decoding television texts in the family living room. The interviewer may also have reinforced any consensualizing process or otherwise exercised an influence over the responses. It is highly probable that the mechanisms of the research project would themselves have consequences. Certainly, the screening of a program such as *Nationwide* outside its normal context of consumption—the home, in the early evening—changes its nature. The adoption of this strategy removed one crucial element from the relationship between a television program and its audience: the choice made to watch it in the first place. Morley was showing *Nationwide* to arbitrarily selected groups of people, some of whom would never have watched it otherwise and cared little about watching it then. Once produced, the audience responses to the program were treated inconsistently; some were interpreted and reworked by the researcher, while others were taken at face value. Unfortunately, the audience comments needed themselves to be treated as texts, and subjected to more sophisticated analysis than they received. And, finally, as Morley himself concedes in *Family Television* (1986, 40–44) he was the victim of crude assumptions about the kinds of relationships he might expect to reveal between the meanings generated and their roots in "deep" social structures such as class. However, and despite all this, *The "Nationwide" Audience* is an important book because it provides us with empirical evidence that the polysemy of the television text is not just a theoretical abstraction, but an active, verifiable, and determinate characteristic. Morley's continuing body of work has greatly advanced our understanding of the social dimension of television discourses, and we will return to it later in this chapter.

Watching with the Audience: Dorothy Hobson and *Crossroads*

The "Nationwide" Audience is a map of the contributing streams to cultural studies at the time it was written; it is determined to "slay the father" of American communication models and "effects" studies; it is heavily influenced by the CCCS/Hall arguments on the nature of texts, readers, and subjects; it marks the point where the encoding/decoding model starts to break down; and it employs elements of the so-called ethnographic approach to audiences and to subcultures that was being developed in the CCCS during the 1970s. Its appropriation of ethnographic methods is anything but thorough, however.

Ethnography is a term used to describe a tradition of work in sociology and anthropology that provides techniques for researchers to enter another culture, participate in it and observe it, and then describe the ways in which it makes sense for those within it. A tall order, it contains all kinds of problems for the researcher who must be sympathetic enough to understand the culture's meaning systems and yet objective enough not to be submerged by them. Stuart Laing (1986, ch. 2) has described how participant-observer accounts of working-class urban cultures became a popular genre in British publishing during the 1950s and 1960s; the work of Phil Cohen and Paul Willis provided the basis for the CCCS ethnographies of urban subcultures in the 1970s.[1] Compared to such research, however, there is actually little that is ethnographic about Morley's method, other than his use of focus interviews with audiences and his attempt to relate their readings of texts to their cultural backgrounds. His strategies of description are still the product of a shotgun wedding between the empirical scientist and the semiotician. Morley's book is, however, among the earliest attempts to appropriate ethnographic methods for a cultural studies approach to audiences. The theoretical and methodological problems this raised will come up again later in this chapter, but I will turn now to the next important moment in the development of this tradition in cultural studies, the publication of Dorothy Hobson's *Crossroads: The Drama of a Soap Opera* in 1982.

Hobson's early work provides some indication of the benefits these methods can produce. In her discussion of housewives and the mass media (primarily radio, in the extract published in *Culture, Media, Language*), she quotes extensively from interviews with women, and uses these quotations as texts to be interrogated, evidence to be understood (Hobson 1980). The *Crossroads* book, however, is more substantial than this. *Crossroads* is an early evening soap opera, set in a motel in the Midlands, and shown in Britain on the commercial channels, not the BBC; it has a regional flavor, with its production company and the bulk of its audience in the Midlands and the North of England. It has been widely acknowledged as the nadir of technical quality in British television drama, and has been the object of warnings from Britain's regulatory authorities about its low standards on a number of occasions. (At the time, the regulatory climate in Britain was extremely interventionist; technical and aesthetic standards could be vigorously policed by statutory industry bodies.) Hobson's book on *Crossroads* is often discussed as if it is a study of the program's audience, but it is important to realize this is only one part of the project. *Crossroads: The Drama of a Soap Opera* was researched at the time when a central character, played by Noele Gordon, was being written out of the program, for what seemed to many of its viewers spurious reasons. Since the soap was seen as irretrievably down-market, many "discriminating" viewers could not have cared less about the damage this decision would inflict on *Crossroads*. But, to the regular (and, presumably, "undiscriminating") viewer, it was an appalling development. Audience reaction was intense, and public pressure on the television production company was severe. Hobson's book exploits this as a moment when the relations among producers, programmers, performers, programs, and audiences were unusually clearly exposed, when the structures that connected them were showing signs of strain, and thus when an observer might learn rather more than usual.

The book begins with a discussion of TV soaps and their history, and then moves into a closely observed study of the production of *Crossroads* itself. Hobson attended production meetings, rehearsals, and taping sessions, and talked to those involved about what she observed. She outlines the nature and effects of production schedules (once one learns of the speed at which episodes are taped, one can understand why the set looks as if it is lit by two fluorescent tubes); and she reveals how those working in the program sustain pride in their professionalism despite the punishing schedule of production. Her approach is sympathetic, but she does not hesitate to draw conclusions about the consequences of the practices and ideologies she observes. It is an eminently readable book: theoretically informed but relatively simply expressed. As a result, *Crossroads: The Drama of a Soap Opera* provides an exemplary account of how the culture industries work, through its examination of the articulation among the broadcasting institutions, the production company, the program makers, and the audience.

Hobson's discussion of the last of these elements, the audience, is my focus here. The key strategic difference between her approach and that of David Morley in *The "Nationwide" Audience* is that instead of bringing audiences into *her* academic researcher's world, she goes into *theirs*. She watches television with her audience subjects, in their own homes, at the normal time. Her research data come from interviews and observations made while watching episodes and from the "long, unstructured conversations" she had with her subjects after the programs finished. She stresses that these interviews were "unstructured" for a reason:

> I wanted viewers to determine what was interesting or what they noticed, or liked, or disliked, about the program and specifically about the episodes which we had watched. I hoped that they would indicate the reasons for the popularity of the program and also areas where they may have been critical. (p. 105)

Like Morley, she was convinced that audiences "work on" television texts to change their specific meanings. But she was not as interested in the process of decoding as she was in assessing the effectiveness of the professional practices of encoding. Hobson's study of production practices, and of the strategic/narrative decisions made in the script and the performance of the episodes, provided her with an idea of what the producers of the program expected of their audience. Her evenings spent watching (the programs she had seen taped) with their eventual audience were intended to enable her to check how closely the assumptions behind the encoding were accepted by the audiences. It turned out not to be as simple as that. She found that while she may have wanted to talk about individual episodes, her subjects' conversation quickly moved to "the program in general":

> It became clear through the process of the study that the audience do not watch programs as separate or individual items, nor even as types of programs, but rather that they build up an understanding of themes over a much wider range of programs and length of time of viewing. (p. 107)

The critic's isolation of the individual television text, then, may misunderstand this mode of television consumption. Hobson also discovered the importance of the specific context within which the family would view the program:

> One of the interesting aspects of watching television *with* the audience is to be part of the atmosphere of watching a program with families and to see that the viewing situation is very different for different people. To watch a program at meal time with the mother of young children is an entirely different experience from watching with a seventy-two-year-old widow whose day is largely structured around television programs. Family situations change both the ability to view with any form of concentration and also the perspective which the audience have on a program. (p. 111)

In this, as in her previous study, Hobson quotes extensively from her subjects, enriching the work with ethnographic details that make the book rewarding and lively. Clearly, the method of watching with the audience and talking at length with them about the program revealed far more than the more formal and artificial methods used in Morley's book. The method has been used quite widely since and to great effect by, among others, John Tulloch.[2]

As Hobson gained an understanding of her audiences' relation to the programs, she became progressively critical of the attitudes of the authorities who regulated television in Britain at the time (and who insisted that *Crossroads* improve its technical standards if it was to continue on the air), and of the production company itself (the members of which seemed to feel, paradoxically, a greater degree of respect for their program than for its audience). Consequently, Hobson becomes increasingly polemical as the book proceeds, arguing that viewers' concern about proposed changes in the series should have been taken more seriously by its producers. She knew, better than the producers, how important the program was to some of its viewers, and had talked to enough of these viewers to know that commonsense explanations of soap operas as "escapism" or "fantasy" were too simplistic. The way in which soaps are interwoven into everyday life is so admirably demonstrated in a "digressive" anecdote from the book that I wish to quote it at length:

> I once sat on a train returning from London to Birmingham when British Rail were running their $1.00 tickets during

> the winter of 1980. Four pensioners sat at a table next to me, complete with their sandwiches and flasks of coffee, and they talked together about many topics of mutual interest. The conversation moved to exchanges about their respective children and grandchildren and names were mentioned. Suddenly, without comment one of the women said, "What about Emily's trouble with Arthur, what do you think about it all?" (This is not remembered verbatim.) The conversation continued about the mess that Emily was in now that it had been found out that he was already married, and how it had seemed too good to be true for her to have found someone like him. How would she be, and how would it all end? As swiftly as the topic had arisen, it had switched back to talking about other topics. The uninitiated or "culturally deprived" would be forgiven for not realizing that the troubles of poor Emily and the misery which Arthur had brought to her were not the problems of the children or relatives of two of the speakers. However, anyone who was aware of the current storyline of the soap opera *Coronation Street* would have known instantly that it was the fate of the fictional characters which were being discussed. Yet from the conversation it was obvious that the speakers were playing a game with the serial. They did not actually believe that the characters existed; they were simply sharing a fantastic interest in the characters outside the serial. How many of us can honestly admit not to having done that ourselves? How many were not saddened at the fate of the "beautiful young Sebastian" as he visibly declined before our eyes in *Brideshead Revisited* during this winter? It is a false critical elitism to allow the "belief" and enjoyment in a fictional character in one program and deny others the right to that belief or enjoyment in another. (p. 125)

Hobson argues strongly for a recognition of the way texts are appropriated by their audiences. Even silly or fantastic stories may connect with a viewer's own life and enrich it: "Stories which seem almost too fantastic for an everyday serial are transformed through a sympathetic audience reading whereby they strip the storyline to the idea behind it and construct an understanding on the skeleton that is left" (p. 136). The assumption that the audience for such programs is culturally impoverished, mere passive consumers, she sees as simply elitist:

> To look at a program like Crossroads and criticize it on the basis of conventional literary/media analysis is obstinately to refuse to understand the relationship it has with its audience. A television program is a three part development—the production process, the program, and the understanding of that program by the audience or consumer—and it is false and elitist criticism to ignore what any member of the audience thinks or feels about a program. (p. 136)

Indeed, she is driven to ask, "Whose program is it anyway?" the title of her penultimate chapter. The ensuing argument about who "owns" the plot of *Crossroads*, and who should decide if a character is to be eliminated, suggests that television producers should be held to have social as well as commercial responsibilities. "Television companies play a contradictory game with their viewers," Hobson says, "by creating an illusion of possession." Can they blame the viewers, she goes on to ask, "for believing that the television company and the programs have something to do with them?" (p. 153). Hobson argues that audiences have "ownership" rights because of the place the program fills in their lives. In particular, she focuses on the uses made of the program by pensioners and the elderly generally, to show how their pleasures are dismissed and denigrated even by those who provide them. The importance of television to the elderly is directly related to the failure of society to provide other kinds of personal contact; as Hobson says, "There *is* something wrong in the lives of many people and the reassurances which they derive from fictional programs should not be underestimated" (pp. 148–49).

Her conclusion is, again, polemical in its attack on elitist modes of television criticism. Possibly, the force of the book's advocacy has enabled some to take it less seriously as a research project than it deserves. Also, one suspects, her untheoretical vocabulary made the book a little unfashionable at the time—as were the objects of her crusade, elderly and female soap audiences. Certainly, while it is often cited, *Crossroads: The Drama of a Soap Opera* is not as widely discussed as Morley's *Nationwide* book. But Hobson can claim to have richly clarified the relations between television and its audience:

> Communication is by no means a one-way process and the contribution which the audience makes to Crossroads is as important as the messages which the program-makers put into the program. In this sense, what the Crossroads audience has revealed is that there can be as many interpretations of the program as the individual viewers bring to it. There is no overall intrinsic message or meaning in the work, but it comes alive and communicates when the viewers add their own interpretations of a program. In criticising the program, those who attack it have missed out on the vital aspect of the appeal of the program to the viewers. It is criticised for its technical or script inadequacies, without seeing that its greatest strength is in its stories and connections with its audience's own experiences. (p. 170)

One would not want to accept such an unqualified claim for the power of the audience over the text (and ideology, for that matter) without argument. However, in such a claim we can see the trunk supporting a number of branches of contemporary cultural studies: the accent on the specific pleasures of the audience that leads to the populism of John Fiske's most recent work, and the concentration on precisely what viewers *do* with a program that motivates Ien Ang's (1985) study of *Dallas*, Janice Radway's (1987) study of feminine romance fiction, David Buckingham's (1987) study of *EastEnders*, John Tulloch and Albert Moran's study of *A Country Practice* (1986), and Bob Hodge and David Tripp's (1986) study of children and television. Hobson's influence may not have been direct in all of the above instances, but it has been profound, not only in her revelation of the gaps in our understanding of the ways in which popular texts and audiences are related, but in her demonstration of the power of a method of research.

Widening the Frame: TV in the Home

David Morley's *Family Television: Cultural Power and Domestic Leisure*, published in 1986, clearly benefits from Hobson's work in its choice of research methods and in its focus on the gender relations within the family as they affect the watching of television. Morley explicitly acknowledges his debt to Hobson and those who followed her, such as Radway (1987) and Modleski (1984). This is a very different project from that of *The "Nationwide" Audience*. The earlier book was still interested in the ways in which audiences understood texts; the text was the central, if implicit, object of study. *Family Television* is interested in the social processes within which television viewing is enclosed; Morley's central thesis is "that the changing patterns of television viewing could only be understood in the overall context of family leisure activity" (p. 13). After Hobson, television viewing was seen as more of a social, even a collective, activity, fully absorbed into everyday routines. Accordingly, Morley shifts his interest from the text to "the domestic viewing context itself—as the framework within which 'readings' of programs are (ordinarily) made" (p. 14). As a result the "unit of consumption" is no longer the individual viewer; it is the family or household. Further, rather than assuming that television viewing somehow supplants family functions, Morley's study reveals how television is adapted to "families' economic and cultural (or psychological) needs" (p. 21). Finally, as Stuart Hall says in his introduction to the book, Morley brings together "two lines of critical enquiry which have tended to be kept in strict isolation—questions of interpretation and questions of use" (p. 9).

Clearly, any investigation into the uses of television within the family must involve some interrogation of the power structure within the family. Inevitably, this will foreground questions of gender and the asymmetrical distribution of power within the (average) family. Morley alerts us to this possibility before outlining procedure, and gender differences are a major element in the ethnographic accounts that follow.

The study is aimed at detailing the "changing uses of television," in different types of families, from different social positions. The focus is on the following issues:

> a) the increasingly varied uses of the household television set(s)—for receiving broadcast television, video games, teletext, etc.;
> b) patterns of differential "commitment" and response to particular types of programming;
> c) the dynamics of television use within the family: how viewing choices are expressed and negotiated within the family; the differential power of particular family members in relation to viewing choices at different times of the day; the ways in which television material is discussed within the family;
> d) the relations between television watching and other dimensions of family life: television as a source of information on leisure choices; leisure interests and work obligations (both inside and outside the home) as determinants of viewing choices (p. 50).

Eighteen families were interviewed in their own homes—first the parents, then the whole family together. Interviews were "unstructured" (but limited to one and a half hours), and Morley accepts, largely, participants' own accounts of what they do. The families surveyed were white, working-class to lower-middle-class, and composed of two parents with two or more children. All owned video recorders. Morley admits this is by no means a representative sample, but he claims, legitimately enough, it is certainly sufficient to provide a foundation upon which to base a more comprehensive study.

Morley is more "ethnographic" in his reporting of this research than in *The "Nationwide" Audience*; he provides fuller descriptions of the family members and their comments, although we still learn very little about each family's social situation or specific characteristics. The book does provide, however, rich evidence of the complexity of patterns of television use and of how deeply embedded this usage is in other social practices. It also provides some ripe examples of real eccentricity:

> This man plans his viewing (and videotaping) with extreme care. At points he sounds almost like a classical utilitarian discussing the maximisation of his pleasure quotient, as he discusses the fine detail of his calculations as to what to watch, and what to tape, in what sequence:
>
> "And like evening times, I look through the paper and I've got all my programs sorted out. I've got it on tonight on BBC because its *Dallas* tonight and I do like *Dallas*, so . . . I don't like *Wogan*, but . . . We started to watch *EastEnders*, didn't we? And then they put *Emmerdale Farm* on, so we've gone for *Emmerdale Farm* 'cause I like that and we record *EastEnders*—so we don't have to miss out. I normally see it on a Sunday anyway. I got it all worked out to tape. I don't mark it [in the paper], but I register what's in there; like tonight, its *Dallas*, then at 9pm its *Widows* and then we've got *Brubaker* on until the news. So the tape's ready to go straight through. What's on at half seven? Oh, *This is Your Life* and *Coronation Street*. *This is Your Life* we have to record to watch *Dallas*. I think BBC is better to record, because it doesn't have the adverts. *This is Your Life* we record because it's only half an hour, whereas *Dallas* is on for an hour, so you only use half an hour of tape.
>
> "Yeah, Tuesday. If you're watching the other program it means you're going to have to cut it off halfway through, and I don't bother, so I watch the news at nine o'clock. . . . Yes, 'cause there's a film at 9pm on Tuesday, so what I do, I record the film so I can watch *Miami Vice* and then watch the film later."
>
> The bottomless pit of this man's desire for programs to watch cannot be entirely fulfilled by broadcast television, and before he became unemployed they were renting a video film practically every night as well as watching broadcast television. (pp. 70–71)

This man never goes out, and Morley perceptively observes that this seems to be related to his loss of employment; in going out, he experiences the loss of total power he has established in his home.

The issue of power within the family comes to dominate the book. Male dominance is clear in most of the families, and takes the most bullying of forms: some men not only chose the programs for the whole family and denigrated the choices of others, but also took possession of the remote control device when they left the room in order to stop anyone switching around the channels in their absence. Women rarely knew how to work the video recorder. Men liked to watch in total silence, while women and children found this oppressive; to resist this regime, women tended to watch the black-and-white set in the kitchen, while the children retreated upstairs. Women had fewer moments of "licensed" leisure, when they were free to give the television their undivided attention; as Hobson found, many women are cooking meals or bathing children at the times when their favorite soaps are on and can watch their favorite shows only in brief bursts. Many women talked of the pleasure of being able to watch afternoon soaps free of this regime, although they also spoke guiltily of this, as if it were an indulgence of which they should be ashamed.

Morley found that gender was a "structural principle working across all the families interviewed" (p. 146). It affected differences within the family over the control of viewing choices, amounts of viewing, the use of videos, "solo" viewing and the guilt aroused by this pleasure, program type preferences, channel preferences, comedy preferences, and a number of other variables. Morley is quick to point out, however, that what may appear to be a set of essential gender differences are in fact "the effects of the particular social roles that these men and women occupy within the home" (p. 146). So, a woman who was the main breadwinner while her husband stayed home caring for the house and children exercised a degree of domestic power and demonstrated viewing preferences more like those of the males in the survey than those of other women.

However, Morley does argue that there are basic differences between the "positioning of men and women within the domestic sphere" that are revealed by this study:

> The essential point here is that the dominant model of gender relations within this society (and certainly within that sub-section of it represented in my sample) is one in which the home is primarily defined for men as a site of leisure—in distinction to the "industrial time" of their employment outside the home—while the home is primarily defined for women as a sphere of work (whether or not they also work outside the home). This simply means that in investigating television viewing in the home one is by definition investigating something which men are better placed to do wholeheartedly, and women seem only to be able to do distractedly and guiltily, because of their continuing sense of their domestic responsibilities. Moreover, this differential position is given a greater significance as the home becomes increasingly defined as the "proper" sphere of leisure, with the decline of public forms of entertainment and the growth of home-based leisure technologies such as video, etc. (p. 147)

His last point is a worrying one: that despite the interrogation of stereotyped gender roles over the last two decades, an entirely new set of social practices now conspire against women's attempts to achieve more power within their domestic situations.

Morley's last chapter does not present a comprehensive summary of his results. Rather, it concentrates on the relationship between television and gender, the way in which the use and control of television in the home is overdetermined by the social construction of gender roles within the family. This concentration nevertheless allows him to discuss the full range of topics he set up at the beginning: program choice, control of program choice, use of the video recorder, and so on. He stresses repeatedly that the patterns he observes are not essential to men and women but to the domestic roles they play, and to the wider construction of masculinity and femininity within the culture. He also admits that gender has assumed a more singular focus for the study than originally intended, and that this does leave out aspects (class and age, for instance) that may well have demanded closer attention (p. 174). Another factor more or less ignored in Morley's reporting of the interviews is education—both its content and the differential access to it: how that affects choices among television genres, forming opinions about what is "good" and worthwhile television—and thus guilt about watching "trivial" melodramas.

As Fiske (1988) has noted, *Family Television* sees Morley move away from the encoding/decoding model of an audience "preference" to the concept of "relevance":

> The preferred reading theory still grants precedence to the text, although it allows the viewer considerable scope to negotiate with or oppose it according to his or her position in the social formation. *Preference* is a textual concept. *Relevance*, however, is a social one: the viewer makes meanings and pleasures from television that are relevant to his or her social allegiances at the moment of viewing; the criteria for relevance *precede* the viewing moment. (p. 247)

Fiske goes on to argue that such a position destroys the category of the audience. One can see what he means. Morley's study directs us to those social forces that produce the audiences, effectively leading us away from the examination of texts and audiences and toward a more wide-ranging study of the practices and discourses of everyday life. This certainly seems to be the direction Fiske has taken as well in his recent work—particularly in his application of de Certeau's theories of popular resistance to analyses of American popular culture.[3] Ethnographic approaches almost inevitably resist restriction to a single arena of discursive contest—such as the audience's response to television. They generate a considerable compulsion to go beyond such a restriction: the conception of a television audience as *only* a television audience. Everyday life is more complex than that. Even John Tulloch's (1989) brief inquiry into his own family's varying responses to television texts generates a series of diverging and ever-widening social histories, refusing simple explanations for their responses, and pursuing the goal of the "thick interpretation of cultures" (p. 200).[4] This "thick" interpretation cannot be achieved through the methods employed by Morley or Hobson. Tulloch's insistence on such a goal is timely, but so far there is virtually no progress toward it within cultural studies.

Text and Audience: Buckingham's *EastEnders*

Tulloch's article is a "note on method" rather than an extended study, and it is provoked by the reading of another recent British study of a text and its audiences, David Buckingham's *Public Secrets: EastEnders and Its Audience* (1987). *EastEnders* is an extraordinarily successful British soap opera that began airing in Britain on the BBC in 1985. Its audience figures comprise nearly a third of the nation, and its characters and performers enjoy almost continuous exposure in a notoriously down-market popular press. Set in a traditional working-class area of London, the East End, it was regarded as more realistic, more lively, and its storylines and subjects as more "contemporary," than any of its competitors on British TV.

Buckingham approaches the relation between the program and its audiences in four separate but related ways: through interviews with the producers, he outlines their understanding of the program and its likely audience; through an extensive textual analysis of specific episodes, he suggests how the audience may produce various versions of the text; through a survey of the marketing and promotion of the program, he discusses the intertextual frame within which its audiences might place *EastEnders;* and finally through interviews with groups of young people he addresses the specific ways in which they make sense of it themselves.

Buckingham's book is sufficiently aware of current debates about the problem of textual meaning and the current revival of the category of the audience to attempt to mark his own work off—often a little spuriously—from that of Hobson or Morley. *Public Secrets'* focus is not essentially theoretical, however, since its main interest is in the popularity of the program itself; this leads to extensive discussion of its texts. Nevertheless, the book does participate in the debates initiated by Hobson and Morley and develops discussions of the ways in which the genre of TV soaps generate their meanings and pleasures, and of the ways in which children understand television soap operas.

The book's first chapter, "Creating the Audience," analyzes the ways in which the producers and the BBC's management initially conceived of the program. In this chapter, Buckingham falls within, and largely reproduces the conclusions of, a strong tradition of production studies.[5] While he establishes that television production "involves the creation, not merely of programs, but also of audiences" (p. 8), his interviews with those responsible for the program reveal the limits of their knowledge about the audience they intend to "create." Relying on instinct and intuition rather than empirically based or analytic knowledge, the producers used the little audience research that actually occurred "largely as a means of confirming beliefs which were already held, and as valuable ammunition in arguing the case with senior management" (p. 14). Paradoxically, the program's producers insist on their instinctive ability to predict their audience's interests while nevertheless making it clear that they do not in any way share those interests. Buckingham's research, like Hobson's, reveals the significant fact that those who make soap opera would never be caught watching one. Hobson (1982) deals at length with television producers' implied contempt for the pleasures they are employed to produce. Buckingham also uncovers this attitude, but, unlike Hobson, does not linger to consider what this might say about the relation between the institution of television and its audiences. Instead, he outlines the corporate planning that mobilized these relatively unexamined assumptions about the TV audience and that influenced the nature of the production:

> Prior to the launch of the BBC's new early evening package, its audience at this time of the day tended to be predominantly middle-aged and middle-class. In order to broaden that audience, *EastEnders* would have to appeal both to younger and older viewers, and also to the working-class audience which traditionally watched

> ITV [the competing commercial network]. The choice of a working-class setting, and the broad age range of the characters thus also made a good deal of sense in terms of ratings.
>
> In addition, *EastEnders* sought to extend the traditional audience for British soaps, which is weighted towards women and towards the elderly. Having a number of strong younger characters, it was argued, meant that the program would have a greater appeal for younger viewers than other British soaps. . . . Strong male characters would also serve to bring in male viewers who were traditionally suspicious of the genre. (p. 16)

As Buckingham's group interviews later discovered, younger viewers categorically refused to identify with the young characters and instead located their interest in the slightly illicit behaviors of the adults. Such details reveal how shaky the production team's assumptions could be, and their unreliability as predictors of audience reaction. As Buckingham says, the producers' conception of the text's relation with its audience was "confused and contradictory" (p. 27), a dead end for anyone hoping to explain *EastEnders'* success in building its audience.

Consequently, Buckingham moves to a more "reader-orientated" approach to explain the audience's active production of meaning. Such a phrase invokes the influence of reader-response and reception theory within literary studies, and Buckingham depends substantially on this tradition in his second chapter. He also acknowledges the debates within the field of media and cultural studies—those surveyed in Chapter 3 and in this present discussion—and situates himself in the (by now) familiar role of one who is in search of a balance between the power of the text and the autonomy of the reader:

> Perhaps the most critical problem . . . is of balancing the "text" and "reader" sides of the equation. On the one hand, there is a danger of favouring the text at the expense of the reader: certain kinds of psychoanalytic theory, for example, regard the text as having almost total power to position

> and even to "construct" the reader, and leave readers very little room to negotiate. Yet, on the other hand, there is a danger of favouring the reader at the expense of the text: certain reception theorists, for example, effectively deny that texts exist at all—instead, all we have to work with is an infinite multiplicity of individual readings. (p. 35)

Following Eco, Buckingham suggests that the problem is exacerbated when we talk about soap opera because it is intrinsically a more "open" form, offering "multiple levels of interpretation." Even with soap operas, however, the possibilities are not unlimited; one can still "talk about readings," says Buckingham, "not as infinitely various, but as differentiated in more or less systematic ways" (p. 37):

> While I would agree that it is ultimately impossible to reduce a soap opera to a single "meaning" . . . it remains possible to specify the ways in which it invites its viewers to produce meaning. If one cannot say what *EastEnders* "means" to its audience, one can at least say a good deal about how it *works*. For example, the ways in which the viewer is allowed or denied access to privileged information—whether we are "let into" secrets or kept guessing—plays a significant part in determining our interpretation. Likewise, the extent to which we are invited to "identify" with particular characters—and the different types of identification which are encouraged—also serves to orientate us towards the text, and enables us to make sense of it, in specific ways. (p. 37)

Buckingham appropriates an aspect of literary reception theory here, in his application of Wolfgang Iser's notion of textual "invitations." From this perspective, texts do not produce or determine meaning, they "invite" their readers to accept particular positions, to explore particular speculations or hypotheses, to share particular information (the "public secrets" of Buckingham's title) denied to some of the characters themselves, to call up memories of earlier events in the serial, their specific knowledge of the program.

Such invitations occur within the narrative itself, within constructions of character, and within the program's constitutive discourses—its particular formations of "common sense." This process does not necessarily work to construct a unitary, noncontradictory reading of the text; rather, the "ways in which [the viewers] are likely to respond to these invitations . . . are potentially extremely variable and, in many cases, contradictory" (p. 83).

Buckingham demonstrates this through a detailed account of the ways in which *EastEnders* "works." Through a process of locating provocations, sites of speculation, and enigmas within the text, Buckingham fixes on determinate moments—not moments where a unitary meaning is irresistibly inscribed, but where only a limited number of options are available if the text is not entirely to be refused. As a by-product of this approach, the richness and contingency of the program is foregrounded—its pleasures made clear in practice if not in theory. Despite this, Buckingham has to concede the partiality even of this exhaustive account:

> Ultimately, textual analysis has distinct limitations: while it may provide a useful means of generating hypotheses, it is clearly incapable of accounting for the ways in which real audiences actually make sense of television. Viewers are not merely "positioned" by television: they are also positioned in society and in history, and will therefore bring different kinds of prior knowledge to the text. As a result, they may refuse to accept, or indeed fail to perceive, the "invitations" which the text offers.
>
> Furthermore, there is also a significant difficulty in defining and isolating the text itself. Indeed, it may well be false to regard any television program as a discrete self-contained "text": the experience of television viewing may more accurately be seen as one of "flow", in which the boundaries between programs have increasingly become blurred. (p. 115)

The invocation of Raymond Williams in the mention of "flow" enables Buckingham to move beyond the text to the intertextual relations that frame its reception. His next chapter examines press reports, the marketing and promotion of the program, and the campaign against *EastEnders* by Britain's moral watchdog, Mary Whitehouse. Buckingham argues that such phenomena influence not only audiences but also the program makers themselves (p. 117), but he concentrates on the question of just what audiences might make of the sensationalized and contradictory press reports any successful TV program attracts—and just how much autonomy audiences might exercise in the process. After this chapter, which is perhaps of less interest to us here than to someone interested in a history of the representations of the program in the British press, Buckingham turns to deal with the audience directly.

Although Buckingham never actually employs the term *ethnographic*, that tradition of audience research underlies this chapter of *Public Secrets*. To discover how a section of the audience responded to the "invitations of the text," Buckingham conducted a series of small group discussions with a total of 60 young people between 7 and 18 years old, all from London. The groups were organized by ages, but the racial mix varied. The discussions lasted one hour and 25 minutes on average, and were conducted in schools or, in a minority of cases, youth clubs. Buckingham describes them as "open-ended," although he directed them with "fairly basic questions" about viewing habits, and about favorite or least favorite *EastEnders* characters:

> Sometimes, generally towards the end of the discussion, I would draw the group's attention to characters or stories which they had failed to mention, at least partly to discover if there were reasons for this. Finally, usually for about the last twenty minutes of the session, I would screen a videotape of the last few scenes from the latest episode of *EastEnders*, occasionally pausing the tape to invite comments from the group. (p. 158)

Buckingham says this constituted a "relatively self-effacing role" for the interviewer, which allowed the group to set its own agenda for discussion. He realizes, of course, that the situation and his role in it were highly artificial, but denies that this had any serious effect on the success of the discussions or on the insights they generated. One would have to accuse Buckingham of naïveté about what might constitute a genuinely "open-ended" discussion, and about the role of the interviewer in ethnographic work, but the research often illuminates the children's relationship to the program.

Unlike Morley, Buckingham actively interprets the children's responses; descriptions of tone and delivery often accompany the quotations from their conversations. As is the case with other work on children and television within this tradition (notably, that of Hodge and Tripp 1986, or that of Patricia Palmer 1986), the conversations are richly revealing. In contrast to, say, Hodge and Tripp's *Children and Television*, *Public Secrets* illuminates the audience's relation to a specific program rather than their general use of the medium, but there are a number of general points that deserve noting. Among them is Buckingham's claim that while the content of the *EastEnders*' episodes may be a source of fascination to the children he interviewed, it is "the process of *revelation*, both within the narrative and in its subsequent reconstruction in discussion, which constitutes much of the pleasure" (p. 166). He found that the children were well aware that information was carefully doled out to them by the narrative, and that revelations of the program's "secrets" were strategically rationed. Far from being victims of the narrative process, they understood its economy, its need for rationing, and enjoyed the pleasures of speculation, anticipation, and revelation/discovery it delivered.

Even among the youngest of the children interviewed, the constructed nature of the program was clearly understood, although the precise mechanisms used in its construction were not. The following conversation is about one of the main adult characters, Angie, who had upset one of this group of 9-year-olds by "swearing"; Vicky, the first speaker, is keen to point out that this is not the fault of the character:

VICKY Angie don't tell them what she's going to say, they tell her what she's got to say.

DB [Buckingham] Who are "they"?
MARK Scriptwriter.
VICKY The description writer, or whatever it was. He comes, he gives them the description, they've got to read it, and they read it over and over till they learn it. . . . She has to say what the description man gives her. She can't say what she wants.
PRESTON Well the description man shouldn't have said it like that, innit? (p. 178)

Buckingham argues, as do Hodge and Tripp (1986) in their more extensive study, that his young viewers did not passively absorb television, nor did they confuse its representation of the world with reality. The children Buckingham talked to were "prepared to grant a degree of credibility to this representation," but they were also "highly critical of what they regarded as its partiality and implausibility" (p. 200). Buckingham sees the degree of critical distance displayed as a crucial factor, and also notes that this was in no way incompatible with the children's "general enjoyment of the program":

> I would argue that this critical distance did not undermine their pleasure, but in fact made certain forms of pleasure possible. . . . The children's comments . . . reveal a complex and shifting combination of different responses. They were by turns moved, deeply involved, amused, bored, mocking and irreverent. The essentially playful way in which they were able to move between these different positions suggests that they had a considerable degree of autonomy in defining their relationship with television. (p. 200)

This chapter's concluding focus is upon children and television, but it also contributes to the body of research that provides empirical evidence of the contingency and variability of audiences' readings of television.

Public Secrets concludes by reiterating its case for the need to approach a popular text from multiple perspectives. These multiple perspectives, however, are not as "multiple" as they might seem. Hall's encoding/decoding model is still visible in Buckingham's method; the major component of his approach has been to examine the dialectic between the determination of meaning by the encoder and the production of meaning by the decoder. So, the project does not take us onto unfamiliar ground. Buckingham's view of the relations between text and audience is orthodox in its rejection of a privileged role for either category in the production of meaning. The only unfamiliar feature in his book is perhaps the explicitness of its use of reception theory, in his insistence on the importance of understanding how a text *works* rather than "means": "that is, *how it enables viewers to produce meaning*" (p. 203). However, as one might have expected in a book engaged in analyzing the audience of a popular TV soap opera, it is most rewarding when it documents specific interactions among audience, text, and everyday lives.

The object of interest implied in the preceding comment is popular culture, everyday life itself, rather than a more restricted interest in television or the mass media. It is also an interest basic to the enterprise of cultural studies. Within this enterprise, ethnographic work has established a firm position, and it is not surprising to see its influence extend (or, more accurately, contract) from the analysis of social groups to the analysis of media audiences. Yet, the transposition from one theoretical objective to another has not been without its costs and its illogicalities. I want to look at the more thorough applications of ethnography to the analysis of urban subcultures in the next chapter, but before continuing with the topic of media audiences I want to address, albeit briefly, the ways in which cultural studies of media audiences have appropriated ethnographic techniques, and ask just what is ethnographic about them.[6]

Media Audiences and Ethnography

The use of the term *ethnography* in this context is itself contentious. Ethnography comes from anthropology; within this discipline it is a written account of a "lengthy social interaction between a scholar and a distant culture":

> Although its focus is often narrowed in the process of writing so as to highlight kinship practices, social institutions, or cultural rituals, that written account is rooted in an effort to observe and to comprehend the entire tapestry of social life. An extensive literature has been elaborated by anthropologists attempting to theorize, among other things, the nature of the relationship between culture and social behaviour, the epistemological status of "data" gathered in the field, the nature of "experience" itself, and the status of explanatory social theories imported from the ethnographer's own cultural universe. . . . Despite these not inconsequential difficulties, however, anthropologists have at least aimed through ethnography to describe the ways in which day-to-day practices of socially situated individuals are always complexly overdetermined by both history and culture. (Radway 1988, 367)

Clearly, this is a very different activity from that practiced by Hobson or Morley. The procedure of interviewing audiences in their homes employs an ethnographic technique, but disconnects it from the purpose for which it was developed. As Radway (1988) argues, ethnographic studies of media audiences have been extremely "narrowly circumscribed," the field of their interest "surveyed and cordoned off by [their] preoccupation with a single medium or genre":

> Even when we have attempted to understand not simply how women read romances or families watch television but also how those activities intersect with, contradict, or ratify other cultural practices carrying out the definition of gender, for example, we have always remained locked within the particular topical field defined by our prior segmentation of the audience of [*sic*] its use of one medium or genre. Consequently, we have often reified or ignored totally other cultural determinants beside the one specifically highlighted. (p. 367)

As a result, the researcher engages not another culture, but an arbitrarily disconnected fragment; this is not merely a problem of detail, but a major disadvantage. The practice of watching TV is separated from all those other social practices that collaborate to make it a meaningful activity. And yet, Radway concludes, this seems not to have occurred to the media researchers themselves: "Ethnographers of media use have . . . tended to rule out as beyond our purview questions of how a single leisure practice intersects with or contradicts others, how it is articulated to our subjects' working lives, or how it is used to contest the dominance of other cultural forms" (p. 367).

Virginia Nightingale (1989) has suggested it makes no sense to use the term *ethnographic* in connection with cultural studies of media audiences. For a start, ethnographic research is simply descriptive rather than critical, and thus not ideally suited to cultural studies' political purposes. Indeed, as she puts it, the practice is logically compromised: it draws on "interpretive procedures to understand texts around which the audience clusters," but it restricts itself merely to "descriptive measures . . . to account for the audience" (p. 53). Further, as she rightly says, the meeting between cultural studies scholars and the "other" culture they are investigating can be as brief as a single one-and-a-half-hour interview in the home. This is hardly a sufficient period to provide a complex understanding ("thick description") of the structure of the subjects' everyday lives—within which their television viewing is, of course, enclosed. The practice of seeking audience readings of texts that have already been "read" by the researchers is fraught with all the contradictions discussed in Chapter 3; additionally, in these studies, the practice is also deployed as a spurious method of authenticating the researcher's reading. As Nightingale puts it, the interviewees' descriptions of their experiences of the text are "co-opted" (p. 55) by the researcher as if these ethnographic data could be relied on, as other data cannot, as utterly authentic. There is a naive trust in the empirical here that could come only from a convert. The most basic problem, however, is the aim of or strategy behind the methods used; comparing some of the work we have looked at in this chapter with Paul Willis's more traditional ethnographies (to be discussed in the following chapter), Nightingale says:

> While the encoding/decoding audience research uses the same research techniques as Willis, their research strategies are quite different. Willis's aim was to demonstrate the working of social process, to explain cultural reproduction through the interlocking of education and the labour process. This type of broad social aim, with its singularity of focus, is missing from the encoding/decoding studies, which concentrate on several, and more limited, aims such as explaining the popularity of the text [Hobson and Tulloch], teaching about British cultural studies [Ang] or demonstrating the operations by which pleasure is encoded in the text [Ang and Buckingham]. (p. 58)

Given the validity of this point, one wonders why the term *ethnography* has become conventionalized in this connection. Nightingale suggests the label's function is to reconnect cultural studies with the studies of community life from which in many ways it originally grew, as well as to confer unity onto the intellectual field of cultural studies through the enclosure of one theoretical tradition within another but hitherto rather separate tradition.

Whatever the reason, a consequence of the ethnographic studies of media audiences has been the revival of interest in less text-based analyses of popular culture, and in the practices of everyday life. Fiske (1988) moves from an interest in the audience to the suggestion that we abolish the category altogether in order to focus on the generation of "meaningful moments" in popular culture; Nightingale (1989) asks for a "mixed genre" method that approaches popular culture from a number of theoretical perspectives, "triangulating" our angles of inspection as community studies research has done in the past; and Radway (1988) returns to the idea of the analysis of "everyday life" as a reorientation for American cultural studies. One hears the wheel turning as we head back to the original targets of cultural studies. Some of these original targets are dealt with in the following chapter. Necessarily if regrettably episodic, its topics include the development of ethnographies within cultural studies that are not entirely circumscribed by a focus on media audiences.

The Audience as Fiction

Before we leave the topic of audiences, however, we should acknowledge that there are other ways of dealing with or conceiving of them. John Hartley has taken a position that opposes the current ethnographic examinations of the audience and raises important issues for us to consider. Hartley makes the legitimate protest that any study of "the *Nationwide* audience" or "the *EastEnders* audience" actually has to invent such an audience in order to study it at all. There is no such social group as "the *EastEnders* audience." We do not live our lives as members of audiences, at least not exclusively so. We might be audiences at one point in our daily lives, but we are many other things besides: workers, commuters, readers, parents, and so on. Nor are we socially defined by our membership in particular audiences; while we might be among the audience of *Days of Our Lives* at one point in our television viewing, we will be among the audience of MTV or *Sixty Minutes* at others. The category of the audience, Hartley argues, is a fiction of those who speak for it, those who research it, those who try to attract it, and those who try to regulate and protect it—the critics, the academics, the television industry, and the broadcasting regulatory bodies.

Hartley begins his article "Invisible Fictions: Television Audiences, Paedocracy, Pleasure" (1987) by considering the idea of the national television audience. If the nation is, in Benedict Anderson's phrase, an "imagined community," an invention in which we all participate, then the national TV audience is too: "one unwarranted, invisible fiction—the imagined community of the nation—is used to invent and explain another: the [national] television audience" (p. 124). This latter fiction is produced by the three major institutions that "invent" television, or, as Hartley puts it, that "construct television discursively": the critical institutions (academics, journalists, and pressure groups), the television industry (networks, stations, producers), and the regulatory bodies within the political/legal system.

All of these institutions produce a different version of

the audience, depending on their needs. The legacy of effects studies on television criticism, for instance, was to install a "commonsense" view of the television audience as helpless, utterly manipulable before the destructive power of television:

> The monster who watches television and then goes on a rampage is a *metaphor*, a creation of criticism. So too are other fictional characters of our times: the woman who watches soap opera and then becomes a distracted decentred housewife (men watch soapies, too, but are rarely accused of catching domesticity as a result); the child who watches television and becomes a zombie (politicians spend most of their waking hours with one eye on the screen, but perhaps we had better not pursue that contrast). (Hartley 1988, 236)

Produced in order to legitimate elite academic criticism of the medium, this is a view of the audience that was once largely shared by regulatory bodies—whose role such a view validated—but it has always been vigorously denied by the television industry—whose interests it threatened. As Hartley (1987) points out, the various versions of the audience are not just imaginative constructs; they are strategic, self-serving fictions "produced institutionally in order for various institutions to take charge of the mechanisms of their own survival":

> Audiences may be imagined empirically, theoretically, or politically, but in all cases the product is a fiction which serves the needs of the imagining institution. In no case is the audience "real", or external to its discursive construction. There is no "actual" audience that lies beyond its production as a category. (p. 125)

Hartley demonstrates what he means by this, taking each of the "imagining institutions" in turn. The critical or scholarly institution is dealt with by way of academic research on audiences, largely the work we have been surveying in this chapter. Hartley points out that Morley's audience was explicitly constructed on a class basis. Morley's research, thus, arbitrarily selected groups of people he then called "an audience" for the purpose of his study; he collected them in a group that would otherwise not have been formed, in a place they would otherwise not have occupied, and asked them to become the audience of a program they may otherwise not have chosen to watch: "Clearly, Morley's audience . . . is an invisible fiction, produced by his project, which was itself a product of academic/critical institutional discourses. . . . It's Morley's *method* that is empirical, not the audience he constructs for his research" (p. 126). Like Morley's, according to Hartley, most academic audience research tends to see audiences as an independently existing social category, possessing intrinsic and observable properties that are more or less the same nationwide. This invention is then taken up by and used within the industry and the regulatory bodies.

The television industry and the regulatory bodies, while often pursuing competing objectives, reveal a surprising degree of similarity in their conception of the audience. For the industry, where the interest is simply in maximizing the number of viewers, and where it is also acknowledged that the audience is "literally unknowable" (p. 129), the solution is to treat audiences as children—to enclose them within what Hartley calls a "paedocratic regime":

> This isn't to say that television is merely infantile, childish, or dedicated to the lowest common denominator—those would be certain mechanisms for losing the audience. On the contrary, broadcasters paedocraticise audiences in the name of pleasure. They appeal to the playful, imaginative, fantasy, irresponsible aspects of adult behaviour. They seek the common personal ground that unites diverse and often directly antagonistic groupings among a given population. What is better, then, than a fictional version of everyone's supposed childlike tendencies which might be understood as predating such social groupings? In short, a fictional image of the positive attributes of childlike pleasures is invented. The desired audience is encouraged to look

> up, expectant, open, willing to be guided and gratified, whenever television as an institution exclaims: "Hi, kids!" (p. 130)

The regulatory bodies, too, see the audience this way: as a group to be protected, their rights defended by broadcasting standards, censorship, and (in the United Kingdom and Australia) interventionary official instruments of broadcasting policy. They see themselves as acting, as it were, *in loco parentis* for the nation as a whole.

Hartley's own version sees the audience as, primarily, the product of the television industry; television sells audiences, after all, to advertisers. It is a product, however, that television producers know very little about, hence their reliance on ratings and on "those imaginary, paedocratised representations of the audience that networks promote throughout the industry":

> Networks minimize their risks by stabilising not demand but supply, but neither networks nor producers know what will "sell"; they don't know who they're talking to and they don't "give the public what it wants" because they don't know. This structural uncertainty at the heart of the television industry means that networks and producers alike are afraid of the audience: afraid of offending it, of inciting it, of inflaming it—above all, afraid of losing it. (p. 135)

In order not to lose the audience, and because they have very little idea of how else to relate to their audience, television programs instruct their audiences in how to understand and enjoy television:

> Since audiences don't exist prior to or outside of television, they need constant hailing and guidance in how-to-be-an-audience—hailing and guidance that are unstintingly given within, and especially between, shows, and in the meta-discourses that surround television, the most prominent among which, of course, are those publications aptly called television guides. (p. 136)

The most obvious example of instruction in "how-to-be-an-audience" is, of course, the laugh track on television sitcoms and variety shows.

The clear tendency in Hartley's argument is textual; seeing audiences as the product of discourses, or the *regimes* constructed through a range of discourses, is to direct attention away from a hypothesized "actual" audience and back to the discourses that call them into being: the criticism, the programs, and government broadcasting policies and regulations. The audience, in Hartley's view, cannot be investigated as a "real" group, ethnographically or otherwise, and so we are ultimately left with the text or, more accurately, the discursive regime within which the texts are produced and received. The notion of audiences as "invisible fictions" throws out a significant challenge to ethnographic research and explanations, and differentiates Hartley's work decisively from that of his former collaborator, John Fiske. Hartley's is currently a minority position, but it usefully complicates current debates on the study of the audience.

Notes

1 This work will be discussed in Chapter 5.

2 I am referring, primarily, to John Tulloch and Albert Moran's work on the Australian soap opera, *Quality Soap: A Country Practice* (1986); a further article in this tradition is Tulloch's "Approaching Audiences: A Note on Method" (1989). There is also Tulloch's most interesting, but so far unpublished, account of discussions of *Dr. Who* with its fans, titled "*Dr. Who*: Approaching the Audience" (n.d.).

3 This is true of much of the argument of *Television Culture* (Fiske 1987b) and of Fiske's two new books on popular culture, *Understanding Popular Culture* (1989b) and *Reading the Popular* (1989a).

4 The phrase "thick interpretation" is derived from Clifford Geertz's (1973) "thick description."

5 For instance, see Tulloch and Alvarado (1983), Alvarado and Buscombe (1978), and Elliott (1972). Hobson's (1982) work on *Crossroads* also falls into this tradition, of course.

6 This question is posed by Virginia Nightingale in her article, "What's Ethnographic about Ethnographic Audience Research?" (1989). Much of the following section is indebted to her article.

5

Ethnographies, Histories, and Sociologies

It is possible to see the arguments around texts and audiences as proceeding from an interrelated, even quite compact, body of ideas. There are other areas in British cultural studies, however, that are not quite so compactly organized, the boundaries of their fields of interest less clearly marked out. In many cases this is due to the complex relation between cultural studies and established disciplines such as history and sociology. In this chapter, I want to indicate some of the benefits cultural studies has drawn from ethnographies of social groups, from the new histories of discourses and institutions, and from the political economies and sociologies of the media industries. Although what follows is only a sampling of these various fields—there is an especially rich tradition of histories of "the popular" that is not considered here—it may usefully extend our view of cultural studies and its breadth of interests.

Ethnography

The Uses of Literacy (Hoggart 1958) is usually regarded as an ethnography of the everyday lives of the northern English working class between the wars. Within the CCCS, there has always been a strong interest in ethnography, producing a far greater range of work than that suggested by the previous chapter's examples from media audience studies. Much of the best work "starts not with a text or a theory (although it is certainly theoretically informed and alert) but with a social group—bikers, schoolboys, housewives—and observes their use of commodities and messages to produce culture, meanings and interpretations" (Batsleer et al. 1985, 145). Over more than two decades, the tradition has taken on numerous forms: the collection and analysis of oral history, Hobson's studies of media audiences, a range of histories of popular movements and class formations, and, perhaps centrally, the analyses of urban subcultures associated with Phil Cohen, Paul Willis, Dick Hebdige, and, in its strongest feminist formation, Angela McRobbie. Having just dealt with the "ethnographic" strategies employed by Morley and Buckingham's audience research in the previous chapter, it may be helpful to demonstrate how vastly different are the strategies employed by those working in the mainstream of cultural studies ethnography.

Paul Willis's study of working-class youths leaving school, *Learning to Labour: How Working Class Kids Get Working Class Jobs* (1977) took three years to research. Willis focused on a group of 12 "nonacademic" working-class boys who had close links with each other and with an "oppositional," rebellious culture in their school. His subjects were studied as a group and as individuals through participant observation, group discussions, informal interviews, and diaries. Willis contacted the group halfway through their penultimate year of school and followed them through their last year and then into their first six months of work. As part of his research method, Willis attended classes with them and worked alongside them at their places of employment; while they were at school he interviewed their parents, junior teachers, senior masters, and careers officers; while they were at work he interviewed their foremen, managers, and shop stewards. He also made comparative studies of five other groups of youths selected from within the same school, from other schools, and from a mixture of class and academic affiliations. The studies are informed by a detailed understanding of the town and the locality. In addition to what it tells us about its subjects, *Learning to Labour* analyzes their school's structures of discipline and control, and the ideological systems from which they were constituted. This is a very different exercise from that of sitting with a family for an hour and a half, or even for a number of such periods, while they watch television.

Just as the media audience studies are inappropriate representatives of the ethnographic tradition within the CCCS, it would also be wrong to see Dick Hebdige's work on subcultures as typical. While Hebdige acknowledges Phil Cohen's influence, there are crucial differences between their work; Cohen's is the more centrally placed in this tradition. Cohen's 1972 article "Subcultural Conflict and Working Class Community" offers a much more rigorously historicized account of subcultural style than has so far appeared in Hebdige's work.[1]

Cohen's subject, initially, is the housing estates in working-class areas of East London that were developed in the 1950s and that, he says, have actively participated in the destruction of a working-class community in those areas. His research in the field led Cohen (1980) to argue that the physical structure of the housing projects actually reframed the ideologies of those who used them:

> The plans are unconsciously modelled on the structure of the middle-class environment, which is based on the concept of *property* and *private ownership*, on individual differences of status, wealth and so on, whereas the structure of the working-class environment is based on the concept of community or collective identity, common lack of ownership, wealth, etc. (p. 81)

The physical form of these new housing estates was, as it were, middle-class; the occupants were not. This disjunction resulted in a deep ideological fissure within the communities they housed: between a nostalgic class loyalty and a bourgeois upward mobility, between an ideology of work and production and one of leisure and consumption, and between the traditional working-class community and its effacement. The contradictions within the larger, "parent," culture had a most forceful impact upon their youth subcultures and manifested themselves in aspects of subcultural style: in the gangs of mods, skinheads, and "crombies" who successively occupied the urban space within and around these housing estates.

Cohen's (1980) analysis of these styles, unlike Hebdige's later analysis, assiduously relates them to the "parent culture" that produced them and from which derive the lived contradictions the subcultural style is designed to resolve "magically":

> The succession of subcultures which this parent culture generated can thus all be considered so many variations on a central theme—the contradiction, at an ideological level, between traditional working-class puritanism and the new hedonism of consumption; at an economic level, between a future as part of the socially mobile elite or as part of the new lumpen proletariat. Mods, parkas, skinheads, crombies all represent, in their different ways, an attempt to retrieve some of the socially cohesive elements destroyed in their parent culture, and to combine these with elements selected from other class fractions, symbolising one or another of the options confronting it. (pp. 82–83)

Cohen goes on to provide examples of how the symbolic structures of subcultural style might be decoded:

> The original mod life-style could be interpreted as an attempt to realize, *but in an imaginary relation*, the conditions of existence of the socially mobile white-collar worker. While the argot and ritual forms of the mods stressed many of the traditional values of their parent culture, their dress and music reflected the hedonistic image of the affluent consumer. . . . The skinheads' . . . life-style . . . represents a systematic inversion of the mods—whereas the mods explored the upwardly mobile option, the skinheads explored the lumpen. . . . [Their] uniform signified a reaction against the contamination of the parent culture by middle class values and a reassertion of the integral values of working-class culture through its most recessive traits—its puritanism and chauvinism. (pp. 83–84)

Unlike Hebdige, however, Cohen does not imply that such a "reading" of subcultural style is in itself sufficient. There are, he says, three necessary levels of subcultural analysis: historical analysis, which "isolates the specific problematic of a particular class fraction"; structural or semiotic analysis of the subsystems of style—largely the analysis of dress, argot (slang), music, and ritual Hebdige employed; and "phenomenological" (or what we might understand as more specifically ethnographic) analysis of "the way the subculture is actually 'lived out' by those who are the bearers and supports of the subculture" (p. 83).

Cohen acknowledges ethnography's obligation to develop a methodology that can protect it against accusations of subjectivity. To understand a subculture without "disappearing" into it is extremely difficult; yet, if one does "disappear" into it, one's statements about it are compromised. Hebdige's (1988) recanting of his *Subculture* thesis implicitly acknowledges a methodological failure: his approach was unable to prevent him writing his own political wishes into his analyses. It is clear that Cohen's (and, later, Willis's) attempts to provide an "objective" rationale for the researcher's practice are justified. However, and as their work suggests, if ethnography is vulnerable to the accusation of being "undertheorized," it is also true that the development of a theory of analytical practice within the field is no easy matter. Operating as ethnographies do, at the point where determinate social conditions become specific lived conditions, it is difficult *not* to privilege "the real," the empirical evidence of one's own eyes and ears, and to allow this category of evidence to overwhelm all others. This runs against the theoretical grain of cultural studies. Nevertheless, under the pressure of "real" evidence, it is tempting— almost irresistibly so—to reject theory as inadequate to deal with the "actual" complexity of the practices of everyday life.

Paul Willis's work provides us with contrasting evidence of the power of such a temptation and of an exemplary resistance to it. *Profane Culture* (1978), his study of two oppositional subcultures (motorbike club members and hippies), was researched under the auspices of the CCCS between 1969 and 1972. Although it was published in book form in 1978, a year after *Learning to Labour,* it represents an earlier example of ethnographic work from the Centre and bears numerous marks of this. "The real" is explicitly privileged in *Profane Culture,* not through a deliberate theoretical argument, but through its insinuation into the validating rhetoric of the book. Within a persuasive and legitimate argument reclaiming the importance of subjective experience for cultural analysis, Willis nevertheless allows "the real" and the theoretical to be opposed as if they were mutually exclusive categories. The hippies' "living out" of their ideas is applauded as "more heroic, . . . fuller, more resonant and honest than [their] dry cerebral statement" (p. 89); the motorbike club members' frank admission of their lack of emotional sympathy with other human beings is preferred over a phony "cerebralised compassion" (p. 30). The intoxicating attraction of the "authentic" looms large in *Profane Culture,* and produces a more romantic identification with its subjects than we find in the more sharply theorized analyses in Hebdige's *Subculture* (1979). The connections Cohen routinely makes between his subcultures and their "parent culture" are not made in *Profane Culture,* either, and Willis's project suffers from this; the sexism of the motorbike culture, for instance, is masked by the absence of such systemic connections.

Willis is not unaware of these theoretical problems, however, and it is clear that the theoretical inconsistencies in *Profane Culture* are not meant to signify a categoric rejection of theory. *Learning to Labour* is as useful an example of a densely theorized practice as *Profane Culture* is of a theoretically compromised one.

Although it was published a year earlier than *Profane Culture,* the research for *Learning to Labour* was conducted between 1972 and 1975, and it is a more sophisticated example of Willis's work. The project studies a group of working-class boys, rebels and "antiacademic" in their school, in order to see how their school experiences equip them for later life. Willis finds that "the lads," as he calls them, determinedly resist the ideologies of the school and that this resistance well prepares them for the unskilled working-class jobs in which they end up. Masculine working-class subcultural codes of work, of earning, and of success enable the boys to choose "happily" not to engage in white-collar, educated, or skilled labor, and to deny that they have any other genuine options. Once within work, they find the shop-floor culture within the factory entirely familiar, structured as it is by the same discourses and power relations as their "counter-school" culture.

A major study, *Learning to Labour* employs ethnography as the primary element within its analysis of cultural forms and social reproduction. Other elements include a sophisticated macropolitical analysis of the workings of ideology and social power within working-class culture, and the analysis of the discourses that structure the ethnographic evidence. Willis, like Hebdige and Cohen, sees the importance of style; for instance, he accounts for the significance the "lads" attribute to smoking through its valorization "as an act of insurrection" that invokes associations "with adult values and practices," the antithesis of the school (p. 19). His emphasis on the way school life is "lived" by these boys enables him to detect how completely their social practices invert its values:

> They construct virtually their own day from what is offered by the school. Truancy is only one relatively unimportant and crude variant of this principle of self-direction which ranges across vast chunks of the syllabus and covers many diverse activities: being free out of class, being in class and doing no work, being in the wrong class, roaming the corridors looking for excitement, being asleep in private. The core skill which articulates these possibilities is being able to get out of any class: the preservation of personal mobility. (p. 27)

The aim of these boys is not to do any school work; some boast of having written nothing all term. By reading the boys' cultural practice from their own point of view, Willis is able to reveal how their apparently aimlessly disruptive behavior has a tactical significance.

While the book contains skilled and illuminating analyses of the functions of discourse (the "masculinity" of physical labor as inscribed in working-class discourse, for instance), it is most important for its diagnosis of the structural nature of these boys' choices and their ultimate class position. As Willis (1977) says, "The difficult thing to explain about how working class kids get working class jobs is why they let themselves" (p. 1), and the answer is finally that they consider their choice to have served their own best interests within the existing class structures. Accurately enough, they see the carrot of credentialism offered to them as a giant con; rather than chase the chimera of middle-class upward mobility, they opt to withdraw from the race and seek unskilled employment. The choice is rewarded by their sense of commonality with their workmates and by their access to the adult male working-class culture that the ability to earn a wage provides. The boys' rejection of qualifications, their contempt for education, their masculinist privileging of physical over mental work, and their ridicule of those who accept the ideologies of the school all reinforce the conviction that their interests will be served by virtually any working-class job and defeated by virtually any middle-class job. A better example of the process of hegemony would be hard to find.

The product of Willis's ethnography, consequently, is a profound critique of the hegemonic function of the education system. His study reveals precisely how the system works, and the last third of *Learning to Labour* attempts to expose its inequities in theory as well as in practice. Willis's "lads," setting up their "counter-school culture," have in fact come to an accurate recognition of their political location; the role for Willis's cultural analysis is to develop his readers' recognition of this in order to advance arguments for socio-political change. This is a complex and important section of the book, but one lengthy quotation may indicate how it depends on and transcends the ethnographic information it has produced:

> Bourdieu and Passeron have argued that the importance of institutionalised knowledge and qualifications lies in social exclusion rather than in technical or humanistic advance. They legitimate and reproduce a class society. A seemingly more democratic currency has replaced real capital as the social arbiter in modern society. Bourdieu and Passeron argue that it is the exclusive "cultural capital"—

> knowledge and skill in the symbolic manipulation of language and figures—of the dominant groups in society which ensures the success of their offspring and thus the reproduction of class position and privilege. This is because educational advancement is controlled through the "fair" meritocratic testing of precisely those skills which "cultural capital" provides.
>
> Insofar as this is an accurate assessment of the role and importance of qualifications, it supports the view that it is unwise for working class kids to place their trust in diplomas and certificates. These things act not to push people up—as in the official account—but to maintain there those who are already at the top. Insofar as knowledge is always biased and shot through with class meaning, the working class student must overcome his inbuilt disadvantage of possessing the wrong class culture and the wrong educational decoders to start with. A few can make it. The class can never follow. It is through a good number trying, however, that the class structure is legitimated. The middle class enjoys its privilege not by virtue of inheritance or birth, but by virtue of an apparently proven greater competence and merit. The refusal to compete, implicit in the counter-school culture, is therefore in this sense a radical act: it refuses to collude in its own educational suppression. (p. 128)

We are, here, a long way from *Profane Culture*'s dismissal of the "cerebral"; there is nothing "dry" about this analysis of the lived conditions Willis's subjects have to negotiate.

Interesting for its thoroughgoing use of Gramscian theories of hegemony at a time when CCCS media studies were more influenced by Althusser, and foreshadowing the complex analyses of ideological formations within popular culture that developed in the mid-1980s, Willis's book is a graphic example of just how useful the employment of ethnographic method can be. It has not merely described a social process, but provided the basis for its social and political analysis.

Such an achievement as that of *Learning to Labour* has not protected ethnography from criticism, however. Richard Johnson (1983, 45–48) has warned against ethnography's unifying tendencies (the suppression of conflicts and contradictions), its sentimental construction of an essential "working-class-ness," and its close identification with empiricist models of culture. This, despite Johnson's close interest in the analysis of lived cultures and the historical construction of subjectivities, and despite his respect for the work that marked Stuart Hall's period as director of the CCCS. Other reservations about the potential subjectivity and (even) intellectual arrogance of ethnographic study come from the editors of *Rewriting English*, themselves CCCS alumni:

> Ethnography has an intensely democratic impulse, which provides a useful check against the temptation—strong for socialists, especially academic ones—to speak too readily on other people's behalf, and an acknowledgement of the obvious but easily neglected truth that any account of an activity that ignores or marginalises the experience of those directly engaged in it can hardly claim much accuracy or authenticity. Yet, ethnography, however enlightened and politically self-conscious, cannot escape the problems affecting all academically based social investigation: how to take account, within the "neutral" forms and procedures of the analysis, of the immensely powerful and pervasive ideologies that shape all practical languages and culture; how and with what authority and on whose behalf to "interpret" the lives, experiences, and meanings of others. (Batsleer et al. 1985, 146)

The democratic impulse and the inevitable effect of ethnographic practice in the academy contradict each other, it would seem.

When we read ethnographic studies, there is always a point at which we need to ask who is speaking, and for whom. It is a problem that refuses to go away; it surfaces in Hebdige as an insouciant confidence in the objective validity of his judgments on style and taste, in Willis as an implicit identification with the group he is studying, and in Buckingham as the denial that the clumsiness of his intervention in the subculture might affect the outcome of his research. As a consequence of the importance of description in ethnographic work, it would seem, implicit assumptions tend to be more difficult to isolate and excise; they are embedded in the experience to be described. As Johnson (1983) says, "Intellectuals may be great at describing *other* people's implicit assumptions, but [are] as 'implicit' as anyone when it comes to their own" (p. 45). Angela McRobbie's (1981) critique of the Birmingham subcultural research makes this abundantly clear.

Focusing on Willis and Hebdige in particular, McRobbie uncovers at least one of the implicit assumptions behind their studies: their privileging of masculine culture. McRobbie (1981) names the significant absence in this body of work—the subject of women's place within the subcultures considered, and the lack of any consideration of women's own subcultures.[2] She notes how the male ethnographers have been "blinded" by their choice of subcultures, with which they have already established an identification:

> Writing about subcultures isn't the same thing as being in one. Nonetheless, it's easy to see how it would be possible in sharing some of the same symbols—the liberating release of rock music, the thrill of speed, or alcohol or even of football—to be blinded to some of their more oppressive features. (p. 114)

As a result, she argues, such studies unconsciously reproduce their subculture's repressive attitude toward women. Willis, for instance, never attempts to go outside the male lineage of his subjects in *Learning to Labour*. Their relationships within the family, with their mothers, female siblings, and girlfriends are all but ignored; yet, as McRobbie (1981) says, working-class culture includes the bedroom and the breakfast table as well as the school and the workplace (p. 115).

McRobbie's criticism of Hebdige is more substantive, bearing on the ideological function of the subcultural styles he examines. Subcultural style is predominantly masculine; indeed, McRobbie says, "subculture's best kept secret" is "its claiming of style as a male but never unambiguously masculine prerogative":

> This is not to say that women are denied style, rather that the style of a subculture is primarily that of its men. Linked to this are the collective celebrations of itself through its rituals of stylish public self-display and of its (at least temporary) sexual self-sufficiency. (p. 117)

McRobbie indicates how the writing of women into the argument of *Subculture* might radically revise it; if subcultures reproduce the dominant structures of gender relations in their primarily masculine styles, then Hebdige's argument about the oppositional and resistant force of these styles is compromised. McRobbie's article reminds us of the problems remaining in ethnographic method, as well as the durability of conservative constructions of gender.

Contentious though it may be, and fashionable though it is in contemporary media studies, ethnographic work is nevertheless an important element in the enterprise of cultural studies. Within the history of the CCCS, it has occupied a strategic role, making links with descriptive social anthropology and with "history from below." Hall (1980a) notes this link himself, and glosses the various enterprises falling into the category of "the new social history—for example, the oral history movement, the work of Centerprise and *History Workshop*, a great deal of feminist historical writing . . . and that whole body of work inspired by Thompson's *The Making*" (p. 24).

Historians and Cultural Studies

Tony Bennett (1986b, 11) has claimed that Left historians' elitist neglect of popular culture as a field of inquiry during the 1950s effectively delivered the area to the various participants in the mass culture debates outlined in Chapter 2. From there it was rescued by Hoggart and others, and incorporated into the territory of cultural studies. Popular culture, even the concept of "culture" itself, has remained a site of disputation between historians and cultural studies analysts ever since. Despite the importance of the *category* of history to the developing protocols of cultural studies, the field's relation with the academic profession—the discipline and institution—of history has never been without tension or ambiguity.

E. P. Thompson and his *The Making of the English Working Class* (1978a) plays a key role in this relationship. *The Making* not only constructs the English working class, "calling it up" through the writing of its story, it also ushers in a new kind of history. Instead of focusing on the elite and the powerful, Thompson's history places its distinctive emphasis on those who lived ordinary lives but who nevertheless participated in, and were the agents and victims of, historical processes. This is not a history of political parties and legislation but of cultural formations and social relations—particularly those within popular culture.

Notwithstanding its wider ramifications in questioning the construction of history, the bulk of the work to proceed from this reorientation of British social history is, in a sense, internal to the discipline; it deals with substantive issues within British social history and historiography and, despite its admitted importance in these areas, need not concern us here. However, at its outer reaches, one would have expected such an intellectual movement within the discipline of history to have been nicely consonant with intellectual movements within cultural studies from the late 1960s into the 1980s. And yet that has not been the case. It is true that Richard Johnson's period as director of the CCCS coincided with a more broadly historical conception of the Centre's work. It is also true that the new history shared many of its key orientations with work going on in cultural studies, such as "the centrality of the notion of experience and the consequent assertion of the agency of the individual within history" (Johnson 1979a, 65). Thompson's stated aim of examining "the peculiarities of the English"—just what was distinctive about British social development in comparison with that of other countries—is also quoted as a CCCS objective under both Johnson (1980) and Hall (1980a). But there were crucial differences between the two movements: most notably, the new history was suspicious of cultural studies' theoretical interests (readers will recall the *History Workshop* controversy from Chapter 2), and the new history ultimately served humanist rather than materialist ideologies. Further, although the new history's emphasis on experience enabled it to cooperate with ethnographic research, its implicit empiricism set it in opposition to structuralist/semiotic notions of textual analysis. Even while some post-Thompsonian social histories became almost Foucauldian in their emphasis on discourse and ideology (see, e.g., Cunningham 1980), Thompson himself maintained his opposition to European theory in virtually all its forms—but especially in its Althusserian guise.

English historians' resistance to theory, and their suspicion of those who come from outside their discipline (or even beyond their shores), has not entirely disappeared even now. A residual wariness is still apparent in their concentration on nineteenth-century (rather than twentieth-century) social histories of popular culture, and in the continuing resistance to the kinds of textual analysis now readily and usefully undertaken by sociologists (such as, for instance, Tony Bennett's [1986a] analysis of the Blackpool Pleasure Beach). This is not the whole story, however. As a result of Left historians' reconsideration of popular cultural formations, we now have theoretically and politically informed histories of popular movements, and of popular pastimes such as cricket and football. The best of such studies give the lie to the claim that history is "untheorized." Hugh Cunningham's (1982) history of leisure in mid-Victorian England is theoretically sophisticated and richly argued; Gareth Stedman-Jones's (1982) work has consistently focused on institutions, their discourses, and their ideologies. Although Tony Bennett (1986b, 18) accuses Chas Critcher of a left-wing populism that forever chases an "authentic" but now "lost" popular culture, Critcher's (1982) history of football is clearly aware of more than empiricist approaches. In this short section dealing with the rise of football hooliganism in Britain since the Second World War, he recalls the work of Cohen, Willis, and Hebdige:

> If the mainstream attitude to "football hooliganism" has been to deny its connections with the game, it may be overreacting to locate it wholly within the game. Rather we need to understand more fully this relationship between

> the game and more general cultural pressures to which some sections of the working class are subjected. The fusion of the "skinhead" phenomenon and "football hooliganism" may have provided a moment when some of those relationships become clear: how football appeared as an element alongside other cultural experiences like housing redevelopment and the break-up of the traditional neighbourhood, frustrated expectations in education and employment, the commercialisation of leisure, the "threat" posed by immigration. (p. 230)

Here the split between history and cultural studies is negotiated in a generally representative fashion, by way of the need to explain the popular movement as a cultural formation—acknowledging the usefulness of the kind of cultural theory Thompson eschewed.

Predictably, perhaps, an area where the new history and cultural studies meet relatively productively is media history. There is a strong tradition of media history in Britain; it includes a number of orthodox histories of media institutions and industries, such as George Perry's *The Great British Picture Show* (1975), as well as more Gramscian accounts, such as Scannell and Cardiff's (1982) study of the BBC. The most substantial of the press and broadcasting histories to have emerged from the combination of media sociology, the new history, and cultural studies is James Curran and Jean Seaton's magisterial *Power Without Responsibility: The Press and Broadcasting in Britain*. Published in 1981, with a revised edition in 1985, *Power Without Responsibility* is influenced, curiously, by both E. P. Thompson and Antonio Gramsci. It provides a model for the kind of work that is now much more firmly established within cultural studies: the cultural history that succeeds in relating institutional, industrial, political, and ideological analysis to produce a complex, and often deliberately disjunctive, account of cultural production.

Curran's history of the press ties the content of the papers to ideological and regulatory conditions as well as to the economic conditions of ownership and control. He offers a critique of previous press histories that questions the democratic consequences assumed to flow from the free market and the role of advertising, and that demonstrates how the press in Britain has not merely reflected dominant social attitudes but produced a conservative version of them. At its best, this history accurately describes not only the politicoeconomic structures within which the press operates, but the textual forms that assist in reinforcing these structures:

> In a[n] indirect way, the press reinforced attachment to the status quo by the way in which it tended to depict reality. Its focus on political and state office as the seat of power decentred capital and masked the central influence of business and financial elites. By reporting the news in terms of discrete and disconnected events, it encouraged acceptance of the social structure as natural—the way things are. Its expanding entertainment content also tended to portray life as relatively unchanging, a panorama of individual drama determined by the laws of human nature and the randomness of fate. By thus blocking out alternative, structural explanations of how society operates, the human interest stories of the popular press have contributed as much as its political commentary to sustaining the extraordinarily resilient consensus of post-war Britain. (p. 120)

Within this passage there are many lines of agreement between Curran and Seaton's view of social process within the media and those taken by, say, the majority of CCCS studies of the media at the time. Indeed, Curran and Seaton acknowledge the work of the CCCS, praising *Policing the Crisis* (Hall et al. 1978) and endorsing cultural studies' Althusserian view of the media's "relative autonomy": "The media do not merely express the interests of the ruling class, rather they have an independent function in ordering the world. The media do not merely 'reflect' social reality; they increasingly help to make it" (p. 281).

Nevertheless, Curran and Seaton's historical and sociological pedigrees tell in the end; they ultimately resist a full appropriation of cultural studies approaches as internally contradictory and unscientific (pp. 278–80). The book concludes, however, by similarly questioning the bases of the authors' own tradition of mass communication research:

> The empirical evidence of the pluralists [here, defenders of market forces, and also cultural studies theorists] gives powerful backing to the determinists' [here, the mainstream of British political economies of the media] conviction that the media exert an important and uncontrolled influence. Yet the deterministic explanation in terms of class manipulation and exploitation is too mechanistic, obscuring a series of complex relationships which have yet to be explained. (p. 282)

The work of explaining these relationships has largely proceeded through the application of Gramscian theories of hegemony within cultural studies, and this will be addressed in Chapter 6. The argument over class and the media's determination of reality will be taken up again in the next section, which deals with political economies and sociologies of the media, and their relation to cultural studies.

The final area I wish to touch on here is one that receives significant influences from outside Britain: from European appropriations of post-Freudian theory that examine the cultural construction of consciousness, and from the work of Michel Foucault, which sees history as the product of ways of thinking about things, of discourse. Foucault's histories of sexuality, or of such institutions as the prison or the hospital, are histories of ways of thinking about the body and gender, or about the relation between the individual and the state. The links between such an enterprise and Williams's originating enterprise in *Culture and Society* (1966) should be clear: in both cases, we are looking at a history of the social production and the social function not only of certain ideas, but also of certain kinds of consciousness. In the cultural studies of the early 1980s, the construction of such a history was the objective of a number of analyses of English educational institutions and the disciplinary discourses flourishing within them.

As we have seen, cultural studies soon separated itself from literary studies—despite the close links between its theoretical influences and those of literary studies, and despite the fact that many of those who worked in cultural studies had literary training. When it came time to apply the new history and to exploit the new theoretical influences from Europe that made it possible to examine institutional discourse as a serial historical text, it was probably inevitable that the discipline of English should be a target for such analysis. Widdowson's collection, *Re-reading English* (1982), draws heavily on the main institutional locations of cultural studies—CCCS and the Open University—for its contributors, who then interrogate the main institutional locations of literary studies. The volume offers histories of the rise of English as an academic discipline, accounts of theoretical issues within it, alternative models of critical analysis, and suggestions for future directions. It is the explanation, however, of English as the product of volatile "ensembles of cultural and ideological pressures" (p. 8) that is the strategic move; it makes "English studies" the subject of discursive analysis and thus turns the tables rather neatly on a discipline that has made everything else the object of *its* modes of analysis.

Brian Doyle's (1982) chapter, "The Hidden History of English Studies," examines the foundation of the discipline, its enclosure within ideas of the nation, and its implication into the structure of gender relations within what he calls "the national family." What most interests Doyle is how English has carefully erased the traces of its own history and naturalized itself as a discipline and as a tradition of texts. The main objective of Doyle's piece is to reverse the process—to historicize the institution of English studies, and to provoke such critiques of its practices and assumptions as are presented in the subsequent chapters of *Re-reading English*. This work is continued by a subsequent volume in the same series, *Rewriting English* (Batsleer et al. 1985), which develops some of the suggestions in Widdowson's collection, by tracing the "politics of literacy and literature outside the institutions of literary criticism and of English in higher education." Beginning with the 1930s, this book examines historical shifts in the constitutive discourses of English in British schools, before looking at a range of working-class and women's writing—the relations, as they put it, between genre and gender—across a broader historical range.

Francis Mulhern's *The "Moment" of Scrutiny* (1979) also deals with an aspect of the discursive and institutional history of the 1930s. Although emanating from English literary studies, this has become a widely used and respected book within cultural studies. Its subject is *Scrutiny*, the influential English literary journal produced by a group dominated by F. R. Leavis from 1932 to the early 1950s, and reprinted in both collected and selected form in the 1960s. Leavis and *Scrutiny* play ambiguous roles within British cultural histories from the Left. *Scrutiny* took on the social and political battles the Left neglected during the 1930s and thus deserves admiration; on the other hand, its championing of a particularly petit-bourgeois, evaluative, and moralistic version of textual criticism has made it anathema to Marxist literary and cultural scholars. Yet, there was common ground between the two traditions; Williams himself suggested that the exploration of such territory was an objective of his involvement in the journal *Politics and Letters* (see the section on Williams in Chapter 2). As Mulhern points out, *Scrutiny* actually opened up space for the analysis of such cultural institutions as itself, although this space was ultimately to be occupied by the work of Raymond Williams and, among others, the CCCS.

Mulhern's book is an exemplary history of the journal: its contributors; its cultural, institutional, and political contexts; and its ideological function. Enclosed within an analysis of the rise of English that provides interesting comparisons to Doyle's, Mulhern's account of *Scrutiny* resembles Scannell and Cardiff's institutional histories: its territory is crisscrossed by contradictions, anomalies, and the complex relations between individuals and their social and ideological contexts. Mulhern's (1979) objective, as he puts it, is to "analyse the conditions in which the journal came into being": "the elaboration and modifications of its discourse over its life-time, the objective functions that it performed in the culture of mid-century England—and so, to define and assess what is called here the 'moment' of *Scrutiny*" (p. ix).

The driving impulse behind *The "Moment" of Scrutiny* seems to be the need to understand the journal's curiously ambiguous relationship with the Left and with practical politics—both of which *Scrutiny* kept at arm's length. As the account becomes less traditionally historical and more discursive in its focus and analysis, the ideological underpinnings of the *Scrutiny* line—and the reasons for its ultimate opposition to the Left—are more clearly revealed. Mulhern concludes his history by arguing that the version of literary criticism institutionalized and disseminated through *Scrutiny* is a discourse "whose foremost general cultural function is the repression of politics":

> This discourse has done much to shape, and still sustains, England's cultivated, politically philistine . . . intelligentsia; it is reproduced . . . by the entire national educational system: it is a key element in the cultural "formula" of bourgeois Britain, part of an ensemble of cultural *domination*. (p. 331)

It is significant that these histories of the role of English, of literary studies, and of a tradition of textual practice uncover cultural studies' roots in literary studies. It is as if the new methodologies have to prove their penetrative force by discovering their own origins. These histories also foreground the problem of aesthetics—still a key item in literary categories, and still an issue waiting to be addressed properly within cultural studies. In this regard, the historicizing of the discipline of English has a strategic value in that it also historicizes, "denaturalizes," the aesthetic categories it has privileged. Deployed in this way, history is anything but disinterested; within contemporary cultural studies, it can operate as a highly polemical strategy of discovery.

The analysis of cultural institutions, and of the discourses that constitute them and enable them to function, is a major development within cultural studies and of profound significance. Within this development, the category of history has become crucial and its definition and uses contested, but it has radically extended the purpose and power of cultural studies research.

Sociology, Cultural Studies, and Media Institutions

Another kind of institutional analysis, this time directed at the media industries, has also exerted a significant influence on the nature of cultural studies' accounts of cultural production. This has not come from within cultural studies, however, but from the British media sociologies of the 1970s.

During the early 1970s, there was an exceptionally strong revival of British media work outside of, and at times competing with, the work of the cultural studies centers. Where cultural studies research was preoccupied with the analysis of the text and the processes of its encoding or decoding, other traditions focused their interests elsewhere. The two most influential and long-lasting traditions, and the ones I want to deal with in this section, are characterized by the politically and sociologically informed analysis of the economic conditions determining media institutions' activities and the application of ethnographic methods to study the media as a workplace, as an industrial culture.

In British media analysis, the boundary between the practices of political economy and sociology has become quite porous; Marxist sociologists have presented what amounts to a political economy of the media in order to demonstrate the importance of the ownership of media outlets. As we shall see when we look at an example of Murdock and Golding's work, some media sociologists invoke classical Marxist theory in order to claim ownership as the most crucial aspect of the relationship between the media and society. The power of media owners is not untrammeled, however; it is mediated by those who work in the institutions and industries they control. The extent, then, of the owners' control of their media cannot be determined without knowledge of how it affects those who work for them. Consequently, ethnographies of the working lives of media professionals also assumed a strategic importance within arguments about the power of the media and the economic or structural basis of that power.

Over this period, cultural studies reserved some of its most bitter criticism for sociology's political economies of the media. Cultural studies accused the tradition of economism, of a blind adherence to the traditional Marxist base/superstructure model of society, of a "top-down" version of ideology that sees cultural effects flowing inevitably from economic conditions of ownership and control. Most of these accusations were vigorously denied, of course, and countered with criticism of cultural studies' textual determinism or its cavalier dismissal of the industrial conditions and the economic decisions that govern the media institutions. While it was widely referred to and often exploited as a source for convenient empirical detail, media sociology was rarely taken on as a model for cultural studies practice. Even in the 1980s there were still strong pockets of resistance to the tradition (Johnson 1983, 27).

Because of the history of antagonism between the two approaches, I am wary of appearing to minimize or perhaps elide the differences between British cultural studies and British political economies of the media by dealing with the latter in a book on the former. However, these political economies do represent a strong and coherent tradition within British media studies that exerted an important, if contested, influence on cultural studies in the 1970s, and can be seen to exert an even more profound and certainly less bitterly contested influence within cultural studies now. In this section, I want to recognize this influence by indicating, if only very briefly, the kind of information it produced: my "exemplary" text is Graham Murdock and Peter Golding's "Capitalism, Communication and Class Relations" (1977).

The authors begin this article by glossing the kinds of questions their approach throws into relief—at least at the time of writing:

> questions about the relations between communications entrepreneurs and the capitalist class, about the relations between ownership and control within the communications industries, about the processes through which the dominant ideology is translated into cultural commodities; and about the dynamics of reception and the extent to

which members of subordinate groups adopt the dominant ideas as their own. (p. 15)

Murdock and Golding take the classical Marxist line in seeing the economic structure of the society as the sphere most requiring close analysis if we are to understand history. They regret that the economic determinants of culture have been relegated to the background in cultural studies textual analysis. Murdock and Golding, like Marx, insist that "property ownership, economic control, and class power" are "inextricably tied together"—even in such areas of cultural production as the media (p. 28).

Their political economy of the media argues that those who own the media control the way it produces culture; and those who control cultural production are themselves enclosed within a dominant capitalist class in whose interests the media represent reality. Therefore, to focus simply on the media's representations of the real, the product of these relationships, is to ignore the structure that determines their very existence. Responding to the accusation that their explanation of the connection between the media and class power is a little mechanical, Murdock and Golding point out that their conception of this connection is (like Raymond Williams's) that of a subtle process of "setting limits, exerting pressures, and closing off options" (p. 16) Against the accusation that they are reviving the crude dichotomy between base and superstructure, with its insistence on the decisive role played by the economic base, Murdock and Golding stress the dynamism and interrelatedness of the system they describe while nevertheless insisting on the importance of understanding the processes of material production *before* "intellectual production," or the economic bases before the cultural bases (p. 17). While Murdock and Golding do make concessions to the cultural field, they also make it clear that they are critical of "top-heavy analyses in which an elaborate economy of cultural forces [i.e., texts] balances insecurely on a schematic account of economic forces shaping their production" (p. 19). In their brief critique of a Stuart Hall article, Murdock and Golding suggest that Hall fails to understand that questions "of resources and of loss and profit play a central role in structuring both the processes and products of television production, including the output of news and current affairs." "Economics," they conclude, "is clearly not the only factor in play, but equally it cannot be ignored" (p. 19).[3]

Murdock and Golding's specific project in the article I am examining is to explain how ideological influence "from above" (p. 20) takes place, and to demonstrate that the "control over material resources and their changing distribution are *ultimately* the most powerful of the many levers operating in cultural production" (p. 20). The ensuing analysis of the movement in media ownership from "concentration to conglomeration"—the increasing concentration of media ownership into the hands of an ever smaller number of individuals, and the increasing interconnection between media industries and other sectors of business—is powerful and important. They trace the agglomeration of media companies and the effective reduction in the number of owners; when this process is seen in conjunction with the commercial diversification of media companies—which therefore expands their sphere of influence throughout the business and financial sector—we have persuasive evidence of how media owners might be stitched into the interests of an elite capitalist class fraction. In a later article, Murdock (1982) provides more detailed evidence of this alignment, again delivered persuasively.

While this style of argument has now been assimilated into all varieties of media studies, it was resisted by representatives of both the culturalist and the structuralist paradigms in the cultural studies of the 1970s. The culturalists rejected its implicit denial of individual agency or power within media institutions, while the structuralists insisted that the primary determining force came from culture or ideology, which framed the definition of interests produced by owners, industry workers, and audiences alike. Culturalist skepticism could be somewhat ameliorated, however, by the results of another branch of media sociology that complemented and responded to the political economies: these were the occupational sociologies that examined how the internal workings of media institutions complicated the economic determinations described by Murdock and others. Their focus was on the way in which the owners' control of the media was expressed, mediated, or countervailed by the social structures within the specific institution.

This is a rich tradition, drawing on American occupational sociologies as well as ethnography. Initially, British work concentrated on the production of news, publishing such accounts of media professions as Jeremy Tunstall's *Journalists at Work* (1971), Phillip Elliott's *The Making of a Television Series: A Case Study in the Sociology of Culture* (1972), and Philip Schlesinger's *Putting Reality Together: BBC News* (1978) (see also Elliott 1977 for an overview of this kind of work in sociology).

Putting Reality Together presents an intelligent history of the institution of news, and offers a sociological account of this institution—an account consonant with that offered within British political economies and in some cases explicitly opposed to that likely to be produced within cultural studies. The book's theoretical allegiances are declared in a privileging of the economic determinants of the institution, and of the demands of the industry against more textually based procedures. Most significantly, for our purposes here, Schlesinger's book establishes the importance of industrial/institutional work practices and professional ideologies as factors in the media's production of culture.

Putting Reality Together provides a number of work-practice studies, showing how the cultures of the newsrooms produce certain effects on the news they publish: for instance, how the practices of news gathering themselves naturalize action, pace, and immediacy as intrinsic to the profession and thus discriminate against more considered, researched, and reflective journalism. The work-practice studies may not reveal evidence of direct intervention by media owners, but they do reveal how conservative the forces are that shape media production at the shop-floor level. This may not in all instances substantiate the political economists' structural accounts, but the ideological effects are certainly no different from those proposed by Murdock and Golding.

Cultural studies, although explicitly differentiated from the tradition that produced Schlesinger's book, has nevertheless benefited from it. There have been a number of production studies of particular programs or groups of texts; in addition to those examined in some detail in Chapter 4, there are Tulloch's two studies (with Manuel Alvarado on *Dr. Who*, 1983, and with Albert Moran on *A Country Practice*, 1986) and Manuel Alvarado and Edward Buscombe's (1978) study of the stylish British private eye show, *Hazell*. In general, the ethnographic studies have found a relatively uncontested place within cultural studies media research, but one cannot say this of the political economies. Poststructuralist cultural studies still finds it hard to admit their importance, even when the current interest in cultural policy, in the role of government and institutions in the formation and execution of policies in education, the media, the environment, and so on, seems directly continuous with much of the work within this tradition.

But, we must not overemphasize this schism; there have always been moments of cooperation, co-option, even a merging of the two traditions. Murdock's (1976) research into urban adolescents, for instance, was included in the CCCS *Resistance Through Rituals* collection; the first issue of *Media, Culture and Society* carried a manifesto that advocated the amelioration of theoretical differences, and an editorial board that included representatives from both traditions;[4] and Nicholas Garnham (1987) provided one of the lead articles for the first issue of *Cultural Studies*. In fact, one can see how the theoretical directions taken by the two traditions have converged over the years. Cultural studies is now more interested in the political/economic conditions surrounding the institutions that produce culture; courses on media institutions now accompany courses on media text analysis within colleges and universities, and issues of ownership and control are taken seriously even by those who do not accept them as the *ultimate* factors in the relation between the media and society. Critiques of cultural studies have had their effect on changes in practice, and in the seriousness with which the processes and mechanisms of cultural production are now taken. Cultural studies is gradually finding ways to make use of sociological approaches, albeit through modifying their definitions of ideology and adopting Gramscian notions of hegemony rather than the more instrumental notions identified with the early political economies. In turn, political economists have been able to add cultural studies' textual and discursive analysis to their repertoire of methods; as we have seen, institutions can be investigated as discursive entities, and this is particularly useful, for instance, in the analysis of news values. Murdock (1989) has himself recently attempted to develop the common ground between the two positions, by arguing that neither approach—alone—can be considered entirely sufficient.

The 1980s can be seen as a decade when cultural studies became more interested in the analysis of institutions, both as powerful locations for the establishment of dominant discourses and as political and economic formations that also shape and determine cultural production. Nevertheless, that does not constitute a merger between cultural studies and sociology. There are more differences to divide a Graham Murdock and a Richard Johnson than the hoary old specter of economism. The natures of their interests in the media are fundamentally different. As James Carey (1989) has argued in relation to the work of the CCCS, cultural studies has not developed the study of the mass media as a subject or as a discipline—the ultimate goal of sociologies of the media. Rather, the media are "centered" as a "site on which to engage the general question of social theory: How is it . . . that societies manage to produce and reproduce themselves?" (p. 110). The answers cultural studies theorists provide to this general question also differentiate them from the sociologists and the historians surveyed in this chapter. This is largely due to the models of culture and ideology employed. It is to this question, then, we must finally turn: to the ways in which the category of ideology is understood and used within cultural studies—ways that differentiate it from the humanistic insistence on the individual agency of the historians and from the "top-down" economic determinism of the political economists. This will take us across a mine field of slippery concepts.

Notes

1 Originally published in *Working Papers in Cultural Studies* in 1972, this article is available in extracted form in *Culture, Media, Language*. Subsequent citations to Cohen (1980) refer to page numbers in this later version.

2 To see what such a consideration might be like, see McRobbie and Garber's (1976) contribution to *Resistance Through Rituals*; it is followed by an elaboration by Powell and Clarke (1976).

3 In such statements they are representative of their tradition. One need only turn to the second issue of *Media, Culture and Society* (Vol. 1, No. 2, 1979), an issue devoted to the political economy of the media, to hear the same notes struck in Nicholas Garnham's editorial. Garnham praises the empirical tradition for having, at least, "recognised the mass media as economic activities," and dismisses the "culturalist" attempt to see "culture as opposed to the economic" (pp. 19–20).

4 This piece is titled "Consciousness of Class and Consciousness of Generation" (January 1979, 192–208).

6

Ideology

Ideology is the most important conceptual category in cultural studies. Indeed, according to James Carey (1989), "British cultural studies could be described just as easily and perhaps more accurately as ideological studies for they assimilate, in a variety of complex ways, culture to ideology" (p. 97). This assimilation has been so complete that even the distinction between culture and ideology seems a strategic rather than a substantive one at times. Consequently, one can understand the antagonism between cultural studies and the political economists/sociologists we have just been discussing. For the latter group, ideology's function is instrumental—to misrepresent "the real," and to mask any political struggle; for cultural studies, ideology is the very site of struggle. While there is certainly some truth in the claim that cultural studies succeeds only too well in its attempt to separate the cultural from the economic, one can see why the study of everyday life might resist the suggestion that the analysis of economic forces provides a sufficient explanation of the workings of culture and ideology. Nevertheless, Johnson (1979b) usefully reminds us that the economistic recovery of a base/superstructure model of society is not necessarily opposed to cultural studies versions of ideology; he makes the significant distinction, however, that within cultural relations "the outcomes of ideology or consciousness are not determined in the same kind of way as in economic or political relations" (p. 234). This argument emphasizes the importance of understanding just how ideology, culture, and consciousness are related and thus how any "outcomes" of their relationship might be analyzed.,

This is not a simple matter, however. The category of ideology is still a major theoretical problem, within both cultural studies and Marxist theory in general. It is not unusual for cultural studies' adoption of Althusserian models of ideology in the 1970s to be represented as utterly deterministic, utterly mechanical. Within such accounts, the similarities between Althusser and Gramsci are glossed over and the differences are exaggerated to legitimate the adaptation of Gramsci's theory of hegemony as a necessary correction to Althusserianism. However, just as Althusser's theoretical dominance during the 1970s produced numerous critiques and ultimate revision,[1] it is likely the more recent use of Gramsci will be similarly revised. Accordingly, even the relatively widely accepted positions canvassed in this chapter must be understood as provisional.

Nonetheless, we can construct something of an orthodox history of cultural studies' use of the category of ideology, beginning with the appropriation of Althusserian theory during the 1970s and the gradual incorporation of Gramscian theories of hegemony to resolve the culturalism/structuralism split. Significantly, Gramsci sees ideology as a site of particularly vigorous contestation, and the popular culture as a source of considerable resistance to hegemonic formation. In the late 1980s, this view of popular culture, coupled with the development of the notion of pleasure as a force that may oppose the workings of ideology and with postmodernist theories that privilege sensation over meaning, has encouraged something of a retreat from ideology as the all-powerful determining force it seemed to be in the 1970s. I wish to sketch out this theoretical narrative in this final chapter, a chapter that will, necessarily, both recall and amplify the discussions of ideology presented in earlier chapters.

The Return of the Repressed

I will begin with what is possibly the most comprehensive attempt to formulate a cultural studies orthodoxy on ideology so far, Stuart Hall's "The Rediscovery of 'Ideology': The

Return of the 'Repressed' in Media Studies" (1982). This article knits together the major European theoretical influences on cultural studies—Saussure, Lévi-Strauss, Barthes, Lacan, Althusser, Gramsci—within a history of ideology's "repression" and recovery in media research. Some of Hall's early explanatory maneuvers have been repeated in this book, so the following does not need to be a full account. Nor, it should be said, is the article itself able to present a full account of the workings of ideology across the whole spectrum of cultural studies' interests. Hall provides, predominantly, an account of ideology within the text, treating the function of ideology within the construction of everyday life as a secondary concern. He does, however, distance himself from a simple structuralist appropriation of Althusser, and his adoption of a theory of hegemony represents a significant shift away from the predominantly textualist theoretical formation of both his own work at the time (1981) and the field of study itself.

"The Return of the Repressed" deals specifically with the study of the media, and nominates three distinct phases in media research from the 1920s to the present. Hall concentrates on the break between the second and third phases; the second phase (roughly from the 1940s to the 1960s) is dominated by the sociological approaches of "mainstream" American behavioral science, while the third phase (from the late 1960s to the present) sees the development of "an alternative, 'critical' paradigm" (p. 56). Hall charts this paradigm shift as one marked not only by differences in methods or research procedures, but also by differences in political and theoretical orientations. The category of ideology is the key to these differences: "The simplest way to characterize the shift from 'mainstream' to 'critical' perspectives is in terms of the movement from, essentially, a behavioural to an ideological perspective" (p. 56). Within the behavioral perspective, ideology was "repressed"; within the "critical" (i.e., for our purposes, cultural studies) tradition, it was recovered as the central category that connected the media to society. Hall's article concludes by outlining the ways in which the function of ideology is understood within this critical tradition.

The first phase of media research (from the 1920s to the 1940s) can be exemplified by the work of the Frankfurt school, and indeed by the British variant in the "culture and civilization" tradition we met in Chapter 2. Researchers in this phase saw the media as a powerful and largely unmediated force that had entirely negative effects on mass culture. This diagnosis was ultimately rejected, Hall suggests, by the second phase: mainstream American mass communication research in the 1960s. This body of work questioned the earlier assumptions of media power—most important, television's potential to produce either positive or negative effects independently. Because it employed a very simple idea of media messages, and of social structure, American mass communication research was able to see the media as unproblematically reflective of society. If society was composed of a plurality of different groups, then this plurality would naturally be expressed within the media—as in other aspects of democratic society. If all social groups had access to the media, as they presumably did in all democratic countries, then their interests were in no danger of being ignored or suppressed. Capitalist democracies were congratulated for becoming "pluralist" societies, in which all points of view contributed to the forming of cultural values—a broadly consensual formation founded on the tolerance and incorporation of difference.

The Frankfurt school's warnings about the manipulative potential of mass culture were made redundant by pluralism; mass communication theorists even announced an "end to ideology," the abolition of unresolvable social or political conflicts (p. 60). Although there was little attempt to interrogate the processes that produced the normative consensus upon which pluralism rested, there was no doubt that it *was* formed and that the media played an unproblematic role within it:

> At the broader level, the media were held to be largely reflective or expressive of an achieved consensus. The finding that, after all, the media were not very influential was predicated on the belief that, in its wider cultural sense, the media largely reinforced those values and norms which

> had already achieved a wide consensual foundation. Since the consensus was a "good thing", those reinforcing effects of the media were given a benign and positive reading. (p. 61)

Hall goes on to explain that this comfortable faith in consensus was soon dealt a powerful blow by deviance theory, which focused on those who were *not* included within the consensual definitions of the normal and the acceptable. Deviance theory revealed pluralism to be a sham, its norms serving the interests of a discriminatory definition of society and actively participating in the subordination of groups that did not fit this definition. While the definitions of specific groups as deviant were characteristically justified through reference to *natural* conditions—as with the ill, the insane, or the deformed—this did not explain the deviant status attributed to blacks, the poor, political demonstrators and so on. Deviance theory revealed that the "differentiations between 'deviant' and 'consensus' formations were not natural but socially defined"; furthermore, they were "historically variable" (p. 62). (As noted earlier in this book, the treatment of environmentalists over the last few years has demonstrated this "historical variability.") A benign and democratic process now stood exposed as a cultural power game in which the "consensus ascribers" defined the rules and thus determined the result.

Consensus was, then, constructed: it was a form of social order that entailed the "enforcement of social, political and legal discipline," and that necessarily served "the given dispositions of class, power, and authority" (p. 63). This understood, the next question to be asked was "whether the consensus did indeed spontaneously simply arise or whether it was the result of a complex process of social construction and legitimation" (p. 63). This, in turn, raised questions about the role of the media in such a process:

> For if the media were not simply reflective or "expressive" of an already achieved consensus, but instead tended to reproduce those very definitions of the situation which favoured and legitimated the existing structure of things,

> then what had seemed at first as merely a reinforcing role had now to be reconceptualised in terms of the media's role in the process of consensus formation. (pp. 63–64)

The formation of the "definitions of the situation" was itself a process that deserved analysis; if definitions could vary, and if they tended to be produced in ways that favored the existing social order, then the supposedly reflective role of the media, and indeed of language, needed to be reassessed. This reassessment inevitably led to the conclusion that "reality could no longer be viewed as simply a given set of facts: it was the result of a particular way of constructing reality" (p. 64).

The construction of "the real" through the media, consequently, returned to the foreground, replacing the idea of reflection as the major issue in critical media research. A casualty of such a focus was the pluralist model of social order, which saw "the real," as it were, naturally emerging rather than produced by representation and cultural power widely dispersed throughout the society rather than concentrated within dominant interests. The critical paradigm not only challenged the "naturalness" of the real, but also argued that the media were a key mechanism for the maintenance and exercise of centralized cultural power—responsible for "influencing, shaping, and determining [an individual's] very wants" (p. 65). This influence was not exercised through the direct transmission of instructions from A to B, but rather through the ideological shaping and structuring of media representations of the world, of "the real," of the "natural":

> [This was] a way of representing the order of things which endowed its limiting perspectives with that natural or divine inevitability which makes them appear universal, natural and coterminous with "reality" itself. This movement—towards the winning of a universal validity and legitimacy for accounts of the world which are partial and particular, and towards the grounding of these particular constructions in the taken-for-grantedness of "the real"—is indeed the characteristic and defining mechanism of "the ideological". (p. 65)

This return of ideology to the agenda of media research opens the way for discussion of the cultural function of ideological processes. Hall suggests these inquiries took place on two fronts: the first was the territory of cultural reception, and focuses on the elaboration of ideology in language(s); the second was the articulation of ideology into social formations, the territory of cultural production.

Hall begins with language, drawing on post-Saussurean structuralist appropriations of semiotic models that use the language system as an analogy for all signifying structures—social practices, narratives, myths. As we saw in Chapter 1, Saussure argues that, since meaning is not inherent in things, it has to be attributed culturally. Further, "different kinds of meanings can be attributed to the same events." Hall asks how this process of attribution is structured: How does one meaning win credibility and acceptance while alternative meanings are down-graded and marginalized?

> Two questions followed from this. First, how did a dominant discourse warrant itself as *the* account, and sustain a limit, ban or proscription over alternative or competing definitions? Second, how did the institutions which were responsible for describing and explaining the events of the world—in modern societies, the mass media, *par excellence*—succeed in maintaining a preferred or delimited range of meanings in the dominant systems of communication? How was this active work of privileging or giving preference practically accomplished? (pp. 67–68)

Both questions are about the "politics of signification," the ways in which the social practice of making meanings is controlled and determined. Neither question has yet been categorically answered; however, the attempts to provide answers have focused on the relation between ideology and discourse, and between ideology and institutional structures.

The account Hall goes on to develop focuses on the media's use of their power to "signify events in a particular way" (p. 69), and stresses the fact that this ideological power is always contested: ideology becomes a site of struggle and a prize to be won, not a permanent possession of dominant groups. But he also reminds the reader that ideology has deeper roots than the social practices of media production; it structures the most basic systems of cultural organization. (In Chapter 1, I used the definition of gender as an example of this.) Every culture has its own "forms of episodic thinking" that provide its members with "the taken-for-granted elements" of their "practical knowledge" (p. 73). This "common sense" is rarely made explicit, and is often in fact unconscious, but it too is built upon a comprehensive foundation of ideological premises.[2]

A feature of the "way things are signified" to us is the invisibility of the process of signification itself. Propositions about the world implied within a news report (the superiority of capitalism over other social systems, for instance) become merely descriptive statements—"facts of the case" (p. 74). The effect of ideology in media messages is to efface itself, allowing the messages to appear as natural and spontaneous presentations of "reality." Hall talks of this phenomenon as "the reality effect." Not only do we, in general, understand reality as "a result or effect of how things had been signified," but we also "recognize" specific representations of reality as obvious. The circle closes, as this recognition effectively validates the representation:

> But this recognition effect was not a recognition of the reality behind the words, but a sort of confirmation of the obviousness, the taken-for-grantedness of the way the discourse was organized and of the underlying premises on which the statement in fact depended. If one regards the laws of a capitalist economy as fixed and immutable, then its notions acquire a natural inevitability. Any statement which is so embedded will thus appear to be merely a statement about "how things really are". Discourse, in short, had the effect of sustaining certain "closures", of establishing certain systems of equivalence between what could be assumed about the world and what could be said to be true. "True" means credible, or at least capable of winning credibility as a statement of fact. New, problematic or troubling events, which breached the taken-for-granted

> expectancies about how the world should be, could then be "explained" by extending to them the forms of explanation which had served "for all practical purposes", in other cases. In this sense, Althusser was subsequently to argue that ideology, as opposed to science, moved constantly within a closed circle, producing, not knowledge, but a recognition of the things we already knew. It did so because it took as an already established fact exactly the premises which ought to have been put in question. (p. 75)

Hall highlights a number of concepts that follow from this "reality effect." First is the idea of naturalization—the representation of an event or a discourse such that it is legitimated by nature rather than problematized by history. Second is the polysemy of language, which held that the same set of signifiers could produce different meanings and thus made the effect of naturalization something to be worked at, produced. And third is the fact that meaning, once it is seen in this contingent way, "must be the result . . . of a social struggle" (p. 77). Before taking up this last point, Hall warns against collapsing the notion of ideology into that of language. They are not the same thing, and ideology must be articulated through language. Second, he notes that the struggle over meaning is not to be reduced to a class struggle:

> Though discourses could become an arena of social struggle, and all discourses entailed certain definite premises about the world, this was not the same thing as ascribing ideologies to classes in a fixed, necessary or determinate way. Ideological terms and elements do not necessarily belong in this definite way to classes; and they do not necessarily and inevitably flow from class positions. (p. 80)

Just as cultural studies theorists have resisted a reduction of the cultural to its economic determinants, this view of discourse and ideology is reluctant to equate them with class affiliations.

The reason, in both cases, is the insistence on the "relative autonomy"—in the first place, of culture, and in the second place, of ideology—of cultural forms from economic conditions:

> The fact that one could not read off the ideological position of a social group or individual from class position, but that one would have to take into account how the struggle over meaning was conducted, meant that ideology ceased to be a mere reflection of struggles taking place or determined elsewhere. . . . It gave to ideology a relative independence or "relative autonomy". Ideologies ceased to be simply the dependent variable in social struggle; instead, ideological struggle acquired a specificity and a pertinence of its own—needing to be analysed in its own terms, and with real effects on the outcomes of particular struggles. (p. 82)

Hall provides us with an example of this social struggle over meaning. In his brief account of the British general election of 1979, he reveals the power exercised through the "definitions of the situation," highlighting the ideological effects of discourse while proposing that Thatcher's electoral victory was the profoundly material effect of a successful ideological bid to redefine the situation. He sets the scene by noting how closely the British working class had been aligned with the Labour party and the union movement until the prevailing definitions of this relationship were seriously challenged. The challenge hit at the heart of a hitherto "natural" alignment and replaced it with another equally "natural" construction of the union movement:

> The theory that the working class was permanently and inevitably attached to democratic socialism, the Labour Party and the trade unions movement, for example, could not survive a period in which the intensity of the Thatcher campaigns preceding the General Election of 1979 made strategic and decisive inroads, precisely into major sectors of the working class. . . . And one of the key turning-points in the ideological struggle was the way the revolt of the lower-paid public service workers against inflation, in the "Winter of Discontent" of 1978–9, was successfully signified, not as a defence of eroded living standards and

> differentials, but as a callous and inhuman exercise of overweening "trade-union power", directed against the defenceless sick, aged, dying and indeed the dead but unburied "members of the ordinary public." (p. 83)

In the final pages of his essay, Hall turns from language to the role of ideology within the social formation—social practices, class and other social groups, institutions. Here, too, he resists a reduction of the notion of ideological dominance to class domination. The idea that dominance was imposed by one class upon all the others was always vulnerable to the contention that ideological dominance had to be understood as something accomplished at the unconscious as well as the conscious level:

> [We need] to see it as a property of the system of relations involved, rather than as the overt and intentional biases of individuals; and to recognise its play in the very activity of regulation and exclusion which functioned through language and discourse before an adequate conception of dominance could be theoretically secured. (p. 85)

The classical Marxist notion that the "ruling ideas" are those of the "ruling classes" is consequently jettisoned for the "enlarged concept of hegemony":

> Hegemony implied that the dominance of certain formations was secured, not by ideological compulsion, but by cultural leadership. It circumscribed all those processes by means of which a dominant class alliance or ruling bloc, which has effectively secured mastery over the primary economic processes in society, extends and expands its mastery over society in such a way that it can transform and re-fashion its ways of life, its *mores* and conceptualisation, its very form and level of culture and civilisation in a direction which, while not directly paying immediate profits to the narrow interests of any particular class, favours the development and expansion of the dominant social and productive system of life as a whole. The critical point about this conception of "leadership"—which

> was Gramsci's most distinguished contribution—is that hegemony is understood as accomplished, not without the due measure of legal and legitimate compulsion, but principally by means of winning the active consent of those classes and groups who were subordinated within it. (p. 85)

As Hall goes on to say, this last point is crucial. A weakness in the Marxist accounts of ideology had always been their failure to account for the "free consent of the governed to the leadership of the governing classes." While they had understood that political power was exercised by the dominant groups within a society, they had not understood that this was achieved through a *combination* of the maintenance of the cultural power of the minority and the active or inactive consent of the powerless majority. Hegemony managed to explain both processes.

This returns us to the problem foregrounded at the beginning of Hall's article, how to account for the production of consensus. As Hall says, the pluralists were right to focus on the media's consensual role, but wrong to assume that it simply reflected a consensus already existing out there in society. Rather, he says, the media institutions actually manufacture consent. It is still very difficult, nevertheless, to explain exactly how this process occurs, because media institutions are generally free of direct compulsion and constraint and "yet freely articulate themselves systematically around definitions of the situation which favour the hegemony of the powerful" (p. 86). There is a structural relation that means the media can prize their independence from, but comply with, dominant definitions. Hall explains it this way:

> Now consider the media—the means of representation. To be impartial and independent in their daily operations, they cannot be seen to take directives from the powerful, or consciously to be bending their accounts of the world to square with dominant definitions. But they must be sensitive to, and can only survive legitimately by operating

> within, the general boundaries or framework of "what everyone agrees" to: the consensus. . . . But, in orienting themselves in "the consensus" and, at the same time, attempting to shape up the consensus, operating on it in a formative fashion, the media become part and parcel of that dialectical process of the "production of consent"—shaping the consensus while reflecting it—which orientates them within the field of force of the dominant social interests represented within the state. (p. 87)

An important point to note here is that this process affects both state-owned and commercial media institutions; Hall's reference to the state is not meant to be taken too literally.[3] Further, the role of the media in constructing consent is not to be understood in terms of any "bias" or deliberate "distortion" in its representation of events:

> When in phrasing a question, in the era of monetarism, a broadcasting interviewer simply takes it for granted that rising wage demands are the sole cause of inflation, he is both "freely formulating a question" on behalf of the public and establishing a logic which is compatible with the dominant interests in society. . . . This is a simple instance, but its point is to reinforce the argument that, in the critical paradigm, ideology is a function of the discourse and of the logic of social processes, rather than an intention of the agent. (p. 88)

This notion is often the most difficult to accept—that the broadcaster mentioned above will, unwittingly if not inevitably, "speak" the dominant discourse. As we have seen throughout this book, the dialectic between autonomy and determination structures the articulation of ideology within language and within institutions. This makes it necessary to insist that the broadcaster might indeed frame his or her own specific view of the "truth," but will do so from within an ideological framework that itself prefers some "truths" and excludes others.

Hall concludes by reminding his reader that there is much work to be done in this area, and that the critical paradigm's position is by no means fully developed or secure.

The Turn to Gramsci

Hall's seminal essay centers on media research, and only briefly examines the theoretical problems of outlining the function of ideology within popular culture in general. It says little about the relations between the individual subject and ideological structures. This aspect of cultural studies' notions of ideology has been frequently criticized:

> The Althusserian drift of much early cultural studies work . . . would reduce [the individual subject] to the status of a mere personification of a given structure, "spoken" by the discourses which cross the space of his subjectivity. However, it is not simply Althusser who is at issue here; much of the psychoanalytic work on the theory of ideology generates an equally passive notion of subjectivity, in which the subject is precisely "spoken" by the discourses which constitute that person. I want to try to formulate a position from which we can see the person actively producing meanings from the restricted range of cultural resources which his or her structural position has allowed them access to. (Morley 1986, 43)

This is from Morley's *Family Television*. The fact that the issue is raised there underlines a key point: that the theoretical problems of the category of ideology underlie the key debates within *all* the areas we have canvassed so far—within the study of texts, of audiences, of subjectivities, of institutions, and of the construction of everyday life. While the culturalism/structuralism split may have now dissolved, the three-way split of economic versus cultural determination versus individual agency still dominates, in one form or another, arguments about the formation of culture and the role of ideology. The power of the idea of hegemony is that it appears to accommodate all sides of this theoretical triangle: Gramsci's work, while prefiguring Althusser's emphasis on the determining role of ideology and the state, offers a more complex definition of popular culture and of ideological struggle. In Gramsci's view, popular culture is the battleground upon which dominant views secure hegemony; further, it is a permanent battleground, the parameters of which are partly defined by economic conditions, but that specializes in political struggle expressed at an ideological, representational level.

Tony Bennett offers an account of the turn to Gramsci in the introduction to *Popular Culture and Social Relations* (Bennett et al. 1986). He outlines the strategic benefits of a theory of hegemony for the study of popular culture. He begins by noting that the culturalist and structuralist traditions in cultural studies, however else they may have differed, both saw culture as governed by dominant ideologies. Disputes prospered over explanations of the maintenance of this dominance, and the precise diagnosis of its structure and effects, but culture was "divided into two opposing cultural and ideological camps—bourgeois and working class." Bennett suggests that Gramsci's radicalism within traditional Marxism lies in his resistance to this orthodox class-based formulation, and indeed to this orthodox view of ideology:

> Where Gramsci departed from the earlier Marxist tradition was in arguing that the cultural and ideological relations between ruling and subordinate classes in capitalist societies consist less in the *domination* of the latter by the former than in the struggle for *hegemony*—that is, for moral, cultural, intellectual and, thereby, political leadership over the whole of the society—between the ruling class and, as the principal subordinate class, the working class. (Bennett et al. 1986, xiv)

This is not a cosmetic or merely a terminological shift. The idea of hegemony does not suggest that domination is achieved by manipulating the worldview of the masses. Rather, it argues that in order for cultural leadership to be achieved, the dominant group has to engage in negotiations with opposing groups, classes, and values—and that these negotiations must result in some *genuine* accommodation.

That is, hegemony is not maintained through the obliteration of the opposition but through the *articulation* of opposing interests into the political affiliations of the hegemonic group. There has to be some change in the political orientation of the dominant group in order to convince those it will lead to accept this leadership. Any simple opposition, such as that between the bourgeoisie and the working class, is dissolved by such a process:

> As a consequence of its accommodating elements of opposing class cultures, "bourgeois culture" ceases to be purely or entirely bourgeois. It becomes, instead, a mobile combination of cultural and ideological elements derived from different class locations which are, but only provisionally and for the duration of a specific historical conjuncture, affiliated to bourgeois values, interests and objectives. By the same token, of course, the members of subordinate classes never encounter or are oppressed by a dominant ideology in some pure or class essentialist form; bourgeois ideology is encountered only in the compromised forms it must take in order to provide some accommodation for opposing class values. (p. xv)

Hegemony offers a more subtle and flexible explanation than previous formulations because it aims to account for domination as something that is won, not automatically delivered by way of the class structure. Where Althusser's assessment of ideology could be accused of a rigidity that discounted any possibility of change, Gramsci's version is able to concentrate precisely on explaining the process of change. It is consequently a much more optimistic theory, implying a gradual historical alignment of bourgeois hegemony with working-class interests. Most important, while Gramsci's account clearly recognizes the function of the state and of public culture, it also foregrounds the ideological role of the representation of "common sense," the power of the "taken-for-granted," and thus the importance of the entire field of popular culture.

Bennett stresses the fact that Gramsci actually defines popular culture by acknowledging the very contradictions that have been ignored in many previous definitions; in Gramsci's view, popular culture is both dominated and oppositional, determined and spontaneous:

> To the degree that it is implicated in the struggle for hegemony . . . the field of popular culture is structured by the attempt of the ruling class to win hegemony and by the forms of opposition to this endeavour. As such, it consists not simply of an imposed mass culture that is coincident with dominant ideology, nor simply of spontaneously oppositional cultures, but is rather an area of negotiation between the two within which—in different particular types of popular culture—dominant, subordinate and oppositional cultural and ideological values and elements are "mixed" in different permutations. (pp. xv–xvi)

This holds the competing forces within the popular in balance, avoiding the reductionism and economism of other descriptions while still insisting on the importance of popular culture as the field upon which political power is negotiated and legitimated.

Bennett notes a number of advantages the theory of hegemony has delivered to cultural analysis. First, and as we have seen already, it has disposed of a class essentialism that linked all cultural expression to a class basis. Second, it has made it possible to examine popular culture without necessarily taking a position for or against its particular manifestations (that is, without being critically elitist or uncritically populist). Third, it has underlined how *movable* the "political and ideological articulations of cultural practices" can be: a specific cultural practice does not carry a particular ideological significance eternally, and so it is theoretically possible to produce, for instance, a feminist version of Hollywood romance. This "opens up the field of popular culture as one of enormous political possibilities" (p. xvi). And finally, Bennett argues, the attack on class reductionism allows for due account to be taken "of the relative separation of different regions of cultural struggle (class, race, gender)" (p. xvi). There is certainly still much to be done in this area, but Gramsci does provide an integrating framework that, notwithstanding its totalizing tendencies, admits difference and contradiction as essential constituents of culture and ideology.

It is possible, as Chantal Mouffe (1981) has noted, to see Gramsci as having anticipated Althusser in a number of areas: interest in the "material nature of ideology, its existence as the necessary level of all social formations and its function as the producer of subjects" (p. 227) occurs within Gramsci's writings but is only fully formulated much later by Althusser. The crucial difference between them lies in the central role negotiation and change play within Gramsci's model of society. Mouffe describes how Gramsci envisaged the process of intellectual and thus political reform through the transformation of ideologies. It is a process in which various elements within an ideological system are rearranged and then integrated, or "articulated," into a new system:

> According to [Gramsci], an ideological system consists in a particular type of articulation of ideological elements to which a certain "relative weight" is attributed. The objective of ideological struggle is not to reject the system and all its elements but to rearticulate it, to break it down to its basic elements and then to sift through past conceptions to see which ones, with some changes of content, can serve to express the new situation. Once this is done the chosen elements are finally rearticulated into another system. (p. 231)

As Mouffe points out, such a process cannot be understood as reducible solely to class interests. Rather, the transformed ideological system will draw its elements from varying sources, all contributing to a common "worldview" that passes for the organic and natural expression of the whole bloc of dominant and consenting groups.

The turn to Gramsci reaffirms the importance of understanding ideology, but categorically withdraws from the installation of a monolithic or mechanical explanation of its workings. This more historically contingent and negotiated view reinforces claims for concrete practical analysis of ideological formations within cultures, as against a mechanical "reading off" of ideological meanings from cultural forms. Hegemony describes the attempt to produce uniformity and coherence, but it also implies that such attempts must always, eventually and necessarily, fail. Therefore the analysis of cultural forms and practices should involve a search for "contradictions, taboos, displacements in a culture" that might fracture the fiction of homogeneity. As Richard Johnson (1979b) has noted, Gramsci's view of the relation between the base and the superstructure is unique because it assumes, as its very ground, the existence of "massive disjunctions and unevenness." As a consequence of the incompleteness of any hegemonic tenure, there is always some residue of previous formations, surviving "concrete features of a society that cannot be grasped as the dominant mode of production and its conditions of existence" (p. 233), but that still need to be explained.[4] Since the turn to Gramsci, cultural studies is better equipped to provide such explanations.

The Retreat from Ideology: Resistance, Pleasure, and Postmodernisms

Readers might remember how vigorously cultural studies resisted the political economists' "top-down" version of ideology; such a view marginalized the cultural into a mere effect of other forces and reduced the subject to a mere junction box within a complex but remote communications system. Cultural studies has been, constitutionally, much happier with "bottom-up" versions of ideology; such versions attribute power to the subject and to the subcultural group to intervene in the signifying and political systems, and to produce change. Culturalism clearly adhered to such a view, and many structuralist interrogations of Althusserian ideology indicated their sympathy with it too. Gramsci's theory of hegemony does seem uniquely well designed for its ultimate destiny as the consensual principle within cultural studies' conceptions of ideology. It does allow for power to flow "bottom-up," and severely qualifies the economistic assumptions of the effectiveness of power imposed from the "top-down." It is not alone, however, in its role as a support for theories of resistance to ideological domination. The latter half of the 1980s was marked by a proliferation of interest in the ways in which ideologies *fail* to determine, *fail* to interpellate the subject, *fail* to prefer readings. We have already seen how such a function has been served by the appropriation of ethnography within audience studies; there are other locations as well.

Michel de Certeau is an influence in this area. In *The Practice of Everyday Life* (1984), de Certeau emphasizes the tactics employed by subordinated groups to win small victories from larger, more powerful, and ultimately determining systems. De Certeau argues that while members of popular culture cannot gain control of the production of culture, they do control its consumption—the ways in which it is used. As do ethnographic audience researchers, de Certeau emphasizes how creative popular culture is, how its members continually seek out ways of operating that serve their own interests while appearing to acknowledge the interests of the dominant group. If popular culture has to "make do" with what is offered to it, it still has the potential to "make over" these offerings to its own ends. De Certeau suggests that much of this "making do" with, and "making over" of, cultural forms and products is subversive; it represents the victory of the weak over the strong. Examples of the kinds of practices in which such subversions operate include reading, shopping, cooking, even renting an apartment:

> [Renting] transforms another person's property into a space borrowed for a moment by a transient. Renters make comparable changes in an apartment they furnish with their acts and memories; as do speakers, in the language into which they insert both the messages of their native tongue and, through their accent, through their own "turns of phrase" etc, their own history. (p. xxi)

When de Certeau talks of renting a house as an insinuation of oneself into another's place, he is choosing to emphasize not the economic power the landlord has over the tenant, but the tenant's power to change the nature of the space itself: in addition to simply living in the apartment, the tenant can repaint, move the furniture, redecorate, change the garden, fill the premises with friends, or offend the neighbors by playing loud music or having parties. Through such tactics, the tenant will actively serve his or her own ends and implicitly challenge the power of ownership enjoyed by the landlord; this, while still paying rent and thus serving the landlord's economic interests. Shopping, similarly, offers little opportunity for the denial of the economic relationship between buyer and seller, but buyers can invent their own uses for the products they purchase; youth subcultures provide particularly rich examples of the appropriation of everyday objects for scandalous use. Even window-shopping can be seen as a "making over" of the pleasure of buying into the pleasures of the spectacle, of the imagination.[5]

De Certeau discusses a particularly clear example of "bottom-up" power: the use of employer's time by the employee—"la perruque," which means "the wig." "La perruque" may be the personal phone call on the work phone, using the machine shop to make home furniture in the lunch hour, or the appropriation of office stationery. It has the practical effect of saving the employee money, and the additional pleasure (for the employee) of costing the employer money. It also has the ideological effect of resistance: it undermines a system that is meant to discipline the worker. The cooperative code of silence observed by other workers aware of the operation of "la perruque" actively subverts the cellular, competitive regime essential to the maintenance of discipline within the workplace.

One can see the similarity between de Certeau's approach and that taken by, say, Hebdige in *Subculture: The Meaning of Style* (1979). In both cases, a process of *bricolage* makes over cultural forms and practices in order to produce moments of resistance, opposition, subversion. The raw materials of subcultural dress styles are mass-produced, commercially marketed garments; their combination in a range of subcultural styles from skinheads to gothic punks offends and subverts conventional notions of fashion. Such a phenomenon would not surprise de Certeau; indeed, he implies that, within popular culture generally, the imposition of a system of control almost inevitably invites its subversion. Examples of this are not hard to locate. For many school pupils in Britain and Australia, for instance, uniforms are compulsory. Their actual function, however, is not only to serve as a sign of the institution and of the pupil's submersion in it; they also operate as the chosen battleground on which students test and challenge school authority by their creative modification of the uniform's details—the length of the skirt, the color of the shirt, the cut of the trousers, the width of the tie, the outlawed decoration or hairstyle, and so on. Thus, while cultural structures are strategically organized to control the kinds of meanings and pleasures we produce, they are always vulnerable to the possibility that we may actually use these structures to produce subversive, resistant effects.

De Certeau's work has been appropriated by cultural studies and, as we have seen earlier, is particularly evident in John Fiske's recent writings. Fiske (1988) defends its usefulness by claiming that "we have for too long simplistically equated power with social determination and have neglected to explore how resistant, evasive, scandalising bottom-up power actually operates" (p. 249). He argues that now we need to extend our understanding of "the forces of domination and their effectivity" to those measures "we" use to deal with them, every day. Fiske is by no means the only one to have turned his attention to the other side of the ideological coin. He is supported in this not only by the example of de Certeau but also by the two major competing theoretical issues of the late 1980s: the role of pleasure, and the postmodernist postulation of the disconnection between the signified and the signifier.

The introduction of pleasure as a category separate from ideology has changed the landscape of cultural studies. Within earlier formations, the pleasures of popular culture were seen to be the sugared pill of ideology and were interrogated for the politics they administered. Giving oneself over to the sensory pleasures of popular film, television, or music was surrendering to the "enslaving violence of the agreeable" (Bourdieu, quoted in Mercer 1986, 60). There has been a competing perspective, however, that has gathered force more recently and that draws on a number of different influences. First, Bakhtin's theory of "the carnivalesque" has been widely and often carelessly adapted to conceive popular culture as, intrinsically, a source of resistance—its illicit, denigrated pleasures not only offending but also subverting the control of its masters.[6] One can see how this might dovetail with Brechtian notions of the popular as somehow organic and authentic, the natural source of opposition to bourgeois domination.[7] The appropriation of "the carnivalesque" has been attacked as a misunderstanding of Bakhtin's (1968) original idea, an idea specific to a particular discussion of Rabelais, and as a romantic populism that grossly exaggerates the political power of popular pleasures (see Bennett 1986b, 14–15). It certainly commits the essentialist error of attributing particular ideologies to particular cultural forms and particular class formations. Nevertheless, the proposition that popular culture systematically produces events, attitudes, and modes of entertainment that break conventions and challenge their founding assumptions has considerable force. Television, as Hartley (1982) has pointed out, is a medium that can be both mundane and scandalous. As I have argued elsewhere, among the pleasures television offers is the spectacle of its formulas, its formal regimes, being fractured: examples of such spectacles occur particularly in live TV, in technical hitches and foul-ups (visible in domesticated form in such programs as *Foul-Ups, Bleeps and Blunders*), but also in transgressive and parodic TV drama such as *Soap* or the early episodes of *Moonlighting*, anarchic TV comedy such as *The Young Ones*, or the various incarnations of the *Saturday Night Live* satire and variety concept (Turner 1989). If the spectacle of the boundaries being transgressed *is* among the distinctive pleasures of popular TV, one can understand the continuing interest in notions of transgression and the carnivalesque.

The second, and perhaps more important, influence is from Roland Barthes, who has separated one aspect of pleasure entirely from ideology. *Jouissance* is the physical pleasure Barthes says may be produced by the literary text. Barthes (1975) likens *jouissance* to orgasm; it is an overwhelming expression of the body and is thus beyond ideology, a product of nature rather than of culture.[8] Barthes's initial suggestion has been widely taken up; the body has been separated off and made the location for the last stand, as it were, against cultural determination. The idea releases other potentials as well—of addressing areas of experience that have been left out of the accounts so far: sexual pleasure, for one, but also laughter, or the visceral pleasures some find on roller coasters and others find watching car chases on movie screens. It does seem logical to assume that there may be pleasures the body will produce irrespective of ideology; ideology comes into the picture in determining our understanding of these pleasures.

All of this represents, potentially at least, a radical *volte face* for Marxist cultural analysis. Barthes's notion calls up something very similar to the romantic ideal of the essential individual who experiences such pleasure, and who does so beyond the appeal of ideology. If the body, as the location of pleasure, is seen to be separable from "a subject" that is constructed through language and ideology, then we have reached the limits of theories of ideology. The ramifications of this notion of pleasure have only just begun to be appreciated and, as Colin Mercer (1986) says, require much more development:

> Any analysis of the pleasure, the modes of persuasion, the consent operative within a given cultural form would have to displace the search for an ideological, political, economic or, indeed, subjective *meaning* and establish the coordinates of this "formidable underside". And I think that we have to take the concept of *jouissance* (orgasm, enjoyment, loss of stasis) with a pinch of salt as a sort of a "nudge" in a certain direction because what we are really concerned with here is a restructuring of the theoretical horizon within which a cultural form is perceived. (p. 55)

We have already seen how this "nudge in a certain direction" has been taken. In previous chapters it has been implicated in the focus on the ambiguity of the text, on semiotic excess within textual studies; in the recovery of the polysemy of the message in audience studies; and in the insistence on the subjective experience of everyday life within ethnographies. All these strategies attempt to account, in one way or another, for a dimension of the subjective experience of cultural forms and practices that is in some way resistant to dominant ideologies.

Fiske's *Television Culture* (1987b) represents the most uncompromising use of this understanding of pleasure (see the review by Bee, 1989); it celebrates popular television as playfully resistant to ideological control. Television is a "semiotic democracy" that recognizes the rights of consumers to make what sense they will of the pleasures on offer, and rewards them through a process of "empowerment." And yet pleasure is also hegemonic, inscribing the subject into a message that is marked by its structured polysemy—as well as by its negotiated character. The need to recognize the importance of such pleasures as those produced by ritual or spectacle, or to acknowledge the textual openness of "live" television or of the new forms such as the music video, paints Fiske into a corner. His view of the popular becomes so optimistic, so celebratory, that there seems little need to worry about the function of representation in reproducing the *status quo*. Though we must retain a sense of the transgressive or tactical possibilities of popular culture, it is also essential to retain a sense of the frame within which they are produced, within which even the carnivalesque must be licensed. One does not ask for a return to the analyses of a decade ago, which took an elitist critical view of popular pleasures in order to see them as the uncomplicated bearers of dominant ideologies. However, one might argue that it is important to acknowledge that the pleasure of popular culture cannot lie outside hegemonic ideological formations; pleasure must be implicated in the ways in which hegemony is secured and maintained. As Mercer (1986) says, it is "absolutely crucial" that we attempt to understand this, that we "engage with" the "currency" of popular culture, "with the terms of its persistence, its acceptability and its popularity." It is crucial, he concludes, that we "engage with the specific ways in which we *consent* to the forms of popular culture"(p. 50). Pleasure, whether ideologically or physically produced, is among the means of production of this consent.

The relations among pleasure, cultural power, desire, and popular culture have not so far been adequately theorized;

they constitute a key issue for cultural studies in the future. As Terry Lovell (1980) has said, too much of the work on pleasure so far has concentrated on individual desires and pleasures, omitting those that derive from and create shared, collective experiences: "collective utopias, social wish fulfilment and social aspirations" (p. 61). We simply do not know how pleasure aligns us with or supports us against dominant views of the world. We do not even know how texts produce all their varieties of pleasure, although this has not prevented many of us from naming what we think are the particular pleasures of specific texts. We can say pleasure must not be understood as either "solidly ideological/repressive or solidly liberatory"; furthermore, there is "no *general* form of pleasure with ascertainable political and cultural effects" (Mercer 1986, 67). There are, however, numerous particular cases we need to examine. At the moment, it would seem, the possibilities most interesting to cultural studies are those that suggest a resistance to, rather than a reproduction of, dominant ideologies.

Further collaborating in the convergence of critiques of the very nature of dominance and hegemony is the current interest in the postmodern. Notoriously vague in its definition, the key aspects of postmodernism that concern me here are its postulation of the disconnection between the signified and the signifier; the free play of the signifier privileging the power of the reader to decode the message in his or her own interests; and its celebration of the popular. One can easily see how this would coincide with the "bottom-up" analyses dealt with above, ascribing more cultural power to the consumer and delimiting the determining influence of the economic, the political, the ideological. Within cultural studies it has taken on a specific inflection.

Georgina Born (1987) suggests there is a "postmodern perspective" in contemporary cultural studies:

> Postmodern cultural studies . . . started out with a special interest in popular culture, a primary orientation towards *consumption* and an overwhelming *optimism* of tone. In

> reaction to the pessimism of the mass culture critique, and the Adornian-Horkheimer stress on the cultural commodity as exchange value, postmodernists celebrate use value, the reality of purpose and meaning in commercial popular culture. Writers have turned positively to leisure, to pop texts, wanting to understand (buzz words) "pleasure", "desire", and the "romance" of their consumption. . . . The point is to blast open the view of commercial cultural goods as closed, univocal and aesthetically impoverished—hence the references to post-structuralist notions of the "end of the author", indeterminate reading, and the fragmented but active reading subject; to reception aesthetics; and, from semiotics, to the idea of cultural texts as polysemic, open, grasped through a "struggle for the sign". (p. 60)

While Born admires much of the work she mentions, she also worries about the romantic populism within the "postmodern perspective" that encourages its authors to invoke the politics of subversion and resistance automatically within the texts they examine. Born suggests that implicit in Iain Chambers and Dick Hebdige's work, and in the work of Angela McRobbie as well, is an unexamined assumption that the simple consumption of popular culture is itself subversive (p. 61). Chambers (1986) himself would argue that his work is part of a corrective, polemical enterprise, complicating the "presumed coherence of ideology, texts and images" in order to "rediscover the details of the bits that go into their making":

> We can no longer overlook the heterogeneous surface activities of everyday life, they too are real. It is there that signs and representations (whether writing or advertising, photography or pornography) are encountered, inhabited and invested with sense. So, to explain them by simply referring to the logic of a deep structure or the mechanisms of a totality, where "any reality, once described, is struck off the inventory" (Jean-Paul Sartre), invariably privileges the mechanical and the reductive. A horizontal vista of mobile meanings, shifting connections, temporary encounters, a world of inter-textual richness and detail, needs to be

> inserted into the critical model. Complexity needs to be respected. (pp. 212–13)

There is nothing automatic about the generation of meaning here; however, it must be admitted that Chambers is more vulnerable to Georgina Born's criticism in his treatment of popular music cultures in *Urban Rhythms* (1985).

Born's article deals with popular music, but the same problem she raises in that context—the romantic invocation of a subversive "popular"—can be seen to affect cultural studies treatments of a whole range of popular textual forms: from women's romance fiction to soap operas to music video clips. Music videos have been particularly vulnerable to this, as the apparent openness of their form—their frequent resistance to interpretation coupled with the specificity of their visual and musical pleasures—has been presumed to reproduce a radical and subversive politics.[9] The optimism of such a view worries Born, and one can see why. The fact that we can produce our own pleasures from the material at hand may be a comfort, but it does not entirely free us from the forces that determine how we conceive of our pleasures, what material is at hand in the first place, and which interests (besides our own) our pleasures may be serving.

The movements I have been noting in this section generate a democratizing impulse, emphasizing the creative power of "the popular" over the forces that attempt to contain it. It could be argued that the pendulum's swing away from containment to resistance has reached the end of its arc, leading to a retreat from the category and effectivity of ideology altogether. The trajectory of this pendulum movement is, of course, hotly debated within cultural studies at the moment—both in its effect on the reading of specific cultural forms (such as the music videos) and in its theoretical implications. Certainly, it is no easier to suggest a commonly held definition of the workings of ideology now than it would have been ten years ago. While Gramsci has solved one set of problems, his redefinition of popular culture has opened up a new set. All are agreed, however, that what is being pursued is not simple; any theory that attempts to differentiate, or construct relations, between culture and ideology has to recognize not only the complexity of relations to be articulated but also the importance of describing the relative weight each element is given in specific historical conjunctures. It is a challenge, but there are few more significant tasks left in contemporary scholarship in the humanities.

Notes

1 See Johnson (1979b, 230–37) for one example, but for a more extended and more sophisticated case, see Lovell (1980).

2 Hall uses the example of an industrial dispute to demonstrate this, drawing out the premises that framed the media representation of attitudes toward workers, toward the British auto firm, Leyland, and toward the logic of industrial production.

3 In fact, the guide to this usage would be Althusser's notion of ideological state apparatuses (the education system, the law, and so on) in *Lenin and Philosophy* (1971).

4 Readers will remember the discussion in Chapter 2 of the way Raymond Williams dealt with this problem in *Marxism and Literature* (1977), by the introduction of the residual and emergent formations of hegemony.

5 Fiske et al. talk about this in their analysis of Australian popular culture, *Myths of Oz* (1987, ch. 5), and Fiske further develops the idea of transgression in shopping in his *Reading the Popular* (1989a) and *Understanding the Popular* (1989b).

6 This rested on an account of certain traditional festivals within medieval culture that were particularly scandalous in their treatment of conventions, religious observances, and other proprieties. Festivals such as the Feast of Fools were licensed moments of excess when the "popular" could express and recognize its opposition to the classes that suppressed it.

7 This set of problems is examined in my "*Perfect Match*: Ambiguity, Spectacle and the Popular" (1987).

8 This account is necessarily brief here, but a simple application of Barthesian notions of pleasure to television can be found in Fiske (1987b, ch. 12).

9 See, for instance, the exchange among John Fiske, Bob Hodge, and myself on the oppositional potential within video clips in the *Australian Journal of Cultural Studies* (Vol. 2, No. 1, 1984, 110–26).

Conclusion

Cultural studies does present a radical challenge to the orthodoxies within the humanities and social sciences. It has enabled the crossing of disciplinary borders and the reframing of our ways of knowing so that we might acknowledge the complexity and importance of the idea of culture. Cultural studies' commitment to understanding the construction of everyday life has the admirable objective of doing so in order to change our lives for the better. Not all academic pursuits have such a practical political objective. Cultural studies' democratizing interest in the naturalization of social inequities and divisions has recovered valuable resources for the cultural analyst: disregarded evidence, subjective experiences, and denigrated social practices. The retrieval and legitimation of the very subject matter of cultural studies has been a complicated and contentious task, however, and it is not yet over. There are continuing controversies as the field defines itself and as it becomes increasingly sensitive to the breadth of the material it must consider, the comprehensiveness of the processes it seeks to explain. No single method or theoretical approach can be asked to take on all of cultural studies' responsibilities.

A great deal of the recent work in cultural studies demonstrates this breadth of interests and methods. I have already mentioned Stuart Laing's *The Representation of Working Class Life, 1959–64* (1986) as a good example of such cultural studies practice now. Laing employs textual analysis in his examination of representations of the working class in stage plays, television, films, and fiction. He also describes the key political, social, and ideological debates that framed and discursively structured the representations in which he is most interested. All of this is, in turn, placed within a social history of British life at the time. The examination of representations unravels the network of discourses of "working-classness" of the time so they may then be connected to their broader cultural and political meanings. However provisionally, Laing's book offers an idea of what cultural studies of the future looks like. In fact, most of the recent work surveyed in this book has moved constantly between the analysis of formal and symbolic structures (such as texts) and of social processes, practices, and institutions. As we enter the 1990s, it is clear that the main interest of cultural studies is no longer simply in texts, or even in institutions or social practices; rather, it lies in the investigation of those complex processes that articulate any or all such elements within and into culture.

This book has outlined a number of theoretical areas where debates will continue to prosper: the definition and function of ideology, the relation between ideology and pleasure, the place of textual analysis and the role of the audience—all need to be dealt with in the future. Some problems are more pressing than others, however. The argument around pleasure and resistance seems to have (over)corrected any prejudice against the popular through the privileging of pleasure over ideology. It is time now for the use of the term *pleasure* to be scrutinized more carefully, for its varieties of power and effect to be defined more scrupulously. The late-1980s discovery of the postmodern has yet, in my view, to justify the considerable attention it has received, or the considerable support it has lent to an evacuation of politics from cultural studies analysis. The hunt for the postmodern text may well be serving as something of a diversion from other key problems. Cultural studies needs to consider what it should do with notions of value, with qualitative discrimination among the texts and practices of popular culture. Most of us do make private value judgments about our favorite television shows, for instance, although we may not expect them to be of interest to anyone else. The new theories of pleasure have certainly revived our sense of the importance of such judgments. It does seem, now the ghosts of the culture and civilization tradition have been laid, that the idea of what is meant by "good" and "bad" in popular culture is probably ripe for review and consideration. A further challenge for cultural studies is to find a way to intervene in the formation of public culture—perhaps through playing a more active part in the framing of state cultural policy. And finally, in this wish list of issues for the future, the close theoretical and methodological relationship between cultural studies research and social sciences research must be further acknowledged and cooperatively developed.

The practice of cultural studies has the potential to challenge the way we think about the world. My own experience in the field has taught me rather to expect revelations, occasionally to understand suddenly what lies beneath those images, sounds, gestures I had taken for granted. If readers find that the work presented in this book has helped bring them to such moments of recognition, I will be well pleased. But I would also hope that readers will follow the ideas in this book beyond its pages, particularly into appropriations of cultural studies other than the British. Theory can be culturally specific too, and there are very different inflections in the work coming out of France, the United States, Australia, and Canada from those outlined in this book. This, then, has been an introduction to cultural studies; the next step is to develop the relationship and see what benefits this brings.

Bibliography

Allen, Robert, ed. 1987. *Channels of Discourse: Television and Contemporary Criticism*. London: Methuen.

Althusser, Louis. 1971. "On Ideology and Ideological State Apparatuses." In *Lenin and Philosophy and Other Essays*. New York: Monthly Review Press.

Alvarado, Manuel, and Edward Buscombe. 1978. *Hazell: The Making of a TV Series*. London: BFI.

Ang, I. 1985. *Watching* Dallas: *Soap Opera and the Melodramatic Imagination*. London: Methuen.

Armes, Roy. 1989. *On Video*. London: Routledge.

Bakhtin, Mikhail. 1968. *Rabelais and His World*. Cambridge: MIT Press.

Barnett, Anthony. 1976. "Raymond Williams and Marxism: A Rejoinder to Terry Eagleton." *New Left Review* 99: 47–66.

Barthes, Roland. 1973. *Mythologies*. London: Paladin.

———. 1975. *The Pleasure of the Text*. New York: Hill Wang.

———. 1977. *Image-Music-Text*. London: Fontana.

Batsleer, Janet, Tony Davies, Rebecca O'Rourke, and Chris Weedon. 1985. *Rewriting English: Cultural Politics of Gender and Class*. London: Methuen.

Bee, Jim. 1989. "First Citizen of the Semiotic Democracy?" *Cultural Studies* 3(3): 353–59.

Bennett, Tony. 1981. *Popular Culture: Themes and Issues*. Milton Keynes: Open University Press.

———. 1986a. "Hegemony, Ideology, Pleasure: Blackpool." In *Popular Culture and Social Relations*, ed. Tony Bennett, Colin Mercer, and Janet Woollacott, 135–54. Milton Keynes: Open University Press.

———. 1986b. "The Politics of 'the Popular' and Popular Culture." In *Popular Culture and Social Relations*, ed. Tony Bennett, Colin Mercer, and Janet Woollacott, 6–21. Milton Keynes: Open University Press.

Bennett, Tony, Susan Boyd-Bowman, Colin Mercer, and Janet

Woollacott, eds. 1981. *Popular Television and Film*. London: BFI.
Bennett, Tony, Graham Martin, Colin Mercer, and Janet Woollacott, eds. 1981. *Culture, Ideology and Social Process: A Reader*. London: Open University Press.
Bennett, Tony, Colin Mercer, and Janet Woollacott, eds. 1986. *Popular Culture and Social Relations*. Milton Keynes: Open University Press.
Bennett, Tony, and Janet Woollacott. 1988. *Bond and Beyond: The Political Career of a Popular Hero*. London: Macmillan.
Born, Georgina. 1987. "Modern Music Culture: On Shock, Pop and Synthesis." *New Formations* 1(2): 51–78.
Bourdieu, Pierre, and Jean-Claude Passeron. 1977. *Reproduction in Education, Society and Culture*. London: Sage.
Brunsdon, Charlotte, and David Morley. 1978. *Everyday Television: Nationwide*. London: BFI.
Buckingham, David. 1987. *Public Secrets: EastEnders and Its Audience*. London: BFI.
Carey, James W. 1989. *Communication and Culture: Essays on Media and Society*. Boston: Unwin Hyman.
Certeau, Michel de. 1984. *The Practice of Everyday Life*. Berkeley: University of California Press.
Chambers, Iain. 1985. *Urban Rhythms: Pop Music and Popular Culture*. London: Macmillan.
———. 1986. *Popular Culture: The Metropolitan Experience*. London: Methuen.
Clarke, John, Chas Critcher, and Richard Johnson, eds. 1979. *Working Class Culture: Studies in History and Theory*. London: Hutchinson.
Cohen, Phil. 1980. "Subcultural Conflict and Working-Class Community." In *Culture, Media, Language*, ed. Stuart Hall, Dorothy Hobson, Andrew Lowe, and Paul Willis, 78–87. London: Hutchinson. (Originally published as *Working Papers in Cultural Studies* 2, 1972.)
Cohen, Stanley, and Jock Young, eds. 1980. *The Manufacture of News: Social Problems, Deviance and the Mass Media* (rev. ed.). London: Constable.
Connell, Ian. 1980. "Television News and the Social Contract." In *Culture, Media, Language*, ed. Stuart Hall, Dorothy Hobson, Andrew Lowe, and Paul Willis, 139–56. London: Hutchinson.
Coward, Ros. 1984. *Female Desire: Women's Sexuality Today*. London: Paladin.
Crisell, Andrew. 1986. *Understanding Radio*. London: Methuen.
Critcher, Chas. 1979. "Sociology, Cultural Studies and the Post-War Working-Class." In *Working Class Culture: Studies in History and Theory*, ed. John Clarke, Chas Critcher, and Richard Johnson, 13–40. London: Hutchinson.
———. 1982. "Football since the War." In *Popular Culture: Past and Present*, ed. Bernard Waites, Tony Bennett, and Graham Martin, 219–41. London: Croom Helm.

Culler, Jonathan. 1976. *Saussure*. London: Fontana/Collins.
Cunningham, Hugh. 1980. *Leisure in the Industrial Revolution*. London: Croom Helm.
———. 1982. "Class and Leisure in Mid-Victorian England." In *Popular Culture: Past and Present*, ed. Bernard Waites, Tony Bennett, and Graham Martin, 64–91. London: Croom Helm.
Curran, James, Michael Gurevitch, and Janet Woollacott, eds. 1977. *Mass Communication and Society*. London: Edward Arnold.
———. 1982. "The Study of the Media: Theoretical Approaches." In *Culture, Society and the Media*, ed. Michael Gurevitch, Tony Bennett, James Curran, and Janet Woollacott, 11–29. London: Methuen.
Curran, James, and Jean Seaton. 1985. *Power Without Responsibility: The Press and Broadcasting in Britain*. 2nd ed. London: Methuen.
Doyle, Brian. 1982. "The Hidden History of English Studies." In *Re-reading English*, ed. Peter Widdowson, 17–31. London: Methuen.
Dyer, Gillian. 1982. *Advertising as Communication*. London: Methuen.
Dyer, Richard. 1982. *Stars*. London: BFI.
———. 1986. *Heavenly Bodies: Film Stars and Society*. London: BFI.
Eagleton, Terry. 1978. *Criticism and Ideology*. London: Verso.
Eco, Umberto. 1966. *The Bond Affair*. London: Macdonald.
Eliot, Thomas Stearns. 1948. *Notes Towards a Definition of Culture*. London: Faber.
Elliott, Philip. 1972. *The Making of a Television Series: A Case Study in the Sociology of Culture*. London: Constable.
———. 1977. "Media Organisations and Occupations: An Overview." In *Mass Communication and Society*, ed. James Curran, Michael Gurevitch, and Janet Woollacott, 142–73. London: Edward Arnold.
Ellis, John. 1982. *Visible Fictions: Cinema, Television, Video*. London: Routledge & Kegan Paul.
Fiske, John. 1982. *Introduction to Communication Studies*. London: Methuen.
———. 1986. "Television and Popular Culture: Reflections on British and Australian Critical Practice." *Critical Studies in Mass Communication* 3, 200–216.
———. 1987a. "British Cultural Studies and Television Criticism." In *Channels of Discourse: Television and Contemporary Criticism*, ed. Robert Allen, 254–90. London: Methuen.
———. 1987b. *Television Culture*. London: Methuen.
———. 1988. "Meaningful Moments." *Critical Studies in Mass Communication*, Sept., 246–50.
———. 1989a. *Reading the Popular*. Boston: Unwin Hyman.
———. 1989b. *Understanding Popular Culture*. Boston: Unwin Hyman.
Fiske, John, and John Hartley. 1978. *Reading Television*. London: Methuen.
Fiske, John, Bob Hodge, and Graeme Turner. 1987. *Myths of Oz: Reading Australian Popular Culture*. Sydney: Allen & Unwin.

Foucault, Michel. 1979. *Discipline and Punish: The Birth of the Prison*, trans. Alan Sheridan. Harmondsworth: Peregrine.

Garnham, Nicholas. 1987. "Concepts of Culture: Public Policy and the Cultural Industries." *Cultural Studies* 1(1): 23–38.

Geertz, Clifford. 1973. *The Interpretation of Cultures*. New York: Basic Books.

Glasgow Media Group. 1976. *Bad News*. London: Routledge & Kegan Paul.

———. 1980. *More Bad News*. London: Routledge & Kegan Paul.

———. 1982. *Really Bad News*. London: Writers & Readers.

Green, Michael. 1982. "The Centre for Contemporary Cultural Studies." In *Re-reading English*, ed. Peter Widdowson, 77–90. London: Methuen.

Grimshaw, Roger, Dorothy Hobson, and Paul Willis. 1980. "Introduction to Ethnography at the Centre." In *Culture, Media, Language*, ed. Stuart Hall, Dorothy Hobson, Andrew Lowe, and Paul Willis, 73–77. London: Hutchinson.

Grossberg, Lawrence. 1988. "It's a Sin." In *It's a Sin: Essays on Postmodernism, Politics and Culture*, ed. Lawrence Grossberg, Tony Fry, Ann Curthoys, and Paul Patton. Sydney: Power.

Gurevitch, Michael, Tony Bennett, James Curran, and Janet Woollacott, eds. 1982. *Culture, Society and the Media*. London: Methuen.

Hall, Stuart. 1971. "Deviancy, Politics and the Media." CCCS stenciled paper, No. 11.

———. 1975. "Television as a Medium and Its Relation to Culture." CCCS stenciled paper, No. 34.

———. 1977. "Culture, the Media and the 'Ideological Effect.' " In *Mass Communication and Society*, ed. James Curran, Michael Gurevitch, and Janet Woollacott, 315–48. London: Edward Arnold.

———. 1980a. "Cultural Studies and the Centre: Some Problematics and Problems." In *Culture, Media, Language*, ed. Stuart Hall, Dorothy Hobson, Andrew Lowe, and Paul Willis, 15–47. London: Hutchinson.

———. 1980b. "The Determination of News Photographs." In *The Manufacture of News: Social Problems, Deviance and the Mass Media*, ed. Stanley Cohen and Jock Young, 226–43. London: Constable.

———. 1980c. "Encoding/Decoding." In *Culture, Media, Language*, ed. Stuart Hall, Dorothy Hobson, Andrew Lowe, and Paul Willis, 128–38. London: Hutchinson.

———. 1980d. "Introduction to Media Studies at the Centre." In *Culture, Media, Language*, ed. Stuart Hall, Dorothy Hobson, Andrew Lowe, and Paul Willis, 117–21. London: Hutchinson.

———. 1980e. "Recent Developments in Theories of Language and Ideology: A Critical Note." In *Culture, Media, Language*, ed. Stuart Hall, Dorothy Hobson, Andrew Lowe, and Paul Willis, 157–62. London: Hutchinson.

———. 1981. "Cultural Studies: Two Paradigms." In *Culture, Ideology and Social Process: A Reader*, ed. Tony Bennett, Graham Martin, Colin Mercer, and Janet Woollacott, 19–37. London: Open University Press.

———. 1982. "The Rediscovery of 'Ideology': The Return of the 'Repressed' in Media Studies." In *Culture, Society and the Media*, ed. Michael Gurevitch, Tony Bennett, James Curran, and Janet Woollacott, 56–90. London: Methuen.

———. 1986. "Popular Culture and the State." In *Popular Culture and Social Relations*, ed. Tony Bennett, Colin Mercer, and Janet Woollacott, 22–49. Milton Keynes: Open University Press.

Hall, Stuart, Ian Connell, and Lidia Curti. 1981. "The Unity of Current Affairs Television." In *Popular Television and Film*, ed. Tony Bennett, Susan Boyd-Bowman, Colin Mercer, and Janet Woollacott, 88–117. London: BFI.

Hall, Stuart, Chas Critcher, Tony Jefferson, John Clarke, and Brian Roberts. 1978. *Policing the Crisis: Mugging, the State, and Law and Order*. London: Macmillan.

Hall, Stuart, Dorothy Hobson, Andrew Lowe, and Paul Willis, eds. 1980. *Culture, Media, Language*. London: Hutchinson.

Hall, Stuart, and Tony Jefferson, eds. 1976. *Resistance Through Rituals: Youth Subcultures in Post-War Britain*. London: Hutchinson.

Hall, Stuart, and Paddy Whannel. 1967. *The Popular Arts*. Boston: Beacon. First published in 1964.

Halloran, J., P. Elliott, and G. Murdock. 1970. *Demonstrations and Communications*. London: Penguin.

Harland, Richard. 1987. *Superstructuralism: The Philosophy of Structuralism and Post-Structuralism*. London: Methuen.

Hartley, John. 1982. *Understanding News*. London: Methuen.

———. 1983. "Encouraging Signs: Television and the Power of Dirt, Speech and Scandalous Categories." *Australian Journal of Cultural Studies* 1(2): 62–82.

———. 1987. "Invisible Fictions: Television Audiences, Paedocracy, Pleasure." *Textual Practice* 1(2): 121–38.

———. 1988. "The Real World of Audiences." *Critical Studies in Mass Communication*, Sept., 234–38.

Hawkes, Terence. 1977. *Structuralism and Semiotics*. London: Methuen.

Heath, Stephen. 1985. "*Jaws*, Ideology and Film Theory." In *Movies and Methods*, Vol. II, ed. Bill Nichols, 509–16. London: University of California Press.

Heath, Stephen, and Colin McCabe. 1971. *Signs of the Times: Introductory Readings in Textual Semiotics*. London: Cambridge University Press.

Heath, Stephen, and Gillian Skirrow. 1986. "An Interview with Raymond Williams." In *Studies in Entertainment: Critical Approaches to Mass Culture*, ed. Tania Modleski, 3–17. Bloomington: Indiana University Press.

Hebdige, Dick. 1979. *Subculture: The Meaning of Style*. London: Methuen.

———. 1988. *Hiding in the Light: On Images and Things*. London: Routledge.

Hobson, Dorothy. 1980. "Housewives and the Mass Media." In *Culture, Media, Language*, ed. Stuart Hall, Dorothy Hobson, Andrew Lowe, and Paul Willis, 105–14. London: Hutchinson.

———. 1982. *Crossroads: The Drama of a Soap Opera*. London: Methuen.

Hodge, Bob, and David Tripp. 1986. *Children and Television: A Semiotic Approach*. London: Polity.

Hoggart, Richard. 1958. *The Uses of Literacy*. London: Penguin, 1958.

Humm, Peter, Paul Sigant, and Peter Widdowson, eds. 1986. *Popular Fictions: Essays in Literature and History*. London: Methuen.

Johnson, Lesley. 1987. "Raymond Williams: A Marxist View of Culture." In *Creating Culture: Profiles in the Study of Culture*, ed. Diane J. Austin-Broos. Sydney: Allen & Unwin.

Johnson, Richard. 1978. "Edward Thompson, Eugene Genovese, and Socialist-Humanist History." *History Workshop* 6: 79–100.

———. 1979a. "Culture and the Historians." In *Working Class Culture: Studies in History and Theory*, ed. John Clarke, Chas Critcher, and Richard Johnson, 41–71. London: Hutchinson.

———. 1979b. "Three Problematics: Elements of a Theory of Working Class Culture." In *Working Class Culture: Studies in History and Theory*, ed. John Clarke, Chas Critcher, and Richard Johnson, 201–37. London: Hutchinson.

———. 1980. "Barrington Moore, Perry Anderson and English Social Development." In *Culture, Media, Language*, ed. Stuart Hall, Dorothy Hobson, Andrew Lowe, and Paul Willis, 48–70. London: Hutchinson.

———. 1983. "What Is Cultural Studies Anyway?" CCCS stenciled paper, No. 74.

Laing, Stuart. 1986. *Representations of Working-Class Life, 1959–64*. London: Macmillan.

Leavis, F. R., and Denys Thompson. 1933. *Culture and Environment*. London: Chatto & Windus.

Leavis, Q. D. 1932. *Fiction and the Reading Public*. London: Chatto & Windus.

Lévi-Strauss, Claude. 1966. *The Savage Mind*. London: Wiedenfeld & Nicholson.

Lovell, Terry. 1980. *Pictures of Reality: Aesthetics, Politics and Pleasure*. London: BFI.

McCabe, Colin. 1981. "Realism and the Cinema: Notes on Some Brechtian Theses." In *Popular Television and Film*, ed. Tony Bennett, Susan Boyd-Bowman, Colin Mercer, and Janet Woollacott, 216–35. London: BFI.

McRobbie, Angela. 1981. "Settling Accounts with Subcultures: A Feminist Critique." In *Culture, Ideology and Social Process: A*

Reader, ed. Tony Bennett, Graham Martin, Colin Mercer, and Janet Woollacott, 112–24. London: Open University Press.

———. 1982. "*Jackie:* An Ideology of Adolescent Femininity." In *Popular Culture: Past and Present*, ed. Bernard Waites, Tony Bennett, and Graham Martin, 262–83. London: Croom Helm.

———. 1984. "Dance and Social Fantasy." In *Gender and Generation*, ed. Angela McRobbie and Mica Nava, 130–61. London: Macmillan.

McRobbie, Angela, and Jenny Garber. 1976. "Girls and Subcultures: An Exploration." In *Resistance Through Rituals: Youth Subcultures in Post-War Britain*, ed. Stuart Hall and Tony Jefferson, 209–22. London: Hutchinson.

McRobbie, Angela, and Mica Nava, eds. 1984. *Gender and Generation*. London: Macmillan.

Mercer, Colin. 1986. "Complicit Pleasures." In *Popular Culture and Social Relations*, ed. Tony Bennett, Colin Mercer, and Janet Woollacott, 50–68. Milton Keynes: Open University Press.

Modleski, Tania. 1984. *Loving with a Vengeance: Mass-Produced Fantasies for Women*. London: Methuen.

———, ed. 1986. *Studies in Entertainment: Critical Approaches to Mass Culture*. Bloomington: Indiana University Press.

———. 1988. *The Women Who Knew Too Much: Hitchcock and Feminist Theory*. London: Methuen.

Morley, David. 1980a. *The "Nationwide" Audience*. London: BFI.

———. 1980b. "Texts, Readers, Subjects." In *Culture, Media, Language*, ed. Stuart Hall, Dorothy Hobson, Andrew Lowe, and Paul Willis, 63–173. London: Hutchinson.

———. 1986. *Family Television: Cultural Power and Domestic Leisure*. London: Comedia.

Mouffe, Chantal. 1981. "Hegemony and Ideology in Gramsci." In *Culture, Ideology and Social Process: A Reader*, ed. Tony Bennett, Graham Martin, Colin Mercer, and Janet Woollacott, 219–34. London: Open University Press.

Mulhern, Francis. 1979. *The "Moment" of Scrutiny*. London: NLB.

Mulvey, Laura. 1975. "Visual Pleasure and Narrative Cinema." *Screen* 16(3). (Reprinted in *Movies and Methods*, Vol. II, ed. Bill Nichols. London: University of California Press, 1985.)

Murdock, Graham. 1976. "Consciousness of Class and Consciousness of Generation." In *Resistance Through Rituals: Youth Subcultures in Post-War Britain*, ed. Stuart Hall and Tony Jefferson, 192–208. London: Hutchinson.

———. 1982. "Large Corporations and the Control of the Communications Industries." In *Culture, Society and the Media*, ed. Michael Gurevitch, Tony Bennett, James Curran, and Janet Woollacott, 118–50. London: Methuen.

———. 1989. "Cultural Studies at the Crossroads." *Australian Journal of Communication* 16: 37–49.

Murdock, Graham, and Peter Golding. 1977. "Capitalism, Communication and Class Relations." In *Mass Communication and*

Society, ed. James Curran, Michael Gurevitch, and Janet Woollacott, 12–43. London: Edward Arnold.

Nelson, Cary, and Lawrence Grossberg, eds. 1988. *Marxism and the Interpretation of Culture*. Urbana: University of Illinois Press.

Nightingale, Virginia. 1989. "What's Ethnographic about Ethnographic Audience Research?" *Australian Journal of Communication* 16: 50–63.

O'Sullivan, Tim, Danny Saunders, John Hartley, and John Fiske. 1983. *Key Concepts in Communication*. London: Methuen.

Palmer, Patricia. 1986. *The Lively Audience*. Sydney: Allen & Unwin.

Perry, George. 1975. *The Great British Picture Show*. London: Paladin.

Powell, Rachel, and John Clarke. 1976. "A Note on Marginality." In *Resistance Through Rituals: Youth Subcultures in Post-War Britain*, ed. Stuart Hall and Tony Jefferson, 223–29. London: Hutchinson.

Radway, Janice. 1987. *Reading the Romance: Women, Patriarchy and Popular Literature*. London: Verso. First published in 1986.

———. 1988. "Reception Study: Ethnography and the Problems of Dispersed Audiences and Nomadic Subjects." *Cultural Studies* 2(3): 359–76.

Saussure, Ferdinand de. 1960. *Course in General Linguistics*, trans. Wade Baskin. London: Peter Owen.

Scannell, Paddy, and David Cardiff. 1982. "Serving the Nation: Public Service Broadcasting Before the War." In *Popular Culture: Past and Present*, ed. Bernard Waites, Tony Bennett, and Graham Martin, 161–88. London: Croom Helm.

Schlesinger, Philip. 1978. *Putting "Reality" Together: BBC News*. London: Constable. (Revised edition published 1987, London: Methuen.)

Showalter, Elaine. 1987. *The Female Malady: Women, Madness and English Culture, 1830–1980*. London: Virago.

Stedman-Jones, Gareth. 1982. "Working-Class Culture and Working-Class Politics in London, 1870–1900: Notes on the Remaking of a Working-Class." In *Popular Culture: Past and Present*, ed. Bernard Waites, Tony Bennett, and Graham Martin, 92–121. London: Croom Helm.

Thompson, Denys, ed. 1973. *Discrimination and Popular Culture*. Rev. ed. London: Penguin. First published in 1964.

Thompson, E. P. 1978a. *The Making of the English Working Class*. London: Penguin. First published in 1963.

———. 1978b. *The Poverty of Theory and Other Essays*. London: Merlin.

Tulloch, John. 1989. "Approaching Audiences: A Note on Method." In *Australian Television: Programs, Pleasures and Politics*, ed. John Tulloch and Graeme Turner, 187–201. Sydney: Allen & Unwin.

———. n.d. "*Dr. Who*: Approaching the Audience." Unpublished paper.

Tulloch, John, and Manuel Alvarado. 1983. *Doctor Who: The Unfolding Text*. London: Macmillan.

Tulloch, John, and Albert Moran. 1986. *Quality Soap: A Country Practice*. Sydney: Currency.

Tulloch, John, and Graeme Turner, eds. 1989. *Australian Television: Programs, Pleasures and Politics*. Sydney: Allen & Unwin.

Tunstall, Jeremy. 1971. *Journalists at Work*. London: Constable.

Turner, Graeme. 1987. "*Perfect Match*: Ambiguity, Spectacle and the Popular." *Australian Journal of Cultural Studies* 4(2): 79–94.

———. 1988. *Film as Social Practice*. London: Routledge.

———. 1989. "Transgressive Television: From *IMT* to *Perfect Match*." In *Australian Television: Programs, Pleasures and Politics*, ed. John Tulloch and Graeme Turner, 25–37. Sydney: Allen & Unwin.

Waites, Bernard, Tony Bennett, and Graham Martin, eds. 1982. *Popular Culture: Past and Present*. London: Croom Helm.

Weedon, Chris, Andrew Tolson, and Frank Mort. 1980. "Theories of Language and Subjectivity." In *Culture, Media, Language*, ed. Stuart Hall, Dorothy Hobson, Andrew Lowe, and Paul Willis, 195–216. London: Hutchinson.

Widdowson, Peter, ed., 1982. *Re-reading English*. London: Methuen.

Williams, Raymond. 1962. *Communications*. London: Penguin.

———. 1966. *Culture and Society 1780–1950*. London: Penguin. First published in 1958.

———. 1974. *Television: Technology and Cultural Form*. London: Fontana/Collins.

———. 1975. *The Long Revolution*. London: Penguin. First published in 1961.

———. 1977. *Marxism and Literature*. London: Oxford University Press.

Williamson, Judith. 1978. *Decoding Advertisements: Ideology and Meaning in Advertising*. London: Marion Boyars.

———. 1987. *Consuming Passions*. London: Marion Boyars.

Winship, Janice. 1980. "Advertising in Women's Magazines: 1956–74." CCCS stenciled paper, No. 59.

Willis, Paul. 1977. *Learning to Labour: How Working Class Kids Get Working Class Jobs*. London: Saxon House.

———. 1978. *Profane Culture*. London: Routledge & Kegan Paul.

———. 1979. "Shop Floor Culture, Masculinity and the Wage Form." In *Working Class Culture: Studies in History and Theory*, ed. John Clarke, Chas Critcher, and Richard Johnson, 185–98. London: Hutchinson.

———. 1980. "Notes on Method." In *Culture, Media, Language*, ed. Stuart Hall, Dorothy Hobson, Andrew Lowe, and Paul Willis, 88–95. London: Hutchinson.

About the Author

Graeme Turner is associate professor in the Department of English at the University of Queensland, Brisbane, Australia. One of the leading figures in Australian cultural studies, he was a founding editor of the *Australian Journal of Cultural Studies* and is currently an editor of *Cultural Studies*. Among his publications are a study of Australian film and fiction, *National Fictions: Literature, Film and the Construction of Australian Narrative*; a cultural studies introduction to popular film, *Film as Social Practice*; a study of Australian popular culture, *Myths of Oz: Reading Australian Popular Culture* (with John Fiske and Bob Hodge); and (with John Tulloch) a collection of articles on Australian television, *Australian Television: Programs, Pleasures and Politics*. He used to relax by playing rock and roll in bars, but has to admit that these days his liveliest audience is his three small children.

Index